THE CORPORATE
GARDENER

HOW DOES
YOUR BUSINESS GROW?

By

Paul G. Allman

iUniverse, Inc.
Bloomington

iUniverse books may be ordered through booksellers or by contacting:

iUniverse
1663 Liberty Drive
Bloomington, IN 47403
www.iuniverse.com
1-800-Authors (1-800-288-4677)

ISBN: 978-1-4502-8034-1 (sc)
ISBN: 978-1-4502-8035-8 (hc)
ISBN: 978-1-4502-8036-5 (ebook)

Library of Congress Control Number: 2010918817

Printed in the United States of America

iUniverse rev. date: 10/18/2011

CONTENTS

ACKNOWLEDGMENTS

I would like to acknowledge and thank all those whose time and input reinforced the concept that all things can be improved: Sherwood Best, PhD, Kerry Bryant, Jack Cooper, S. Nelson Gray, Kathryn Nirschl, SPHR, Cynthia Sistek-Chandler, EdD, Ron Savage EdD, Dr. Christopher Ullman, and Rev. Everett "Duke" Winser. The precious gift of your time and focused support is reflected in the pages of this book.

I would also like to thank all the participants in the programs I have conduct over the last twenty plus years, who have contributed to the on-going development of the information included in *The Corporate Gardener.* If nothing more, you were a sounding board for my evolving ideas.

And finally a very special thanks to my wife, Sharon Grandinette, whose proofreading patience, endless supply of red pencils, and ongoing encouragement provided invaluable support throughout my writing journey.

INTRODUCTION

In the early 1980s, I was responsible for establishing technical skill training programs for a major aerospace company that had just undergone a government review of workmanship quality. The results of the review were below acceptable standards, and I was hired to develop and conduct skill-based classes to improve and certify the quality of the organization's workforce. The organization had attempted skill development, but it was informal, undocumented, and inconsistent.

Over the next several years I developed a certification and qualification system covering over fifty technical topics, which eventually led to training approximately seven thousand participants annually. The organization's workmanship continued to be reviewed, as many organizations during the eighties went through TQM and, ISO–9000, and companies embraced the emerging focus on organizational processes. The certification and training system consistently received high marks.

Even though my department's focus was on technical training, there was always a great interest in, if not need for, the less technical or "soft skill" training—courses in communication skills, leadership, motivation, and team building.

In 1988, I started my own consulting firm, PTS-Professional Training Services, with a focus on the challenges associated with establishing skill development systems and implementing organization-wide change. PTS also developed over twenty essential core soft-skill courses providing clients an opportunity to select topics and develop a customized management certification program based specifically on their needs.

With the "re-engineering" efforts of the nineties, PTS established continuous process improvement (CPI) programs in several major companies by developing functional resource teams, process improvement teams, and integrating soft-skill courses into each program. Employees became excited about new opportunities to influence their work processes, resulting in visible, documented, and substantial annual savings.

Over the years, I've worked with a wide variety of businesses, such as entertainment, aerospace, manufacturing, health care, and city governments, ranging from Fortune 100 companies to small- and medium-sized organizations. Several "natural" laws seemed to have a great influence on successful outcomes.

First, most people wanted to be a part of something bigger and more lasting than themselves. They wanted to be a part of an organization committed to success. Adapting to, implementing, and managing change was a large part of the equation for success. For change to be effective, it had to be modeled and supported from the top down but, more importantly, experienced and implemented from the bottom up. Individuals at all levels of the organization wanted to feel that their contribution made an impact on the organization's success. First and foremost, it was important that their voice be heard when it came to influencing the issues surrounding their area of performance.

Second, most individuals wanted time-tested fundamentals, not just fad-based flavor-of-the-month initiatives, as they engaged in the change process. They desired training courses that taught practical skills they could implement immediately, while discovering something about themselves in a learning environment that allowed for fun during the process.

Third, to accomplish lasting success, organizations needed participants to establish a belief that learned skills would be modeled, reinforced, and practiced once they returned to the work area. A lot of lip service was given to investing in employees, and participants wanted a chance to show off their new skills. More often than not, they were not given the opportunity. Participants would often ask, "Why isn't my boss attending the training? They don't do what I'm being trained to do, so how can they support me?" Or, "Will there ever be time to apply and perfect skills learned in class, or is learning only secondary to the ongoing demands of the work output?"

Whether implementing a skill development system or a process improvement program, it became clear that two basic issues needed to be on the radar of organizations: ongoing practical investment in the employee skill base and an understanding of the change process to encourage responsibility for improvement at all levels. With these issues in mind, I developed the idea for *The Corporate Gardener*, providing a simple story offering new managers struggling with team dynamics and challenging work assignments an overview of the best in management concepts and practical skills. Written with a focus on first-time managers, *The Corporate Gardener* is also an excellent refresher for more experienced managers seeking guidance on how to mentor less experienced, multigenerational staff members.

Utilizing the concepts of continuous improvement as well as management and leadership theory, *The Corporate Gardner* applies the world of nature and gardening as a metaphor for addressing today's work challenges. As the experienced current workforce transitions into retirement, we have the potential for lost organizational knowledge. Part of the challenge will be getting the older workforce effectively communicating with the new. For the first time in history, generations with extremely varied views, expectations, and values are working together on the same teams. In almost any organization today, one can find twenty-somethings, forty-somethings, and sixty-somethings working together at different levels with varying degrees of authority. In some cases, recent college graduates with little managerial training are overseeing employees old enough to be their parents. Conflict is inevitable, and according to a survey by Lee Hecht Harrison, more than 60 percent of companies report they are experiencing tension among different generations. Imagine how strong and productive organizations would become if both ends of the spectrum could find a way to bridge the generational gap.

At one end of the generational gap are those representing the current management structures designed and implemented by the traditionalists. The character Mrs. Hortensis illustrates this in the book. Although Mrs. Hortensis is far from typical, she shows that it is possible to bridge that gap. On the other end are generation Ys, sometimes referred to as the Millennials. They are the new workforce and are just beginning to shape the way things are done in business and society. Nick represents the generation Y group and those in their early twenties who are full of innovation and fresh ideas and are ultrasavvy when it comes to technology. His journey, guided by Mrs. Hortensis, is a discovery of how he can become more productive in his new position.

This is a journey many will undertake in the next several years. By the year 2011, there will be approximately seventy million Americans in generation Y, making up over 30 percent of the population. While they may certainly be able to run circles around older employees gathering information from the Web or utilizing technology, they lack a sense of the big picture in business, simply because they have not yet accumulated the life experiences to have a mature worldview.

Unlike generations before, generation Y has been nurtured and programmed with multiple activities since they were toddlers. Parents with high expectations showered them with a great deal of attention and pressure to perform. Unlike previous generations, which have struggled with annual reviews, generation Ys have grown up receiving constant feedback and recognition from teachers, parents, and coaches, and they often feel lost without regular communication. They are less likely to respond to the traditional command-and-control type of management still popular in many organizations today. They prefer to solve problems in groups and are perfect candidates for working on process improvement teams, which utilize innovation to challenge existing structures. Their philosophy of speaking their mind leads to a willingness to challenge the status quo.

Generation Ys thrive in environments where creativity and independent thinking are looked upon as positive. While they are typically adept at multitasking, what they seek is effective mentoring that is formal, challenging, and structured. This includes breaking down goals into steps and, where possible, encouraging them to work in groups. It does not mean providing them with all the answers, but rather helping them to stay on track. They respond well to structured and supportive work environments where they can have a say in the way things are done and address their frustrations openly. They don't want to spend a great deal of time talking about things or having meetings. Instead, they want to get involved and do something. Because they are new to the workforce and don't understand all the subtleties of organizational life, ongoing training is key to their success.

Generation Ys are also cost-efficient, having witnessed the financial insecurity that beset earlier generations stung by layoffs and dot-com busts. They believe in their own self-worth and value and, as a result, are not shy about trying to facilitate change in the organizations for which they work.

The Corporate Gardner breathes new life into the sometimes overwhelming topics of leadership development, continuous improvement, management techniques, customer focus, team building, staff development, and interpersonal communication. Through storytelling, the book demonstrates the fundamentals of building a team, developing team members, turning around complex projects, discovering improvement opportunities, and working more effectively and efficiently with staff and management.

The book also addresses the predictions about our economy, which indicate years of continued financial challenges. Corporations that wish to sustain and grow will need to focus more and more on cost-cutting measures, improvement, and efficiency efforts reminiscent of the last similar economic cycle beginning in the early 1990s.

The Corporate Gardner is based on one of the fundamental requirements for effectively managing and leading change efforts: understanding the motives, values, and goals of others. The key message is to understand and accept the differences in people. Clashes among generations are not new, but if we were to summarize the future challenge of managing and leading in organizations, it would be to know how to value the individual, nurture relationships, and streamline existing organizational structures. The reason I chose a novel to explain the complexity of change was to make the principles more understandable and illustrate how simple it can be at times to bring order to apparent irresolvable challenges.

ORGANIZATION OF THE BOOK

The Corporate Gardner is organized based on the typical progression of change, starting from discovery through implementation, to invention. Each chapter addresses the soft skills needed to be successful during the different stages of change. At the end of each chapter is a summary of the key learning points to be used as a quick reference guide for future review, or for easy sharing of the information. The information is presented as if Nick were taking notes after each meeting with Mrs. Hortensis.

Since nature and the garden are the metaphors for understanding organizational issues, I also tried to go beyond just the metaphor and include interesting information about gardening as well.

I have been told that some readers may just want information about leadership and management and may not want to discover it hidden in all the gardening information. However, there are plenty of books on management like that already, so the readers of those books may not be my audience. My experience indicates that people retain and use information that they can identify with and have an interest in.

Gardening is one of the nation's most popular pastimes. One in four Americans indicates that gardening is an important hobby or interest of theirs, spending five or more hours per week tending lawns, flowers, and vegetables. Since many people buy books on leadership and don't even read them, I felt that if several different interests could be merged, the chance of an individual being exposed to a broad overview of management and leadership techniques was more likely.

Combining the existing interest in gardening (26 percent of those aged thirty to forty-four, and 30 percent of forty-five to fifty-nine-year-olds garden) with the complex principles of management provides a convenient bridge to quickly learn and utilize important techniques.

I have also listed some books for further exploration in an appendix at the end of the book, with the information arranged by author under specific subject groupings. This is by no means a complete list. Hopefully, *The Corporate Gardner* will open the door to a library filled with invaluable information for those learning to lead others.

My wish is that readers find the story informative and enjoyable. There are programs that designate a high level of achievement, such as receiving a black belt in martial arts. I hope, going forward, that there is equal recognition in the ever-growing number of *green thumbs* in leadership.

THE LANDSCAPE

"Working smarter, not harder, requires understanding the simple things yet unknown, and developing a desire to discover them."

—Paul Allman

October 9

Nick glanced at his watch and took a deep sigh of relief noticing it was nearing four o'clock in the afternoon. It was Friday, and soon the office staff would be leaving.

At last, the end of another long week and the start of a not-long-enough weekend, Nick thought, frustrated by the lack of staff accountability and their inability to complete work on time. Deadlines were missed and simple tasks routinely behind schedule. Despite the continuous distractions and unnecessary interruptions, he was the only one who got anything done. Nick had sought guidance from upper management but received only constant reminders that results were needed now.

Had he made the wrong choice? Maybe he wasn't cut out to be a manager. Whether a matter of a poor choice or lack of ability, clearly the current work environment was not what Nick expected.

Fresh out of college, Nickolas Avtid had joined BTA Development Corporation three years ago, hoping the company would provide him a career direction. The work was challenging and required organizational skills, plenty of multitasking activities, and the ability to work under pressure to meet demanding deadlines with a real sense of accomplishment when things came together, even though frequently at the last minute.

Nick quickly fit into the organization's fast pace. He had become very successful at rescuing projects headed for trouble and enjoyed being the hero, turning things around *just in the nick of time.* His dedication and contributions had not gone unnoticed, and Nick was asked to manage one of the company's most difficult projects. He knew about the project. Employees referred to it as the "dead-end assignment." A depository for some of the more interesting staff members, it was a work environment full of frustrations where everyone looked out for his or her own interests.

Management had hoped Nick's enthusiasm and talent would somehow rub off, but just the opposite was happening. Since accepting the new position, Nick's last two months had been nothing but a whirlwind of disappointments and now self-doubt. *Maybe I need to start my career over somewhere else. It's clear that no one here wants to follow my directions and do what I tell them to do,* he thought.

All day his work consisted of dealing with petty complaints, answering unnecessary questions, and holding special meetings when individuals didn't follow through. There seemed to be no escape from it. "What good is having an office if you can't close the door and work in peace?" he complained out loud.

One day he had timed the interruptions and discovered they occurred about every six minutes. *How am I supposed to get any work done? I can't recall a time when I wasn't able to figure things out on my own. I don't go running to my boss every few minutes with silly concerns.* He sighed again and looked out into the work area through his office window.

It was a plain window spanning nearly the entire wall, and it provided a panoramic view of his staff's work space: a large room with eight ten-by-ten-foot cubicles clustered together in the center. At the rear of the room was a small alcove near a watercooler.

Directly opposite of Nick's office was the main entrance. Above the door hung an old rectangular clock with a large, round face and small swinging pendulum encased in an antique oak frame. It appeared to be the only thing in the area that was well maintained. Several handprints on the wall were permanent reminders that someone periodically removed the clock, adjusting the time to make sure it was always accurate. It would be a travesty should anyone work a few extra minutes.

The room hadn't been painted in a long while. The ceiling was high, and around the upper edges of the walls were the accumulated smudges of dirt and dust, unbothered for years. There were permanent shadows outlining the florescent light fixtures, as if someone had traced them with a dirty brush.

A ceiling fan hung down in the center of the room stirring the air in an attempt to offer relief from a stale musty smell, but it squeaked and wobbled slightly in its efforts. The distraction of the continuous noise, like the ticking of a clock in a quiet room, had forced Nick to turn it off. There had been complaints about this change, but he figured the others would eventually get used to it. At least that was one distraction he had eliminated.

Nick mentioned to his new boss, Fritz Morgan, that the fan should be repaired and the room needed painting. Mr. Morgan's response was that something might be done next year, but nothing until then.

"First, we need to get the project back on track," his boss grumbled. "There are several progress payments past due, and that's where the money will come from. Focus on getting the work done. Then worry about rewarding individuals with a better work environment."

Nick's boss had been a self-starter with the organization and, much like Nick, found a place where his natural skills could develop. He was a stocky barrel-chested man, barely five foot five, with a deep sharp voice. The few plain suit jackets he wore had a well-worn look, but his appearance was always neat and pressed. Most of the time he was seen with his shirtsleeves rolled up just below the elbows, his tanned arms making a striking contrast to a faded white shirt.

He had been with the organization a long time, earning a reputation for running a tight ship and keeping unnecessary expenses to a minimum. As a mid-level director, he had three managers reporting to him, including Nick.

Mr. Morgan was the only contact Nick ever had with senior management, except when the administrative assistant for the president brought him papers to sign. The forms stated he had received the organization's policy and procedure manuals and agreed to follow them without exception.

Nick's boss was a no-nonsense person, direct and demanding, and he expected his managers to think for themselves. "Just get some results" was his marching slogan and made it clear he wasn't going to babysit anyone. Interaction was limited to asking where weekly reports were or to inform Nick of new restrictions on the budget.

Mr. Morgan felt the project was fairly straightforward and the problem was simple—the group didn't work hard enough. Nick agreed it wasn't that difficult of a project and quickly set about identifying what was preventing the group from moving forward. He presented an outline of key improvement steps, yet no one followed his suggestions.

Nick called a special meeting to remind the group that he was their new boss and that things needed to change. At the meeting he carefully reviewed his detailed recovery plan outlining how to get the project back on track. It went unused.

Nick looked at the clock above the entrance and realized it was a few minutes before five. He wanted to pick up the latest updates from John before he left and quickly headed for his office.

John was a thin man, his face neatly framed with small oval wire-rimmed glasses and graying dark hair carefully parted. Nick had never seen him with his sleeves rolled up or the collar button of his starched shirt undone. He was much older than Nick, had been with the organization twenty-six years, and was part of the project from the beginning. Nick's impression of John was that he had burned out a long time ago and only came to work because he had nothing better to do.

John's meticulous mannerisms were reflected in the thoroughness of his reports, but he spent much of his time correcting others and pointing out how poor their efforts were. He typically kept to himself, and you could set your watch by the predictable things he did. He went to lunch every day at noon, not a minute before or a minute later, usually eating at the same café just down the street. When the clock above the door showed five, he left, not a minute early and not a minute late.

He occasionally excused himself from late afternoon meetings stating, "My contract doesn't extend beyond the hour of five," and he refused to come to work early even if Nick requested a special meeting before the normal start time. Once Nick had suggested a Saturday morning meeting to catch up, and John sternly responded, "That's not what I agreed to twenty-six years ago. Besides, we're not paid for that extra effort. If they won't show their appreciation by compensating *us*, why should we work harder for *them*?" To John, it was all about *us* verses *them*.

His work was steady and predictable, and if you disagreed with John, your facts better be correct. He would always get back to you with some underlined article or company procedure clarifying his point and reminding you to check information before making erroneous statements.

"Hi, John," Nick said, entering his cubicle, "how is the final spreadsheet on the first phase of recovery going? I need the report for Monday's status meeting with Mr. Morgan."

"Almost finished, but it won't be ready by Monday. I didn't receive the input Celeste promised, and the little information she gave me was inaccurate and very poorly done."

"But I told you days ago that I needed the information this Monday!"

"I can't help the fact that no one around here is capable of doing a thorough job," John said, getting up to go home. "I will leave what I have completed on my desk if you want to look at it."

"Why can't anyone do what I ask?" Nick blurted out, probably a little too loud in frustration as he left John's area.

Walking back to his office, Nick noticed Mary in the far corner, eyeing him over the rim of her glasses. Mary was hard for Nick to understand. She had a friendly smile punctuated with plump cheeks and a round face. A nice person, she was probably in her early sixties, liked by everyone, kind, and generous to a fault. Pleasant and unassuming, she was never confrontational or directly took sides during a group conflict. Instead, she quietly negotiated tensions in the group, usually one-on-one in a secretive way.

And there were tensions. Every day there was confusion, miscommunication, shouting, petty disagreements, and accusations. After being with the group only a week, Nick called a meeting and reprimanded everyone on their inability to work as a team. For the next several days, individuals sulked around under a dark cloud of resentment. His attempt to focus them on how they interacted only made things worse.

During the frequent tensions and turmoil, individuals would eventually find their way to Mary for comfort and support. She really didn't say much; she just listened in the way a grandmother would when you fell and scraped your knee or complained about the other kids in the school yard.

Her small cozy work area was at the back of the main room, in an alcove created by support beams for the building. With the watercooler just outside her door, it was a perfect place for individuals to escape. Nick had noticed on his first day that Mary obviously enjoyed visitors because there was a jar of candy on her desk as an offering to those who ventured by.

Some in the group had only recently joined the organization and clearly had no idea what they were supposed to do. That didn't stop them from giving directions or complaining about tasks not being done.

Bill had quickly established a reputation for being direct and demanding. "It's all about the destination, people, let's move" was his favorite saying. Bill was a young, burly, tall mountain of a man, with large hands and a loud voice. His chiseled chin, dark bushy eyebrows, casual dress, and broad shoulders gave him the appearance of a lumberjack. He could be heard frequently bellowing out directions or addressing his concerns to other workers. On more than one occasion Nick had asked Bill not to talk so loud. Bill just shrugged his shoulders and said, "Whatever you say. You're the boss." But nothing really changed in his churlish behavior.

Cindy was also one of the new ones, always neat but plainly dressed in a fashion that reminded Nick of something stylish several decades ago. Even though she was barely in her forties, she wore dresses in various shades of gray perfectly hung several inches below the knees with an off-white blouse covered by a blazer bearing a simple seasonal brooch. Her hair was carefully pinned back and sometimes braided in a practical way.

She had joined the group just a few weeks prior to Nick's arrival. Quiet and polite, she hardly left her desk and made a noticeable effort to avoid any contact with the others. Mr. Morgan had said, "She's some kind of turnaround specialist, and we are lucky to have hired her away from her previous employer." Nick didn't see that at all. He barely noticed her presence. She seemed to prefer working alone and undisturbed.

Her office was like a sanctuary. It was neat and orderly with a small fountain in the corner that gave off a quieting sound as you entered. On the shelf behind her desk she had arranged her books alphabetically and on one of the walls taped flip-chart paper diagramming some sort of system.

Nick had found the neatness of her area interesting. He still hadn't unpacked many of the boxes he brought with him. He figured they could wait until he got around to it or needed something. The first thing Nick had done with his office was to turn the desk at a slight angle so it faced the door and window.

In the corner of his office, next to several stacks of files, was Nick's only embellishment. It was a plant he received from Mary as a welcoming gift. With all the distraction, he hadn't paid it much attention and it was now a shriveled clump of brown curled leaves still clinging to the pot in desperation.

Nick entered his office, noticed the plant, and muttered, "That illustrates this group perfectly," reflecting on what John said about Celeste not providing the information.

Celeste wasn't new to the organization and had been on this project for about a year. She was a stylish dresser and paraded around the office sporting the latest trends, some definitely too short and ill-fitting. Even though slightly overweight, she strutted the halls like any good model walks a runway. Her curled and flamboyantly combed hair changed color frequently, and her hands and neck sported more jewelry than was needed. Sometimes you could hear her coming before you'd see her.

She was someone exciting to be around. If there was any laughter coming from the group you were sure to find Celeste at the center of it.

Her laugh was infectious and continuous. Of course, that was when she was around. She never seemed to be at her desk.

Nick hadn't seen a more disorganized work space. Celeste had accumulated a great deal of stuff randomly scattered about her cubicle. Nick wondered how she managed to find anything in her menagerie of mess. On the filing cabinet next to her desk she displayed a collage of photographs representing the parties, events, and activities she had recently attended. On her computer was a stuffed animal, and Nick had noticed a pencil on her desk with a large eraser shaped like a lightbulb, a dartboard for making decisions, and a small basketball hoop over her trash can. Her office was set up more for fun than work. However, she was always the first to volunteer for new assignments. As of yet, she hadn't turned anything in on time and Nick planned to have a talk with her about follow-through. He kept putting it off because she provided the only positive interaction between members. John frequently complained about her sloppy work efforts, but Nick wasn't quite sure yet how he was going to address the issue with her.

Nick's priority was to keep the project on track, jumping in whenever possible and taking over what wasn't getting done. Recently, he had given Jim specific directions on how to organize a project status meeting. When the slow-moving Jim didn't follow through, Nick took over and completed the arrangements at the last minute. Jim irritated Nick because of his wishy-washy noncommittal attitude. He was in his late thirties and, with broad shoulders, looked capable of taking on any challenge. If Nick hadn't taken charge, the whole project would have been in jeopardy. Later, running into Jim outside his office, he confronted him in front of everyone, making it clear how the project suffered because of his lack of accountability. Jim claimed he didn't know it was his responsibility. Nick found that hard to believe.

Surprisingly, some people resented Nick's support when he jumped in, and this frustrated him. If he had just one other player like himself on the team, it would be so much easier.

Nick was a real sports enthusiast and understood the value of working together as a team. He frequently used sports analogies to remind his group of the importance of teamwork, but it made little difference. In one of his early interventions he reminded everyone that the real success of individuals was through team achievement. Bill had bellowed out, "Yeah, tell that to the number-one golf pro."

Nick had called Bill into his office after the meeting, looked him straight in his eyes, and said, "Let me make this clear. You need to support me in front of the group instead of showing belligerent resistance." Bill said he thought it was funny at the time but would just do as he was told in the future. A real tension was starting to grow between them.

How do you get people to work together as a team? Nick wondered, noticing the clock on the wall that showed it was already after six. From his sports background, he knew that individual talent alone was not what made a team successful. There was something special about a group of individuals who could function effectively together. A cohesive team could actually outperform a disorganized one with more talent.

It certainly wasn't the work. Nick had already determined that the project didn't need to be so difficult. He was beginning to think that working together as a team was more challenging than actually doing the work.

"Why was I asked to be the manager anyway?" he muttered to himself, sensing the emptiness that had come over the work area. "Why can't I just be one of the regular employees again and enjoy doing things without worrying about others?"

Just the other day, the group left early to join a retirement celebration for someone in another department. Nick had overheard Jim saying, "Never miss a chance to celebrate someone getting out of here." Nick realized he had missed every birthday celebration and get-together since he had taken the new assignment.

I've never managed a group of people before. My boss said I would be great at the new position because I was one of the best at what I do. I know my technical skills are strong, but I never received training on how to get people to do what they are supposed to. If I could just get individuals to listen to me and do what I say ...

When Nick first assumed his responsibilities, he thought that by managing others he would be able to accomplish a great deal more. He was realizing that working with people who did not demonstrate commitment and accountability made tasks unnecessarily difficult.

The lack of responsibility demonstrated by Mary, Celeste, Jim, and others was draining Nick of his enthusiasm. *How can I get these people to become more reliable and accept ownership for outcomes?*

Nick was becoming aware that there was something more to managing people than just knowing how to complete assignments. He sensed a need for help but didn't know who to approach or exactly what to ask. He was fearful that if he sought assistance, especially from his boss, he would be perceived as incompetent, and that was something Nick wanted to avoid at all costs.

"Enough of this," Nick said jumping up. "I haven't done anything exciting on a Friday night for a long while. I need to stop letting work influence my life so much and start doing something for me. I need to ..." Nick thought for a minute. "I need to begin exercising again. Tomorrow morning I will start running like I did before I got involved with this stupid project. At least that will help release some of *my* tension."

Nick turned, closed the office door, and went to his desk to write himself a note: *Stop worrying about others and just focus on what you want to do.* He had become one of *them*.

TYPICAL CHALLENGES AND FRUSTRATIONS

A work environment filled with:

- *unnecessary distractions and interruptions.*

- *complaints, confusions, miscommunications, shouting, petty disagreements, and accusations.*

- *a lack of commitment and accountability.*

- *no guidance from management but results that are needed now.*

- *managers who are expected to "think for themselves".*

NEW DIRECTION

- *never managed a group of people before.*

- *first time responsible for directing others.*

- *boss says he will be great because he was one of the best workers.*

- *never received training on how to get people to do what they are supposed to do periodically must remind everyone he is their boss.*

- *current focus is getting the work done and then worrying about rewarding individuals.*

- *still enjoys being the "hero" and providing the extra efforts needed to turn things around just in the nick of time.*

- *contemplating how to get people to work together as a team.*

THE BEGINNING

"Although I am an old man, I am but a young gardener."

—Thomas Jefferson

October 10

A brisk morning wind struck Nick's face as he closed the front door, the surprising jolt awakening his senses and converging his thoughts.

I need to jog and reflect, Nick thought, sitting down on the front steps to lace up a pair of new Air Max 360 running shoes.

He began jogging against the wind, up the street, with his thoughts whirling from the frustrations of a typical workweek. *How do you get people to work together as a team? The way the group is currently approaching their tasks we will never get to where we need to be. Despite the uniqueness of some of the people, we have the capability to turn this project around. I've tried to model the right behavior by doing as much work as I can. Still, we are going nowhere.*

Last night Nick thought about quitting, but he wasn't one to run away from challenges. He had never failed when he put his efforts toward a goal; however, this was different. Before he would just work harder and longer, but this time it involved others.

There must be a solution.

Nick turned and jogged down a long narrow cul-de-sac lane several blocks from where he lived. At the far end he recognized his favorite house. Across from it was a small flower-lined path leading to the city park through a colorful canopy of birch, maple, and oak trees gently swaying from the wind. The home stood out, embraced by the many trees and plants that framed it. It was definitely unique to the neighborhood, sitting in a location thick with vegetation surrounded by newly constructed multilevel condos with minimal, yet well-manicured, landscaping.

Whenever Nick passed this way, he wondered why someone hadn't developed the property. The home sat on what appeared to be several lots, and he knew there was money to be made by subdividing the land. He estimated it could be a small fortune but guessed the owner, Mrs. Hortensis, simply didn't appreciate what she had.

Drawing nearer, his eyes surveyed the area, outlining how the plants and trees cradled the house and created an oasis. Even though it might be underdeveloped, he was grateful no one had changed its look.

As he jogged nearer, Nick recognized Mrs. Hortensis working in her front yard. Having grown up not far from here, Nick had spoken with the older woman many times in the past, yet didn't really know that much about her. Her look was timeless, for as long as Nick could remember she had remained the same. She appeared to be in her late seventies and was always dashing about with shiny silver gray hair in a neat braid dangling beneath a broad straw hat. Her tall and stately posture seemed to command attention from the plants as she purposefully moved from one area to the next wrapped in a faded green gardening apron that was new thirty years ago. Nick enjoyed the predictable friendly wave from her as he jogged by on his way to the park. Sometimes he would stop and stretch, leaning against the oak tree near her front yard, and they would have short conversations, generally about the weather.

Most days, he would encounter her maintaining the vegetative sea surrounding her home. *Just think how much more free time she would have*, Nick thought as he approached, *if she didn't have to keep all this up*. However, the space did emanate a calm, relaxing feeling, giving Nick a sense that the plants had become partners in harmony. *Harmony … that's the atmosphere I wish I could create at work*, Nick thought to himself.

"Hi, Mrs. Hortensis," Nick called out as he slowed his approach and caught his breath. It had been a long time since he had done any exercise; the new project was starting to affect his health.

"Well, hi there, young man. It's been a while since I've seen you out jogging." Mrs. Hortensis waved as she walked over.

He stopped and leaned against the oak tree next to the well-maintained white picket fence separating her property from the rest of the world.

"Isn't it just a beautiful day?" Mrs. Hortensis exclaimed, barely slowing down as she talked. "Nothing like a sunny fall morning to make you want to get out and work in the yard."

"Your yard is inspiring," Nick said. "Every time I come by here it makes me feel in touch with nature. It's hard to put in words … relaxed, I guess."

Mrs. Hortensis smiled as she stopped next to the fence. "I guess all my hard work has had a purpose. Everyone needs a place to relax."

Nick nodded, still catching his breath. "Recently I've become more aware of how important it is to have somewhere to get away from it all."

"We all need that special spot to go and sort things out," Mrs. Hortensis said, looking closely at Nick. "I heard you've been working at Ben Anderson's company. How are things going?"

"Who's Ben Anderson?"

"He started BTA Development Corporation, the company you're working for, some thirty-five years ago. He sold it several years back. Said he wanted to retire and enjoy the good life but passed away seven months after he left. The company was all he had. I'll bet he worked sixteen hours a day, every day."

"He died just after retirement? That sounds like bad timing," Nick said, stretching his back.

"He used to walk by here once in a while after he retired, and we would talk. He said the same thing about the yard, how it made him feel relaxed. He complimented me on the hard work I put into maintaining it and complained that no one wanted to work hard anymore. He was glad he had sold his company, but I felt there was more to the story."

With one hand on the tree, Nick reached behind, grabbed his ankle, and pulled his leg upward to stretch his thigh muscle. "Things haven't changed that much in his company. You are rewarded for dedicating your whole life there. The unspoken motto is 'Work hard and you will go somewhere.' Ironically, I think some of the ones who don't want to work are still there."

Mrs. Hortensis just listened.

"I seem to have most of them on my new project. If Mr. Anderson was around today, he would be very disappointed with their efforts."

"How do you mean?"

"I can't figure out what is going wrong with my group. I wish I could take the same feelings I get …" Nick motioned with his arm, making a sweeping arch as he pointed at her garden, "with the harmony of your yard and replicate it in my work environment."

Nick noticed an interesting look on Mrs. Hortensis's face as he continued. "Sorry, I'm just venting. I don't have anyone to share my frustrations with. Nothing you would be interested in. I need to sort out if I've made the right decision in accepting my new position and if I'm cut out to be a manager."

"Sounds challenging at work," Mrs. Hortensis commented. "Ever done much gardening, Nick?"

"No, I've never really had the time. Besides, I don't have that much space around my condo, and I don't have a green thumb," Nick responded, getting ready to begin jogging again.

"Nonsense," Mrs. Hortensis retorted with a twinkle in her eye. "There is no such thing as a green thumb. If you believe that only a few people can garden, well, then you must think that only a few can manage."

Nick looked at Mrs. Hortensis and wondered what one had to do with the other. "Judging by the progress of my group, I'm one of those people that can't manage. If it weren't for my extra efforts, the group would never get anything done."

"Nonsense," Mrs. Hortensis said again. "You just need to understand some basic principles. Managing a group and gardening are very similar."

Mrs. Hortensis's reply stimulated his curiosity. "Explain that?" he asked.

"Well, the two have a lot in common."

"Are you suggesting that if I were a gardener I would also be a better manager?"

"Something like that," Mrs. Hortensis responded, sensing Nick's hesitation. "How long have these issues been going on with your work group?"

"For quite some time, and unfortunately, the problem seems to get worse every week. I've tried everything. My boss said I should 'get tough,' but at the same time he told me there were individuals that I couldn't challenge. I'm getting mixed messages. I receive no input from upper management, except that they want things fixed *now*. They are always asking me for more and expect me to do it with less." Nick threw up his hands. "I don't see how gardening could help solve that dilemma."

Mrs. Hortensis just smiled. "What's the rest of your morning like?"

"I've nothing really planned," Nick said carefully, "but I have a lot of things I need to get done. I just thought I would take a few minutes to begin exercising again and think about why I dislike work so much. Focus and figure out what to do."

"I need a break. Come join me for a cup of tea and let's talk." Mrs. Hortensis gently tucked her cutting shears in her apron and headed toward her front door, as if to say, "Come on if you want, but I'm going in anyway."

"Are you sure?" Nick called behind her. "I don't want to interrupt anything you might have already planned. Maybe another time would be better?"

Mrs. Hortensis stopped and turned. "First thing you need to learn, young man, is to not be so hesitant. I invited you. I know what my schedule is. Don't be afraid to take advantage of opportunities as they come along. Life is too short."

Nick bristled a little at her abrupt and to-the-point comments. "Okay," he said, deciding to accept her challenge. "Thank you, Mrs. Hortensis." He opened the front gate and headed up the walkway.

Mrs. Hortensis had already reached the front door, entered, and without looking back left it open for him to follow.

NEW INSIGHT

Maybe he wasn't modeling the right behavior by doing as much work as he could himself, like jumping into complete work that others were responsible for.

Harmony ... that's the atmosphere he wished to create at work.

Managing a group and gardening are similar. You just need to understand some basic principles. Principles learned while becoming a better gardener can also assist in becoming a better manager.

Don't be afraid to take advantage of opportunities as they come along. Life is too short.

THE MAGICAL GARDEN

"It is only through awareness and curiosity that we discover the unknown."

—Paul Allman

October 10

Nick had never been inside Mrs. Hortensis's home before and had always wondered what was behind the imposing intricately carved oak and stained-glass front door. As he hurried up the walkway to catch Mrs. Hortensis, Nick made it clear he couldn't stay long.

Her house was built in the craftsman style from the early 1900s. It was large with a wonderful wraparound porch, adorned with handcrafted chairs and hanging flower baskets. The exterior walls were covered with green copper patina shingles, and windows carefully detailed in molding represented an exposed peg-style framing. Every detail conveyed a quality of workmanship illustrating an era where the time to finish a task was not measured by how long one took, but how exact and complete the results were.

It was clear that those who worked on this house had taken immense pride in what they were creating. To them, the house must have represented not just a home but also a functional work of art.

Several Chagall-like stained-glass windows sat on each side of the entry door, and above that was an odd shaped balcony on what appeared to be a second floor where the roof came to a peak. The rain gutters, made of copper, were strategically incorporated into the design of the house and gently blended with the resplendent wood and stone pillars flanking the steps leading to the front door. The entranceway was a portico supporting purple blooming wisterias. The base of the old wisteria plants look liked

16

braided rope with the individual stems intricately woven together creating the appearance of several large trunks. The way the plants had intertwined with the pillars and portico indicated to Nick they had been there a long time, laying down a carpet of purple petals to welcome visitors.

As Nick entered her home, he was immediately struck by the feeling that the garden had followed them inside. Just off the entrance alcove was the living room with high ceilings, massive exposed oak beams, and ornate cherry panels that gave the feeling of being surrounded by nature. Pots of plants were neatly arranged in several corners, and a few hung in baskets from the ceiling.

Mrs. Hortensis interrupted Nick's visual exploration: "What kind of tea do you like?"

"Oh, I don't know … regular tea will do just fine."

"Nonsense," she said clearly and directly, getting Nick's attention, "have you ever had fresh tea from the garden?"

"No, I thought it came from tea bags."

"Well, you're about to discover that some of the best tea can be found right in your own backyard. Let's go and gather some leaves."

As they made their way through her house, Nick noticed photographs from all over the world lining the hallway leading to the kitchen. He thought he recognized Mrs. Hortensis in several, but the pictures had obviously been taken a long time ago.

They entered her backyard off a small porch, and Nick's sense of urgency to get on with the rest of the day disappeared as he took a deep breath in amazement. If the front yard seemed incredible, the green sculptured intricate environment behind her house was *magical*. The garden seemed endless, and Nick quickly realized the property was even bigger than he had originally thought. It was an oasis of ferns, camellias, leucospermums, geraniums, bromeliads, proteas, hydrangeas, grevilleas, and rose bushes, with no boundary fences in sight. It gave the appearance of extending forever! There was a small pond with a large frog fountain in the center, surrounded by herringbone brick and stone pathways leading from the porch only to disappear into the bushes.

"Wow, I've never seen anything like this before. You have such a variety of plants … and colors."

"Colors determine the mood of your garden," Mrs. Hortensis said. "Sometimes they can add complexity and at other times be subtle and simple. Did you know there are over a hundred shades of green?"

Nick just nodded his head and followed her down the stone pathway. Each turn seemed to bring a new flora surprise. "I don't know what insight you have on management, but it's clear you really understand gardening."

Mrs. Hortensis just smiled. "Do you like mint tea?"

"Yeah, that sounds good."

Mrs. Hortensis reached into her well-worn garden apron pocket and pulled out a pair of shears as old as the apron itself. Slowly she bent down and began to cut bunches of leaves. "Smell these," she said, handing Nick a small assemblage. "The first one is spearmint, the next apple mint, and the last is peppermint."

"They all look the same to me."

"Oh, there are differences once you know what to look for," Mrs. Hortensis said with a twinkle in her eye.

And what a difference there was! Nick recognized the spearmint, but the peppermint possessed a deep and unusually fresh fragrance, and the apple mint was mild with just a slight hint of fruit. "I didn't know there were three types of mints."

"Well, there are a lot more than three. Over there is pineapple mint, and one of my favorites, licorice mint. It is also called *Agastache foeniculum*. Over there, bergamot. Down there I have …"

"Whoa! How do you know all this? How do you know the difference? They all look the same!"

Mrs. Hortensis just smiled. "We'll put a little corsican mint in our tea as well." She reached down to cut some ground cover. "And just one big leaf of mint-scented geranium, also known as *pelargonium tomentosum*."

Nick thought she was a bit punctilious using unnecessary fancy names, but each leaf she handed him to smell was different in its own way, yet still similar. Some offered soft velvety leaves and others had small compact blades growing in tight bunches.

"Let me show you a special plant." Mrs. Hortensis led Nick along the path to the far side of the garden, past so many different plants that the journey seemed to take forever.

Mrs. Hortensis stopped and picked a leaf from a medium-sized shrub. "Smell this. We'll just put one of these in our tea for extra flavor."

"Wow, that smells like crushed lemons, or like …" Nick hesitated for a moment, " like fresh lemon pie. How can all that smell come from just one leaf?"

"Its common name is Lemon Verbena, or *Aloysia triphylla*. This plant helps remind me that the greatest gift of the garden is the restoration of the five senses. It's hard to outdo nature when it comes to creating wonderful surprises. Let's go inside and wash these off."

As they walked back to the house, Nick noticed plants he missed the first time. "I wish I could just go out and pick plants like this from my backyard. Are you sure they're safe?"

"Do you mean unsafe because of the pollution in the air or because they are possibly harmful?"

"I wasn't thinking about issues with pollution. I was wondering how you know that the plants aren't toxic. Isn't it safer to buy things already properly packaged?"

Mrs. Hortensis raised her eyebrow. "We could spend all afternoon talking about how native cultures around the world have used different parts of natural plants to make teas, medicines, and lotions. They use plants growing in their backyard to provide food, medicinal cures, fragrance, and—"

"I meant how do you know they're *safe*," Nick interrupted, trying to clarify his point. "I'm sure not all plants are harmless."

"There are over 250,000 species of plants on the earth." Mrs. Hortensis glanced at Nick. "Did you know that 99 percent of all flowering plants have never been tested for their medicinal properties and that a quarter of all prescribed medicines are derived from just forty plants? It's a complex and exciting natural world when you start to try to understand it. A friend and excellent scientist once explained to me that the simplest yeast cell has the same number of components as a Boeing jetliner."

"Do you have a background as a scientist?"

"Yes," Mrs. Hortensis answered. "I worked for over thirty-five years with some of the best scientists in the country and struggled through some interesting situations." She hesitated for a moment, focusing again on Nick. "Enough about me, let's talk about the challenges you're having at work."

Nick began to explain the details of the project as they walked back to the house and into the kitchen.

Mrs. Hortensis turned on the flame below an ornate copper teakettle and then gently washed the plants, carefully removing extra stems and dead leaves. She placed the collection in a unique-shaped ceramic teapot and added hot water from the kettle.

Mrs. Hortensis looked at Nick as she stirred the mixture with a wooden spoon. "Tell me about the people you work with."

Nick began to smell the mint fragrance in the room as he watched the steam escape from the teapot. "There's not that much to tell. Some have been with the organization over thirty years. They're affectionately referred to as the 'short-timers' because some are so close to retirement. They are quite a bunch of characters."

"Really? In what way?"

"John is the worst. He explains, in detail, why every idea the group thinks up *won't* work. He says things like 'We've tried that before,' 'Management won't back us on that,' or 'I'm not paid to do that.' Thank goodness for Celeste. She is willing to try anything, enthusiastic and excited all the time. Several people have complained on occasion about her lack of follow-through, but she never says no and always has a new idea when we need one. Then there is Mary. She is such a flibbertigibbet it's almost impossible to have any kind of serious conversation with her."

Mrs. Hortensis looked at Nick intently.

"There are several in the group who are so new I don't even know their names. One, called Cindy, really keeps to herself and is perfectly happy to sit all day in her office and do her own thing."

"Tell me more about John," Mrs. Hortensis prompted.

"He's actually quite skilled, thorough, and detailed at what he does. He's probably a little too particular about making things perfect, but he does catch the little things that others seem to miss."

"What are his hobbies, needs, goals, and interests?"

Nick thought for a moment and then said, "I have no idea. There is so much work to do that we don't have time to just sit around and talk. In the last two weeks, the group has only been together once, and that was for an emergency crisis meeting I called because we missed another deadline."

"Well, that's where we can start." Mrs. Hortensis raised her index finger and pointed into the air. "You asked earlier how gardening and management could be similar. To be a successful gardener you have to know your plants. Do they need sun, shade, water, special soil, or protection from the wind? The more you know about your plants and how to provide the right environment for them, the more likely they will thrive."

"I apologize for being so blunt—you obviously understand a great deal about plants—but I don't think what happens to plants really applies to management. People can talk to you about their needs. Plants can't talk."

"Oh, but they do," she corrected him. "When plants need more light, they stretch toward the sun. If they need water they droop and beg. It's not what they actually 'say'; it's what you become aware of through observation. The same is true with people. It's more important to be aware of what people *don't* say than what they do say. If you aren't working at understanding the hidden messages in individual and group communication, then you are neglecting to *really* listen," Mrs. Hortensis explained. "Neglect is a problem that can be easily cured."

"I think I'm fairly observant." Nick noticed that Mrs. Hortensis's eyes were focused directly at him.

"As you begin to pay attention to the hidden messages in communication you become more aware of the important needs of the individuals and the group," Mrs. Hortensis shared. "At one time, I had a team with thirty scientists reporting to me."

"That's impressive."

"Early on in my career I assumed that people would come to me with their issues. Some did, and during our conversations, I responded to the words I heard, not to the intent behind the message. I didn't take time to understand the reason underlying the communication. For example, I had an employee once complain to me about the lack of structure in our work environment. I took it personally and began trying to figure out how I could diagram the overall project better and develop procedures to guide activities. Later I learned all she meant was she didn't know when was the appropriate time to contact me about issues. I responded to what I *heard*, not to the *intent* the person had behind the message."

"That takes a lot of effort. If I did that I would spend my whole day figuring out what people were trying to say. When would I get *my* work done?" Nick quipped, letting his voice run up at the end.

"Like I said, neglect is a problem that can be easily cured since it is something that *you* own. Making it a priority, well, that's a different challenge."

Nick took another sip of tea, amazed at its fresh and unique flavor. "I've never really looked at it like that before. Become more aware of how a person is communicating and that might indicate specific needs?"

"Yes. However, just being aware of specific needs is only part of the picture. For a group of individuals to be a *team* they need a bigger vision, a larger purpose. Think of it in gardening terms. The more agreed upon and understood a garden's purpose, the more likely the garden will come together as a whole."

"What you just said makes no sense," Nick blurted out. "What do you mean 'a purpose'? A garden is full of things you plant. The purpose of a bush or a tree is to grow."

Mrs. Hortensis paused a moment and then said calmly, "You first have to determine what type of garden you want. Will it be formal or informal? Will it contain drought-tolerant, native plants, annuals, or perennials? Do you want a garden that attracts songbirds or one that bears fruit? Do you plan to have one that requires daily maintenance or that is fairly self-sustaining?"

"Sounds like a lot of decisions. What does that have to do with purpose?"

"These decisions," Mrs. Hortensis took a breath, "will determine the choices you make later on. Most gardens, like most organizations, are a combination of different elements grouped together for a common purpose. When faced with challenging choices the fundamental question for any staff member should be: what is the purpose of the group?"

Nick thought for a moment. "Everyone knows their assignment on the project. My *purpose* is to make sure everything gets completed on time."

"I asked, 'what is the purpose of your group?' I don't mean in terms of a specific project task, but as a *team*. What part of the organization's mission and vision do they support? How are the organization's values demonstrated and reinforced by the group?"

"You seem to know a lot about working in organizations."

"I learned the hard way. I spent many years managing in a scientific industry where female managers were the exception, not the rule. An important early lesson I learned was that for a group to stay focused, they needed to understand their purpose."

"Purpose and values," Nick said, scratching his head. "Well, I think most people know what they are supposed to do. As far as general purpose or values written down anywhere, our group doesn't have anything like that. I'm not even sure the overall company has anything like that."

"Then, that's where you start."

"You mean write them down? Isn't that going backward? We have a project to do. We have deadlines! Wouldn't defining our values and purpose at this stage be a waste of time?"

"Nonsense," said Mrs. Hortensis. "I think you need to slow down and learn to walk in a planned direction, or you'll continue running in circles. I have two suggestions for you. First, I want you to get to know your group members. I don't mean pry into their lives, but take interest in them as people. Spend time with each one over coffee or during a small break, and just have a conversation with them that is not work-related. Start by sharing your hobbies and interests, but let them do most of the talking."

"What does that have to do with them doing their jobs?" Nick tried his best not to sound agitated.

"Develop a relationship with your workers and learn whether or not you have the right people assigned to the right tasks. You might have some great workers right in front of you who have never been noticed or encouraged to contribute."

Nick shrugged his shoulders.

"You see, Nick, the individuals you manage are a group now. I can put any number of people in a room and they immediately become a group. But, what you want is a *team*. The difference between a group and a team is how individuals work together."

Mrs. Hortensis now had Nick's full attention. The question he was pondering just last night was how to create a team.

"Second, once you get to know your team members, I want you to document your group's purpose and identify your internal customers."

"What and who are internal customers?"

"They are the individuals who are dependent on your team's output. They can be members of the team or individuals in other departments. Ask them for feedback on how you are doing as a team. Ask simple questions, such as whether there is anything that you can do to make their jobs easier."

"I don't know about that," Nick said skeptically. "People would start requesting management to perform all kinds of unnecessary activities. I would only be making more work for myself."

"No, I'm not suggesting that you should do their jobs for them, but through conversations and awareness, try to discover what steps the team could adjust or change that would make activities easier for your internal customers."

"I wish some of the other groups we work with could hear that. I have made so many suggestions, but other departments won't change," Nick complained.

"Nick, stay focused on the things *you* can change and impact and less on what others should do. There are so many aspects of organizational processes that become fixed and inefficient simply because internal customers never ask each other how things could be improved. They just assume that activities have always been done a certain way and never question why they should change. Those who do make suggestions but don't get support join the ranks of the learned hopeless."

23

"The learned what?" Nick questioned.

Mrs. Hortensis grinned. "The learned hopeless. What individuals *learn* is things won't change. Then they lose *hope* that things will ever be different. People just give up and accept work as it is, even though they know it could be better. Over time, many become bitter and frustrated with their jobs and blame the organization for not doing something about it."

Nick nodded in agreement. "That sounds like John. In fact, I think I have several of those in my group."

"Part of the everyday purpose of your team members should be to review frustrations and discover what can be improved. By examining discontent, team members should discover who their internal customers are. Frustrations then become opportunities to improve, and internal customer satisfaction a measure of the group's success."

"A common purpose and internal customers," Nick said reflectively.

"Yes, how well your team supports the overall mission and vision while working with internal customers is demonstrated in what I call 'interdependency handshakes.' Find the missing handshakes and you will solve most of your issues." Mrs. Hortensis placed her hands together simulating a handshake. "I wasn't always just a gardener, you know," Mrs. Hortensis said with a twinkle in her eye. "But it was through gardening that I found the answers to some complex leadership challenges."

"It sure sounds like you know what you are talking about," Nick said. "Could we get together again and talk more about my issues?"

"Yes, but start with the few suggestions I gave you," Mrs. Hortensis said, again raising her hand and pointing her finger in the air.

"How do I do that?" Nick asked, looking for an easy answer.

"You'll figure it out by asking your group to help. Nick, you have to lead, but let them create a mission statement. Something that creates pride, focuses energy, and establishes a sense of accomplishment. It should be memorable, idealistic, clarify a purpose, define direction, and encourage commitment. Why don't we get together in a couple weeks and you can share how things worked out," Mrs. Hortensis offered.

On the jog back home, Nick thought about Mrs. Hortensis's suggestions and decided there was nothing to lose by trying them. He had his doubts that anything would really change because of some gardening metaphors, but the tea was something to remember.

Once home, Nick decided to write down the interesting things they discussed.

WHERE TO START

Successful managers:

- *know the people around them.*

- *spend time understanding needs and interests. The more they know and understand how to provide support, the more likely they will establish the right environment.*

Through observation, they:

- *become aware of what people don't say.*

- *understand the hidden messages in individual and group communication.*

- *really listen. They take time to understand the reason and intent underlying the communication.*

- *become aware of the important needs of individuals and the group.*

PURPOSE

Just being aware of specific needs is only part of the picture. For a group of individuals to be a team, they need to understand a common vision, a larger purpose.

- *Fundamental question: what is the purpose of the team? (not in terms of a specific task, but as a team)*

- *Are the organization's mission, values, and vision supported?*

- *How are they demonstrated and reinforced by the team?*

The difference between a group and a team is:

- *an understood common purpose.*

- *a clear understanding of how individuals can work together to achieve it.*

THE "LEARNED HOPELESS"

Understanding how one contributes to the team purpose prevents individuals from joining the ranks of the "learned hopeless." Individuals who learn things won't change and lose hope that they ever will. People just give up and accept things as they are, even though they know it could be better. Over time, many become bitter and frustrated with their jobs and blame the organization for not doing something to resolve their issues.

STEPS TOWARD BUILDING A TEAM

First: *Take time to get to know your group members.*

- *Take interest in them as people.*

- *Spend time with each one and have a conversation that is not work-related.*

- *Discover whether or not you have the right people assigned to the right tasks based on group needs and individual interests.*

Second: *Identify your internal customers and document your group's purpose.*

- *Who is dependent on your team's output?*

- *Ask for feedback from them on how the team is doing.*

- *Ask simple questions, such as "Is there anything that I can do to make your job easier?"*

- *Create a mission statement for the group. It should be memorable, be idealistic, clarify a purpose, define direction, and encourage commitment.*

- *Discover interdependency handshakes. Find the missing handshakes, and you will solve most of your issues.*

Third: *Review frustrations, and discover what can be improved.*

- *Examine discontent.*

- *Allow time for conversations to discover what steps the team could change that would make activities easier for your internal customers.*

Frustrations should be viewed as opportunities for improvement and internal customer satisfaction a measure of the team's success.

Cultivating Commitment

"My green thumb came only as a result of the mistakes I made while learning to see things from the plant's point of view."

—H. Fred Ale

November 1

The day after visiting Mrs. Hortensis, Nick purchased two plants in four-inch pots, one spearmint and one peppermint. When he inquired about licorice mint, no one in the gardening section of the home-improvement store had any idea what he was talking about and recommended he try a local nursery. He wished he had written down the fancy name Mrs. Hortensis used to help find it.

Several weeks elapsed and the plants were looking utterly maltreated. Nick's project was showing signs of improvement, some deadlines were being met, but Nick was still spending long hours at work. Coming home late one evening, Nick spotted the drooping plants by the back door and realized he had neglected to water them. He remembered what Mrs. Hortensis had said, that thirsty plants would droop and beg for water. He tried soaking them, but nothing seemed to help. Disappointed, he finally threw them away.

Despite the setback with the plants, Nick had made some interesting progress with the project and was eager to talk to Mrs. Hortensis about it.

As usual, Mrs. Hortensis was out working in her garden. She spotted Nick coming and waved.

"Your garden looks as good as ever," Nick said as he approached. "You know, since our last meeting, I can't stop thinking about that tea you made for me."

Mrs. Hortensis smiled. "Let's have another cup and you can fill me in on how things are going at work."

They entered the house and walked down the hallway toward the backyard. This time Nick stopped as they were passing the row of photographs. "Is that a photo of you?"

"Yes, that's me with Dorothy Hodgkin."

"Dorothy Hodgkin?" Nick asked, shrugging his shoulders. "Who's that?"

"She received the Nobel Prize in Chemistry in 1964. By using X-ray diffraction techniques, she modeled vitamin B-12 and insulin structures, which, among other things, allowed pharmaceutical companies to produce human-type insulin. I was her main project leader."

"Yes, I remember you said you worked with some of the best scientists in the world."

Mrs. Hortensis pointed at the photograph. "We met first at Oxford, and later, after I completed my PhD from Cambridge, we taught and worked together."

Nick noticed her diplomas on the wall. "Is that your real name, Doctrina Hortensis?"

Mrs. Hortensis smiled. "It is. I shortened Doctrina to Trina. My father made up the name Doctrina. I was born in Cairo, where he was working in the Egyptian Education Service. He used to say, 'Some day you are going to be either a *doct*or or a balle*rina*.'" Mrs. Hortensis motioned with her arms and legs in a simulated plié.

"I guess that explains the pictures of the pyramids at Giza."

"Yes, if you look closely you can see me on the top of Cheops. There, in the middle. Inside each pyramid is an elaborate narrow stair system, which leads you to the center and the sarcophagus. When I emerged from the center I continued along the side to the edge of the pyramid and climbed to the top."

"You are full of surprises." Nick pointed at another photograph. "Is that the queen of England?"

"Yes, that's Dr. Hodgkin next to her. She became the first woman since Florence Nightingale to be called by the queen into the Order of Merit, Britain's highest royal order. There I am on the left."

"So, was it working with Dr. Hodgkin where you learned about managing project groups?"

"Yes, but it was a process that evolved over time. At first, I thought I needed to be a friend to everyone. When tensions arose, that didn't work. Most of the members of the group I led were men, and many of them were much older than me. You can imagine how a group of technical scientists, all experts in their respective fields, might have treated a young woman in the 1950s—especially one who was trying to manage them. There were those who took advantage of my good nature. Tasks weren't getting done. So I became a task master, a no-nonsense person. Other tensions arose in the group, and a couple of key technicians left. I remember Dorothy calling me into the office one day to tell me we couldn't lose technicians at the rate we were. Dorothy said there were rumors that I was a 'difficult' person to work for. I soon realized that style of management didn't work either."

"So what did you do?"

"Dorothy recommended I do some reading on how to run a group. There wasn't a great deal of information available in the 1950s about managing group dynamics, but I started with B. Jowett's translation of *Aristotle's Politics* and Machiavelli's *The Prince*. The 1937 edition of *The Encyclopedia of Social Sciences* gave me some direction, but the new work in 1954 by Peter Drucker, *The Practice of Management,* was especially helpful. Through his book, I realized that there were several important styles in maintaining group relationships and managing task accomplishments. I also learned that these different styles contributed to constructive team dynamics. The challenge was to determine which style to use and when."

"When you invited me for tea several weeks ago, I wondered if the experiences you had would apply in my type of business," Nick shared.

"Principles of good management are universal. They include planning, organizing, directing, and monitoring living things to accomplish a determined objective. That is why the metaphor of gardening applies perfectly. The skills necessary to grow a living plant and keep it healthy are no different than those required to establish a successful team. In fact, some gardening terms are even used in everyday work life, such as 'transplanting individuals,' 'weeding out the bad,' and 'enjoying the fruits of our labor.' I began to wonder if some of the basic elements of management could be better understood by examining nature. After that realization, the next step was how to utilize any new understandings. I began to examine my management style while gardening and started contemplating what to do about it."

"I wonder how others view my style," Nick wondered out loud.

Mrs. Hortensis shrugged her shoulders. "One of the lessons I discovered is that your style should create a balance within your group. Just like in nature, there is a continuous struggle to develop equilibrium. Your approach should assist the group in speaking the appropriate language at the right time to create the right harmony."

"Language?" Nick looked perplexed.

"In all organizations and groups there are basically two different languages spoken. Under tension, some people react and listen better to one language than the other."

"You mean languages like Spanish, Greek, or Swahili?" Nick asked, puzzled.

"No, those are cultural languages," Mrs. Hortensis said. "I meant behavioral languages."

"Do you mean verbal and nonverbal behavior?"

"That is part of it. More specifically, some people under tension focus on the language of *tasks*: schedules, budgets, goals, objectives, rules, and procedures. Others focus on the language of *people*: support, fears, respect, motivation, inspiration and relationships. Once you begin to understand the subtleties of team dynamics, it becomes clear how the different languages can create conflict and misunderstandings. There were some great research studies done by Blanchard and Hersey in the sixties regarding the situational aspects of management. Knowing how to adjust can determine your leadership effectiveness."

"You just lost me." Nick shook his head.

"To effectively speak different languages implies that a leader knows when and how to shift direction so they are better understood. Many times that requires leaders to go where they are not comfortable going."

"Are you saying a leader has to be uncomfortable to lead?"

"Let's use the analogy of a person trying to speak a foreign language. At first you feel uncomfortable, but ironically those you are communicating with can relax because you are speaking their language. To make *them* feel at ease you had to go where *you* are not."

"I must be a great leader because I am not comfortable with my group at all," Nick said with a grin.

Mrs. Hortensis raised an eyebrow. "That is the beginning, sensing that something needs to change. To me, the true challenge of leadership is knowing how and when to go where you are not comfortable so the team can follow. In other words, at times, you have to manage, and at other times you have to lead."

"Is there a difference?" Nick leaned in closer trying to catch every word.

"Managers deal with the complexity of tasks—schedules, roles, budgets, issues, crises, team dynamics, etc. Leaders deal with the complexity of change—vision, motivation, inspiration, strategic thought, resistance interventions, and so on."

"Hmm," Nick said. "So if I want to change my group I have to go where I'm not comfortable. That's interesting. I wasn't very comfortable interacting with my group the way you suggested when we last met."

"How did that work out?" Mrs. Hortensis turned to walk into the backyard.

Nick followed her. "Well, I called the group together and proposed we identify our internal customers and define our group's purpose. I must admit, I was a bit skeptical. There was some resistance, mostly from John and Bill, but a few volunteered to create something. Ed had just transferred into our group and said he would like to coordinate the effort. Celeste and Cindy agreed to help. Ed is deceptively high-energy and intense for his medium build, impatient at times, but quick minded and very creative. When they finished, the whole group got together and looked at their results. After making some minor changes, from John of course, we posted the final version in our work area."

"Did they post a mission statement?"

"I don't know if you can really call it a mission statement. It is the group's definition of what we do and the way things could be if we worked more effectively together."

"That's a mission statement and vision statement," Mrs. Hortensis responded with a slight grin. "A mission statement explains what a group does, and a vision statement indicates what the group could become."

"So, the group did well?"

She nodded.

"They also posted a quote by Benjamin Disraeli over the door, next to the clock, leading out of our area: *The secret to success is consistency of purpose.*"

"That's a nice quote. Did you acknowledge them for a job well done?" Mrs. Hortensis asked.

"The group said it was gratifying to get together for a noncrisis activity."

"Sometimes that can be one of the hidden benefits of creating a mission statement," Mrs. Hortensis responded, noting Nick didn't answer her question directly. "Just getting together to discuss the team's objectives without specific tasks in mind."

"We decided to make time for more frequent get-togethers and now meet each Monday and Friday. We review tasks and status project activities. The surprising result is that people who didn't talk that much before have started to communicate. I've overheard comments like 'Well, it's part of our group statement' and 'How does that help our internal customers?' There's even talk about creating some kind of award for those best supporting our posted purpose. At least the group is talking."

Mrs. Hortensis nodded. "Margaret Wheatley, in *Leadership and the New Science*, likens a vision statement to an intentional force field that permeates the organization like a wave of energy."

Nick agreed. "She's right. The communication has given the group a new focus and keeps them from dwelling on the tensions."

"Knowing what's expected of you certainly helps in reducing frustrations," Mrs. Hortensis added.

"Originally, I thought I would meet with only a few team members, but it turned out to be so interesting I made time to talk with them all. I started with John. I had no idea that outside of work he was part of a volunteer group that designed and constructed parade floats. I mean, they are gigantic, have mechanical movement, and must meet strict regulations. He showed me photographs of his floats. They won awards six out of the last eight years, including the President's Award for best entry. Now, when John and I are at odds I say, 'If you were working on a float, John, how would you make this feasible?' John fires back, 'Is there an award in it for me?' John's become more comfortable kidding around, and tensions have certainly eased. I even found out that Cindy was in charge of productivity improvement efforts at her last company. She has become quite a resource for us all. It turns out the time she spent alone was used to diagram a flowchart of our processes."

Surrounded by all the beautiful plants in the garden, Nick once again became aware of a calm, relaxing feeling coming over him. "This is what I hope our group finally achieves, a cohesive harmony," he said, pointing and sweeping his hand across the view of the garden. "But I still don't completely understand what all this has to do with management."

"Well, as I was saying earlier," Mrs. Hortensis explained, "about the time some of the photographs on the wall were taken, I was struggling with managing my group. A coworker suggested I take up gardening to 'relax and get my mind off of things.' One of the first books I read was *Herbal Teas, Tisanes and Lotions: A guide to growing and using herbs for making stimulating tonics, soothing infusions and refreshing drinks,* by Ceres. Next, I read Teeguarden's *Chinese Tonic Herbs* and the American Horticultural Society's *Encyclopedia of Gardening.*

"Do you think I can find copies of those books?" Nick asked eagerly, turning to face Mrs. Hortensis.

"I'm sure you can," she said. "I discovered some interesting people through my reading. For example, Gertrude Jekyll. She was an influential British garden designer, writer, and artist who created over four hundred gardens in the UK, Europe, and the USA. She wrote thousands of articles on gardening for *Country Life, The Garden,* and other magazines. She had a wide circle of friends, like John Ruskin, William Morris, and watercolorist Hercules Brabazon. In 1889 she was introduced to the prominent architect Edwin Lutyens and asked him to design a house to fit into her garden."

"That's an interesting approach, a house to *fit in* the garden," Nick said, half-questioning what he heard.

"It was. The resulting masterpiece, *Munstead Wood,* is still in existence in Godalming, Surrey, England, and is now a museum. Jekyll and Lutyens continued to work together and became the standard and definitive word on garden designs."

"I'll bet she would be impressed with your garden," Nick said.

"Thank you, Nick." Mrs. Hortensis stopped and turned toward him, clearly appreciating his acknowledgment. "I learned a lot from her books, which were often illustrated by her own photographs and drawings. She focused on the principles of planting, color grouping, and overall garden design. Everything was based upon her own experiences, and she paid meticulous attention to detail. Jekyll made regular use of a wide range of plants, including her favorites: lavenders, bush and rambler roses, clematis, lilies, hollyhocks, and stachys with clipped yew ferns. Scent was important to her, as were the massing and sweeping of color. Textures and shapes were carefully considered and harmonized. All plants she selected were directly related to the constraints and opportunities of the overall design and space available.

"Was she the creator of garden design?" Nick wondered out loud.

"Not exactly. The theory of garden design can be traced to Vitruvius from the first century BC. Although he had little to say specifically about the design of outdoor space, he put forward the influential theory that the objectives for all design projects were: commodity (*utilitas*), firmness (*firmitas*), and delight (*venustas*). Good principles to keep in mind when you are managing any project."

"How do you remember all that?" Nick asked with enthusiasm. "It's as if you were reading from a book!"

"Nick, the knowledge I've gained about gardening helped to initiate a turning point for me. I started experimenting with that small piece there ..." Mrs. Hortensis pointed to an area just beside the back porch. "And, as I experimented in the garden I began to think. People at work would say things like 'We need to *plant the right seed*, *dig up* issues, *weed out* the bad ideas, get to the *root* cause of things, or *cultivate* trust.' As I reviewed the concepts of gardening and how they could help me in managing others, I began to see the relationship between the skills required in taking a plant from a small seed to a hardy self-sustaining bush, and the *growing* and *cultivating* of work groups. I started contemplating what were the key elements of the growth process, and I wondered how I could introduce them to the team."

"I don't understand," Nick said with a light laughter. "You mean you thought of planting your workers in the garden!"

Mrs. Hortensis laughed. "Well, some of them actually needed, or deserved, just that! I was thinking about basic concepts, like expectations. You don't put a seed in the ground and expect it to start flowering the next day. Even if you are planting a mature plant, it needs time to acclimate. I began by reviewing my expectations to see if they were realistic. Then, I reviewed the degree of understanding of those expectations by team members and the level of support I was giving them."

"What did you use for measurements? How did you know people got it?"

"With growing plants you measure success by size, strength of stem, quantity of fruit, etc. The model I developed focused on commitment. Let's go back inside and I'll show you."

As they sat down at the kitchen table Mrs. Hortensis handed Nick a piece of paper and a pencil.

"Draw a large rectangle near the top of the page and print the word COMMITMENT inside it. Now draw four pillars supporting the box. Each pillar represents a key element of commitment: clarity, skills, influence, and acknowledgment."

"The first pillar is the culmination of my thoughts about expectations. I labeled it CLARITY. You have to be clear in your expectations, and they have to be clearly understood by those for whom you have expectations. Without clarity, responsibilities, outcomes, priorities, and resource requirements are confusing or undefined."

Nick wrote the word "clarity" in the first pillar.

"Once things were clear, I began to look at the team's capabilities. Can a team do the things expected of them? Individual fears can play a big part with this pillar. At first, I believed that if people couldn't perform an assigned task, they would tell me up front. I was wrong.

"The challenge for me became making sure individuals were capable to meet the expectations before I turned them loose. I had to do this carefully so as not to be perceived as a micromanager. Usually just a few simple deliverables or activities to be completed right away gave me enough feedback. I labeled this pillar SKILLS."

Again, Nick filled in the second pillar with the word "skills." It was beginning to make sense.

"The first two pillars fundamentally deal with the task side of group dynamics. But I began to wonder about the people side. What's motivating the desire for someone to commit to anything?"

Nick sat thoughtfully and then said, "Earlier you said in any group there are two languages being spoken."

"That's right, Nick, and the first two pillars of the commitment model focus on *task* language. The next two focus on *people* language. One of the keys to understanding people language lies in the theories of motivation. Within every individual there are extrinsic and intrinsic motivational forces at work. Take Celeste in your group, the one with the toys on her desk, who you see as disorganized. Her extrinsic motivation might be the need to create a workplace with more fun and a less serious environment, but her intrinsic motivational force centers on being liked, belonging to the group, and influencing its direction."

"That's interesting," Nick said.

"Depending on the situation and the individuals, one motivational force may require more emphasis than the other.

"You mean either an extrinsic force or an intrinsic force?"

"Yes. Typical extrinsic forces can be either fear or reward. Fear is experienced through failure, consequences of poor performance, and personal disappointment. Reward is realized through promotions, praise, and more control over work activities. Both of these need to be continually reinforced to obtain the same effect. Intrinsic forces, on the other hand, touch the inner meaning of the individual. Forces, like a sense of contribution, belonging, and being needed."

"So intrinsic forces are better?" Nick suggested.

"Not necessarily better, but more powerfully focused on the very core of motivation. Some of the key intrinsic motivational forces create a sense of pride and ownership. When individuals sense they control the outcomes, tasks are viewed as *their* goal not just the group's goal, and the level of commitment goes up. I labeled this pillar INFLUENCE. Simple interactions or brainstorming sessions can set a group in the right direction. With influence, people begin to take responsibility for success. Finally, the most complicated of the pillars is ACKNOWLEDGMENT."

"What about communication?" Nick blurted out. "That comes up all the time in our group. Lack of communication."

"Well, commitment is built on a solid foundation of communication, that's true. Poor and inadequate communication was stated in John Kotter's book, *Leading Change*, as the chief reason for failed change efforts. I'm suggesting something more specific. Something a person in charge can consciously focus on."

"How about discipline?" Nick asked, punching his fist into his hand. "You have to show them you're the boss or they'll take advantage of you."

"True, you need to establish yourself as the point of authority, but effective discipline isn't about demonstrating to someone that you're the boss. It's about directing and changing behaviors."

"So much for my guesses." Nick smiled as he held up his hands in defeat.

"Those were good guesses. *Acknowledgment* incorporates many of the principles of communication and discipline. Simply put, it means giving meaningful feedback. Suppose your boss called you on the phone and curtly said, "Nick, I need you to come to my office right away! What would you think? Most people would conclude they are in trouble and begin looking for someone or something they could blame. In fact, in some organizations a measure of success is that you haven't been called into the boss's office. No news is good news. When the boss does call, most people expect to hear negative feedback. Many bosses establish this expectation because they don't balance the negative input with the positive. They stay focused on resolving the issue the group is experiencing instead of implementing ideas that could prevent the issue in the first place. For example, instead of focusing on what is wrong, remind people about what is going right and encourage them to do more of it."

"There sure is a lot of negative feedback when I interact with my boss. I wonder at times if he really knows what I actually do." Nick furrowed his brow.

"Do you know how many employees complain about their boss not knowing what they do? Or being able to actually *do* what they do! The pillar of acknowledgment lets people know they are appreciated for what they are doing and that someone is aware they are doing it. Find what is going right, instead of what is going wrong in the organization, and encourage people to do more of it. Model the appropriate behavior, and encourage and reinforce others by giving positive feedback instead of negative."

"You mean I shouldn't tell people when they are doing a bad job?" Nick looked confused."

"No, by all means you should. You are responsible for the safety of your team members and ultimately the success of the group. You must be on the lookout for, and point out, behavior that is going to create issues. However, over time our focus begins to zero in on the things going wrong or the things that could go wrong. We tend not to look for the good things or what is going right, because there is no risk involved. After a while, many just search for and respond to the bad. I don't mean you shouldn't give negative feedback, but try to make sure the criticism is received as constructive."

"So I should just focus on the positive?" Nick asked, still perplexed.

"No, but sandwich the negative input between some positive input. You've heard the saying, 'If you can't say something nice, then don't say anything at all.' If you are pointing out the negative behavior, then find something positive as well."

"I get it. Grow flowering plants on either side of a cactus." Nick smiled.

"That's a good gardening analogy, Nick." Mrs. Hortensis winked.

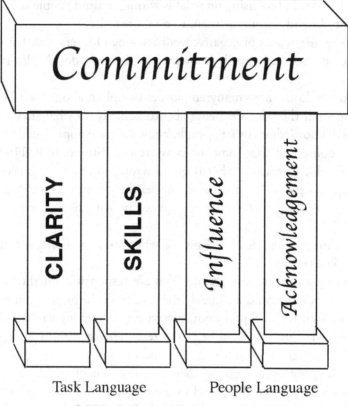

Task Language   People Language

© PTS – Professional Training Services, 1998

"The commitment model became one of my essential tools for measuring group performance. If I observed a lack of enthusiasm, missed deadlines, poor work habits, and unsupportive behavior by the team, I checked each pillar of my model. Have I made expectations clear? Clear from the other's perspective, not just mine? Have we documented the expectations and routinely discussed and adjusted them? Do individuals possess the skills needed to actually perform their assigned tasks? Have the desired behaviors or outcomes been demonstrated at least once? Do I have the right people in the right positions? If not, how am I developing the necessary skills to allow them to succeed? Have I coached and trained where necessary?"

Nick was now writing as fast as he could.

"Nick, do you remember the grapevines on the arbor near the back fence? They would produce grapes if I didn't train them, but I have more grapes and they are easier to access because I support and train them."

Nick was still writing as Mrs. Hortensis continued. "When examining group commitment, first I review the task side of the model. Then I shift my focus to the people side of the issues. Have I allowed the owners to influence the outcome and to take responsibility for success? Finally, have I taken the time to be aware of what my team members are actually doing? Have I consciously reminded them of successes, reinforced what is going right, and encouraged others to do the same?

"But it is important to ensure that there remains a balance. Too much acknowledgment can become superficial and appear phony, and too little acknowledgment and infrequent praise seems artificial and forced. It's much like watering plants. Give them too much water and you will eventually kill them, and where there is not enough water they will slowly die. Remember, just like plants, it's not what people are telling you, it's what you notice by being more aware."

Nick turned over the page on which he was taking notes. He hoped he'd captured what Mrs. Hortensis had shared.

Mrs. Hortensis continued, "So after I check the pillars, I plan what I need to do to rebalance the group. Sometimes I run through the pillars with the whole group and sometimes just with selected individuals."

"Let's go back to what you said a minute ago," Nick said eagerly. "What do you mean by the right people being in the right job?"

"We were about to get some leaves for tea until I made us come back inside," Mrs. Hortensis remarked, getting up from the table slowly. "Let's go back to the garden. I can answer your question better by showing you."

Nick folded the paper carefully and put it in his back pocket. He was glad he had taken notes for later review.

Key points Nick captured:

GROUP DYNAMICS

Two important elements impact group dynamics:

1. *interactive behavior (language) used to maintain group relationships*

2. *interactive behavior (language) used to manage task accomplishments*

Each is necessary and contributes to a successful team. The challenge is to determine which language to focus on and when.

HOW DOES YOUR STYLE BALANCE THE GROUP?

Your interactive style should create a balance within your group. Your approach should assist the group in speaking the appropriate language at the right time to create an interactive harmony.

Under tension, some people react and listen better to one language than another.

Language of people: *support, addressing fears, respect, and meaningful relationships.*

Language of tasks: *schedules, budgets, goals, objectives, rules, and procedures.*

There are several styles important in maintaining group relationships and managing task accomplishments. Each style contributes to constructive team dynamics. The challenge is to determine which style to use and when.

Principles of good management are universal. They include planning, organizing, directing, and monitoring living things to accomplish a determined objective.

TRUE CHALLENGE OF LEADERSHIP

"Flexing" your behavior. The biggest challenge in leadership is knowing how and when to adjust your interaction and manage your behavior in ways you are not comfortable. This will encourage team members to follow your direction.

Managers deal with the complexity of tasks— schedules, roles, budgets, issues, crises, team dynamics, etc.

Leaders deal with the complexity of change— vision, motivation, strategic thought, resistance interventions, and so on.

MISSION, VISION, AND VALUES

Has your group discussed its mission? Where do they fit in the organizational big picture? Sometimes the hidden benefit of creating a mission statement is just getting key individuals or team members together to discuss the team's objectives without specific tasks in mind.

COMMITMENT

You can never work hard enough at making your expectations clear, and a visible measurement of that is commitment. Use the commitment model to examine the understanding of expectations:

First: *Review the task (clarity and skills) side of the model.*

Clarity: *You have to be clear in your expectations, and they have to be clearly understood by those of whom you have expectations.*

Skills: *Make sure individuals are capable of meeting the expectations before turning them loose. Allow for more interaction and feedback, and review early on.*

Second: *Focus on the people (influence and acknowledgment) side of the issues.*

Influence: *When individuals sense they control the outcomes, tasks are viewed as their goal, not just the group's goal. The level of commitment goes up. Sandwich the negative input between some positive input.*

Acknowledgment: *Give meaningful and timely feedback so people know that you appreciate what they are doing and that you are aware that they are doing it. Find what is going right instead of what is going wrong in the organization, and encourage people to do more of it*

MOTIVATIONAL FORCES

Extrinsic forces *come from outside the individual and can be either fear- or reward-based. Since they originate outside the individual, they need to be continually reinforced to obtain the same effect.*

Fear *is experienced as failure, consequences of poor performance, and personal disappointment.*

Reward *is realized as promotions, praise, and more control over work activities.*

Intrinsic forces, *on the other hand, come from within and touch the inner meaning of the individual. These forces are a sense of contribution, belonging, being needed, and pride in their work. This is the real source of motivational force.*

DIVERSITY

"Well-managed environments can support the unusual and the different."

—Paul Allman

November 1

As Mrs. Hortensis and Nick walked through the garden, she pointed out various plants. "Do you see the different micro climates?"

"What do you mean by micro climates?" Nick looked perplexed. "Isolated areas with different temperatures?"

"Sort of. Do you see those big trees off to the left, and then the other area over there in the sunlight?" Mrs. Hortensis swept her arm from side to side, pointing to the back of the garden.

"Yeah."

"Each one is a completely different growing climate," Mrs. Hortensis explained. "Some plants prefer the deep shade of a mountain forest. Others love the desert sun."

"In this yard, there is that much of a difference, from the mountains to the desert?" Nick asked in disbelief.

"There is." Mrs. Hortensis smiled. "Each neighborhood and every yard has physical characteristics that produce slightly varying climates. Some plants may flourish on the east side of the home but die or do poorly on the west. South-facing hillsides collect warmth, and are especially good places for growing selected tropical plants. North-facing hillsides are cooler and thus good for camellias and azaleas."

"That much difference?" Nick shook his head. "There sure are a lot of rules to gardening."

"There are many factors that can determine the success of your garden, but there are only a few key conditions that are important to all plants—such as the amount of sunlight, the type of soil, the amount of watering, and the temperature zone. In addition, some require extra fertilizer, proper air circulation, shelter, and special care. The challenge is to be sure to put the right plant in the right environment. Some plants are extremely durable, like jade plants, and can survive in a wide variety of conditions, while others do well only in a specific climate, like clematis. Plants that struggle in one location may thrive in another. For example, you may find your gardenias blooming for the first time when you move them from a sunny spot with sandy soil to a slightly shaded area with acidic soil."

"How do you determine which plant or people go where?"

"That is a gardener's, as well as a manager's, true challenge. When we were in the kitchen, you asked about having the right people in the right jobs. Just as you place plants in the best environment for them to thrive, you must also put team members in a position where they can succeed and provide them with challenges they can survive. That's why it is so important to become more aware, so you can move individuals toward the appropriate challenges. The commitment model helped me become more aware. It is not a perfect science. At times you can put plants and people in the right conditions and for some reason it may not work out."

"I know," Nick confessed. "After our first meeting, I purchased some mint plants for making tea. They lasted about two weeks and then died. A special deadline came up, and I got busy, left them in the sun, and forgot to water them."

"You're not the first to experience that problem. Good gardening starts with good planning. If you plant carrots in January you'll never have to worry about eating carrots," Mrs. Hortensis quipped. "You shouldn't buy plants until you have a place to put them and a plan to take care of them. The same thing happens to people in organizations all the time. I am amazed at how many new employees are hired without proper orientation or introduction programs. Some employees never fully understand the real purpose of their group and their role in supporting it. They just go about doing their tasks and complaining about issues others should resolve as they voice the lack of support they are receiving. Never focusing on the 'handshakes of interdependability.'"

"Can you explain interdependability handshakes again?" Nick asked with enthusiasm.

"It is understanding who is dependent on the outcome of your actions. In a manufacturing world it would be the next person after you in an assembly line. They can't do their job if you haven't done yours. And how they do their job is *dependent* upon how you do yours. I use a handshake metaphor because it is about seeing others as internal customers and reaching out to them with greetings and support. Drastic improvements in an organization can come about simply by identifying missing handshakes."

"You mean people should go around and shake hands all day," Nick said with a glint in his eye.

"Your humor needs some work." Mrs. Hortensis rolled her eyes. "Even though at times shaking hands would be a good idea, it is a metaphor for how we all relate to each other while accomplishing a common purpose. Remember when we talked about the purpose of your group? It is a simple principle, which even applies to good gardening. What is the purpose of the garden? Do you want to make a barrier to hide a wall or the view of a neighbor's house? Do you want to create a sitting area for reading and relaxation? Or do you want to grow things, which you can harvest like a vegetable garden? Until you understand this simple principle, you will be buying plants only to have them die while you are trying to decide what to do with them. Or they will die when you dig them up to move them because you have found a better spot. Without understanding common purpose, your group's successes will slow, while the actual activity level goes up. Management gets involved in resolving situations to keep things moving and can easily get caught up in the time trap of day-to-day issues."

"I spend a lot of my time doing what others are supposed to do." Nick nodded in agreement.

"As the group leader, your time would be better spent on strategic issues, planning, reinforcing interdependability, and focusing on long-term success."

"The problem is my group can't do things on their own. They usually need me to get involved." Nick was sure that without him nothing would be accomplished.

Mrs. Hortensis ignored his comment. "When I was designing this garden, I searched for plants that had the right color or variation in the leaves to create the right mood. I viewed the garden like an artist views a painting but evaluated the plants like a scientist. Plants were chosen based on the known requirements of the area they would be planted in. These turned out to be good principles to remember when I was hiring people for my group. When hiring individuals, you must wear the hat of both a manager and a leader. They are not synonymous. As a manager, you know what you want to accomplish and create a team with the right capabilities, placing individuals in the right spot to be challenged. You manage by establishing measurements to carefully evaluate the group's objectives, tasks, and progress. A good manager has to analyze and understand processes, create productive redundancy where necessary, and establish documented deliverables for key tasks. As a leader, you need to step back and look at the big picture, become a visionary, and remind individuals of their purpose. Spend time looking ahead to see what are the potential obstacles, and address them before they become an issue. The ongoing balance between being a manager and leader is ultimately what determines your success."

"Whatever you did in this garden has really worked." Nick liked the overgrown look to her garden. Everywhere he turned there were combinations and groupings of bergenia, epimedium, foxglove, geraniums, hostas, and lilies that captured the eye. For the first time, he began to notice the different colored leaves and their unique shapes. Some were striped and variegated; others had bright red underside and silver-gray speckled tops. *So many different shades of green*, Nick thought. *Light green, dark green, yellow green, blue green ...*

Mrs. Hortensis interrupted his thoughts. "What you see is *my* particular style. There are many different gardening styles, just like leadership styles, and you have to select the one that fits you best and supports your purpose. However, there are basic principles common to all styles."

"Do you have a name for your gardening style?"

"I call it controlled chaos." Mrs. Hortensis smiled. "Henry David Thoreau said, 'Gardening is civil and social, but it wants the vigor and freedom of the forest and the outlaw.' For me, a garden should have a natural feel, but it should also look like it has been tamed. It took me years to figure out how to bring those same principles to the workplace. My garden may look free-form, but each plant has a role to play. The fruitless mulberry trees provide a canopy for shade-loving plants, like impatiens, coleus, astibles, and hellebores. They love their shade, and all shade-loving plants thrive in the company of trees. The plants on the hillside provide erosion control, while those along the back of the garden hide the fence. See that mint-leaf eucalyptus tree over there?" Mrs. Hortensis pointed back toward the far side of the garden. "It hides the roof line of the house next door."

Nick moved around looking to see the adjacent houses, but all he could see were plants.

"It helps to create the illusion that there is nothing else here but this garden and that we are in our own world," Mrs. Hortensis said. "In the corporate world, that's known as being focused. Along the back wall of the garden, to the right, I encouraged a thick green drapery of trailing ivy to turn a boundary wall into an asset, instead of allowing it to restrict my vision. It allows us to feel that we are peering into the dim margins of an enchanted forest, with the promise of a more exotic garden beyond."

Nick easily imagined that there wasn't a building within miles and that he was alone with nature.

"I also designed this garden to have something different occurring throughout the year. Every month a different flower, different scent, and different fruit make an appearance. I started by planting a few blooming perennials, like camellias, roses, geraniums, and pyracantha, until eventually, by the end of the year, I had covered each month. Then I started over again."

"Using the gardening metaphor," Nick said dubiously, "are you suggesting that I should have something to change within my group every month?"

"You've got it," Mrs. Hortensis responded, looking straight at Nick.

"How do you find what to change?" Nick was still trying to grasp the concept.

"To use the garden as an example, I began to notice what plants were blooming in the neighborhood and was astonished to see how many were flowering even in the dead of winter. I took small cuttings, went to the nursery, and bought one or two. In the business world they call this benchmarking or best practices, which means to find those who are successful at doing something and then learn from them. The differences you discover are the things you can change."

"But changing so frequently—doesn't that lead to instability?"

"You don't change everything. In my garden, I discovered how different colored foliage could provide a year-round backdrop to showcase the periodic changes. In an organization, this backdrop becomes the procedural foundation of any group. There is always something beautiful to look at because I used foliage colors to give the garden visual bones. Over there, under the trees, I planted a backdrop of shade-tolerant plants that contrast and accentuate the flowering plants. Here it is the month of November and I have red cestrum flowers framed by limelight green pittosporums and dark-leafed camellias. See all the tiny buds patiently waiting their turn to show off?"

Nick could see the small buds, but he couldn't imagine what the flowers would be like. To him they resembled brussels sprouts. "How is finding plants that bloom in winter a gardening metaphor for management?"

Mrs. Hortensis faced Nick directly. "A good manager is responsible for the development of his or her team members. Even when things are challenging, a good manager takes responsibility for team growth."

"I get it." Nick lit up. "When things are at their worst, like in winter, you find those individuals that are blooming, support them, and develop the others."

"There you have it," Mrs. Hortensis said proudly and then pointed to the east. "Over there, closer to the sunny area, I have cream-colored gardenias, rose pink plumerias, yellow daylilies, and blue nemesias." Pointing south: "There, I have the purple flowers of *Tibouchina urvilleana*, the princess flower, comingling with silver junipers. The challenge is creating a balance. In the garden, there is an ecosystem, while in companies there are organizational systems.

"That's the balance you have been talking about," Nick said, indicating he was starting to understand.

Mrs. Hortensis nodded. "The development of your team members is usually put on the back burner under crisis situations. Since many organizations frequently work in a reactive mode, teams eventually become unbalanced. This is especially true when you only measure success in short-term increments."

Nick's head was beginning to swim with all the information.

"Lastly," Mrs. Hortensis said, "I wanted to create a low-maintenance garden that was water wise, so I chose drought-tolerant native plants, like salvia, elderberries, poppies, and hollybushes. There on the hillside I planted *Romneya coulteri*, great for soil erosion control and, as a bonus, all summer long I can enjoy its sweetly scented, poppylike white flowers highlighted with fluffy gold stamens."

"I thought plants only bloomed in the spring and summer."

"Nonsense," Mrs. Hortensis said, gesturing to the back door to move their conversation inside. "With a little research, you can find something unique to bloom every month. Certain areas of the world allow more varieties to grow and gardening is less challenging. We happen to live in one of those climates. But you know, they grow tomatoes all year long in

Iceland using thermal fields near the volcanoes. You just have to have the imagination and take the initiative."

"With so many varieties available, how did you decide what you wanted to plant?" Nick asked with amazement.

Mrs. Hortensis led Nick into the kitchen, turned on the kettle, and began washing the tea leaves she had picked earlier.

"Remember what we said about understanding your purpose? After you are clear about your purpose, it becomes a matter of basic decision making. Making good decisions isn't that hard. If you find yourself struggling, stop and remind yourself of your purpose. Write the purpose down as a goal statement and include what the expected outcome will be, how it will be measured, and when and by whom it will be accomplished."

"Understanding the purpose of your group seems to be rather important," Nick said.

"Yes," Mrs. Hortensis concurred. "Usually, the reason certain decisions are so difficult to make is that we have lost sight of our objective. Once that becomes clear again, it is simply a matter of making a list of those items that impact the objective. This can help us compare and categorize a great deal of information. For example, identify criteria such as 'like to have' or 'must have,' including things 'we can change' and things 'we can't change.'"

"Where do I get the criteria?"

"Focus on developing a list of criteria based upon your purpose. This criteria list should address the elements impacting your objective. For example, in the case of a garden it would be the type of soil, the amount of sunlight, the weather conditions, and the purpose of the plant. The list could also include availability, cost, and hardiness, but the simpler you can make the criteria list, the easier the decision will be."

"Is that how you decided which plants to put in your garden?" Nick looked amazed.

"While building this garden, I made a list of plants that possessed characteristics that fit my criteria. Eventually, I narrowed the list down based on what was easiest to find. I labeled some of the criteria as 'must-have,' meaning at a minimum the solution *must have* these characteristics. Other characteristics were labeled 'nice to have.' After that, it becomes a simple matter of choice."

"So how would that apply in a business situation?"

"There may be certain quality standards or functional requirements in a project that cannot be negotiated. They are the *must-have* criteria. Things that you add to improve the project are usually *nice to have*. For example, you *must have* a car for transportation. It would be *nice to have* one with the latest stereo, plush leather seats, and a convertible. But you can easily meet the *must-have* criteria—car for transportation—without the *nice to have* criteria. The challenge can be understanding whether something is really a must-have or not."

"That made your selection and purchasing of plants easier?" Nick suggested.

"People make selections based on facts but tend to purchase based on emotions. To make sure things kept moving forward, I defined each step as an action that needed to be taken. Instead of just listing plants, I indicated whether I would buy a plant, or research plants, among other things."

"You make it sound so easy."

"It's not easy. The choices you make as a gardener or manager can be complex and confusing. Even with criteria lists, some individuals hesitate to make a choice. They want to be sure and make the right choice. I struggled with that myself early on in my career. Sometimes I would wait and analyze a situation looking for the 'perfect' solution, when all I needed was to just do something, take action, anything to move forward. It was an important lesson for me to learn. Taking steps sometimes would lead me in a new unseen direction. Many times, looking back, I was amazed at how far I had actually progressed. I discovered new directions and accomplished results just because I acted. Have you ever heard the phrase 'beginning is the most important step of whatever you do'? I've used that lesson many times with people, especially if it involved a major step in a project. People tend to overanalyze things. This causes them to freeze themselves, as well as the group, through the inability to take action. While analysis is important, sometimes taking action and allowing the possibilities through movement to take over is important as well. Many times, all you have to do is assist someone to identify the next action in the process and describe that step in terms of the activity needed. The criteria list can help you know when it is time to start responding. If you have met the essential criteria, then begin planning movement toward an outcome."

"I take action on the things I need to do on the project," Nick said proudly, "but sometimes I do put off confronting the people-based issues in my group."

"One of the hidden secrets of successful people is that they have developed the discipline to do things they don't want to do, when they need to do them. They focus on the outcome—move on and through the obstacles. In group dynamics, it is important to see visible action so adjustments can be made and feedback given, allowing progress to be measurable."

Over tea, Nick began to discover more about Mrs. Hortensis as she revealed details from her earlier life. She turned out to be quite a fascinating person. She had spent the early part of her life traveling all over the world and could speak four languages by the time she was his age! Nick felt as though his life had been sheltered and lacking adventure.

Mrs. Hortensis marveled, while traveling through Africa, how local inhabitants used plants growing naturally around them for all kinds of practical purposes. They chewed the peelu bark to keep their gums healthy and teeth white. Certain plants would relax them, and others could stimulate them. Only a simple walk to the side of the road was necessary to find a solution to a skin rash or an upset stomach. "The garden is the poor man's apothecary," Mrs. Hortensis quoted an old German proverb.

She recalled that while living in Sweden, a stroll in the forest became a virtual supermarket of food. Smältron, blueberries, lingonberries, birch bark, and chanterelles all had a purpose. She shared how the people there valued and appreciated nature.

It was during her travels that she had made a promise to herself that someday she would learn more about the plants around her and their uses. It wasn't until she was struggling with managing her work group that she began to explore the world of gardening and begin that journey.

When Nick arrived back home, he made sure he sat down and wrote in his journal what he had learned. He also wrote down a few assignments he wanted to try.

Journal Entries: Meeting November 1

MANAGER'S TRUE CHALLENGE: right people in the right job

- *Each employee understands the real purpose of the team and his or her role in supporting it.*

- *The focus is on handshakes of interdependability. Encourage discussions.*

- *Hire individuals who will accept the responsibility for their development even when things are challenging. Take responsibility for team growth.*

As a **Manager:**

- *Develop a structure for what you want to accomplish.*

- *Analyze and understand processes, create productive redundancy where necessary, and establish documented deliverables for key tasks.*

- *Create a team with the right capabilities.*

- *Direct performance.*

As a **Leader:**

- *Look at the big picture, and become visionary.*

- *Remind group members of their purpose.*

- *Lead them through stages of change. As a leader, your time is better spent on strategic issues, planning, reinforcing interdependability, and focusing on long-term success.*

INTERDEPENDABILITY HANDSHAKES:

Know who is dependent on the outcome of your actions.

The handshake metaphor is about seeing others as internal customers and reaching out to them with proactive interaction and support. Drastic improvements can be accomplished simply by identifying missing handshakes.

BASIC DECISION MAKING

Identify criteria:

- *"Like to have" or "Must have"*

- *Things "we can change" and things "we can't change."*

- *List of criteria based upon your purpose and elements impacting objectives, individuals, and organizations.*

- *Use words that convey action when describing identified criteria to encourage taking the next step.*

A criteria list can assist in taking action and moving forward. Taking steps will sometimes lead to a necessary and new unseen direction.

One of the hidden secrets of successful people is that they have developed the discipline to do things they don't want to do, when they need to do them. They focus on the outcome and move on and through the obstacles.

In group dynamics, it is important to see visible action so that adjustments can be made and feedback given, allowing progress to be measurable.

ASSIGNMENTS:

Meet one-on-one with employees.

- *Review expectations.*
- *Verify skill sets.*
- *Create brainstorming opportunities.*
- *Acknowledge performance (compliment the routine and unexpected).*

Plan strategic time.

Review how decisions are being made within the group.

Let others stretch without the fear of failure. Don't set up individuals to fail, but encourage them to stretch.

ADMIRING THOSE THAT FLOWER

"One of the worst mistakes you can make as a gardener is to think you're in charge."

—Janet Gillespie

December

The next month at work was a whirlwind of excitement for Nick. He had carefully redrawn the four pillars on a piece of cardboard and constructed a sign for his desk. He reviewed each person in his group using the commitment model and found that several didn't know how to perform the tasks they were assigned. Both Bill and Jim were operating under the wrong guidelines. Jim had actually obtained a project description sheet that was three years old. To address this, Nick implemented a cross-training program. First, Nick had Ed standardize the project guidelines. Then Nick met with all the employees to determined who had the appropriate skill sets and assigned individuals to work together following the new guidelines. After a few weeks, Nick sensed that some of the prior tensions in the group were easing. He surmised that some of the old issues could have been attributed to either people covering up what they didn't know or people's frustration over filling in for the experience others lacked.

Nick also conducted two focus group sessions designed to gather input regarding key upcoming steps on the project. He was surprised at some of the feedback. Two employees in accounting, who typically did the minimum required, began discussing tasks in a way that would temporarily increase their workload. Originally, Nick thought that some of the goals might be too challenging, but to his surprise, the whole group was now discussing how the goals could be expanded. Nick could sense a new pride and willingness, not only to contribute, but in taking on new challenges with enthusiasm.

Acknowledgment, the last pillar of the commitment model, had the biggest impact on Nick. He spent extra time reflecting on how he had interacted with group members and realized he fell into the category of a "negative reinforcer." He had reprimanded the group for not working together as a team, demanded that Bill stop talking so loud, and asked John to stop being so critical. Nick could think of several examples of negative feedback he had given but came up short when he tried to think of positive feedback. He hadn't intended to interact with people that way, but there was so much to do and so many pressing deadlines to meet that he found himself putting out fire after fire. In the past, when Nick would walk into a room a hush would come over the conversation as if the people were waiting for something negative to happen. When he would summon someone to his office, you could see sympathy in the eyes of the others as if they expected the worst.

Nick had believed that this approach kept the group on schedule and Mr. Morgan off of his back. There were team members who were doing a good job, but he figured they didn't need recognition from him.

He thought about the acknowledgment pillar for days. How could he implement steps that would remind him to focus on the good that was going on in his group? It was so easy to get caught up in the day-to-day problems and overlook the daily successes.

While out shopping for a new DVD combo recorder/player, the salesperson gave Nick a business card. On the back of the card was a note thanking him for visiting the store and offering a 10 percent discount if he came back and shopped there again. Nick decided he could create something similar as a way to acknowledge individuals for a job well done. He would make a card he could hand out. Each card would be worth a nominal amount to give it some actual value.

Nick went to his boss to get support for the idea.

"Do you know how much something like that could cost?" Mr. Morgan's jaw tightened. "I'm not going to the president with an idea like that. We are looking at reducing expenses, not trying to implement lamebrain ideas on how to spend more money. If I were going to the president with a request, I would be asking for more staff to get us out of the mess we are in. The demand has doubled for support efforts in the last year and the number of employees has gone down. I heard a rumor that Fred is thinking about leaving."

Fred was one of the other managers who worked for Nick's boss and was responsible for implementing project designs during the construction phase. Fred was sensible and practical, and Nick liked working with him.

"Fred's the only really capable person we have around here," Mr. Morgan went on. "I would offer him more money to stay if I could, rather than wasting it on what you're asking for. We are all working long hours and not going anywhere. Besides, your people all have jobs, and that should be thanks enough. Now, where are the status reports on your project?"

Nick got the message. Anything short of focusing on what was needed to get the job done right now was not going to be supported.

Nick too had heard rumors that Fred was leaving. Fred talked with Nick several times during the last month about an offer from another company, and while he liked working here, most of the time it was too chaotic. He doubted that the climate would change soon. "It's the way things are done around here. No one really appreciates or even notices the work you're doing," Fred had said to Nick. "It's the culture. You can't change that."

Fred was good at what he did and could go anywhere he wanted. *If only we could keep Fred and get rid of a few of the others,* Nick thought to himself. *Why is it always the good ones who want to leave?*

When Nick reflected on the demotivating phrases his boss barked out from time to time, it was no wonder Fred wanted to move on:

"Focus on the status of your project right *now.* Looking into the future is idle daydreaming!"

"You know what needs to get done. Just do it."

"All of this feel-good stuff about work is poppycock. That's why it's called 'work' and not 'play'!"

"You're not supposed to like work, you're just supposed to do it."

"Work is a four-letter word, and don't forget it."

"I didn't hire you to babysit you. If you don't want to work, there are plenty of people I can find to do your job."

Despite the poor reception from his boss, Nick continued to give the acknowledgment pillar some thought. He remembered what Mrs. Hortensis had said about support from the top. You may not get it but the people who work for you see you as the top. Start with what you can control and impact, and begin to model the preferred behavior.

A few days later, Nick decided to try one more time with his boss. This time, Nick asked if it would be okay if he funded rewards out of his own pocket.

"Go ahead and waste your money," Mr. Morgan said with a chuckle. "Don't come to me asking for a raise if you're willing to give your money away on those kinds of foolish things!"

Nick had a plan. He gathered a few of the key players in his group and explained the basic idea to them: "I would like to create a way of acknowledging people and the work they do. It won't be worth much money, but it's the thought and recognition that matters. The goal is to focus on what is going right and encourage people to do more of it. We need an identity for this recognition system, something that can explain the purpose of what we are doing, yet is simple to remember."

Cindy suggested that they create an acronym. "Make a word from the first letter of the other words and together they could spell out something catchy."

Nick had the group write down a few key words that summarized what acknowledgment meant to them. Then Nick wrote the words on a flip chart. "This will be the vocabulary to build our name from," he told the group.

The group spent several hours coming up with names and had fun doing it together. Some of the names they created were funny, some way off base, and others just plain ridiculous. Several were okay, but the group was having trouble deciding on a final name. They had narrowed the list down to three:

1. BEST: **B**uilding **E**xcellence through **S**ervice and **T**eamwork.
2. HANDSHAKES: **H**elping **A**nd **N**urturing **D**ependability through **S**ervices **H**andled with **A**ccurate, **K**nowledgeable **E**xperience and **S**upport.
3. STAR: **S**trategic **T**asks **A**ccomplished through meaningful **R**elationships.

There were things they liked about them all. "HANDSHAKES really says what we're trying to do, but it's too long," Ed said.

"BEST sounds too traditional, but I like the positive side about being the 'best,'" Cindy added. Most agreed that STAR was the best name, but the words in the acronym didn't seem to flow well.

Nick remembered reading an article about a voting technique to facilitate group decisions. He shared it with his group. "Achieving true group consensus is difficult and time-consuming. All the same, it's important to air the different points of view and find a way to move forward. Each side during a discussion should have a chance to share and clarify their perspective. After all have been heard, a simple majority vote wins. There were many ways to make group decisions: unilateral decisions, decisions by authority, majority rule, among others.

"A focus discussion followed by a vote allows a group to hear from the minority and give them a chance to 'convince' the group to change. If the majority doesn't change after hearing from those in opposition, then the group moves forward. Before starting the process there must be an agreement that members will support group decisions even if they don't all agree."

Everyone nodded.

After a brief discussion, the group agreed on STAR if they could modify a few of the words. After several rounds of voting they finally arrived at a name: **STAR:** *Successful Teamwork through Acknowledged Results.*

Nick knew Ed had a creative design background and asked if he would make something about the size of a normal business card. Ed came up with a shooting star for a logo. In the middle of the card was STAR in big letters with the acronym spelled out underneath. Along each edge of the card was written *Acknowledgment for Excellent Service.*

Once the group approved the card, Nick had them printed and called the staff together to explain the concept.

"This card will be worth one dollar," Nick said, showing it to everyone. "You can buy something from the company store and I will reimburse you for the number of cards turned in with the receipt. I know it's not a lot of money, but it's my way of acknowledging some of the great work that is going on."

Nick passed one of the cards around so everyone could have a closer look.

"There are several ways you can earn one of these cards. One is by recommending that I acknowledge someone for doing their job well—an individual who is making things easier for our internal customers. Staff members who are going out of their way to create a handshake of interdependability should be rewarded. Both the person making the recommendation and the individual being acknowledged will receive a card. I will also become more aware of those contributing to our success and acknowledge them on the spot with a card. You can also submit ideas for improvements and I will give you a card, just for making suggestions."

"You mean any suggestion?" John skeptically challenged.

"Yes, John, *any* suggestion. What I'm hoping is that we find ideas that will improve our processes and discover and improve areas where there are missing handshakes between those we should be supporting." Nick scanned the room. "Have any of you been frustrated doing your jobs?"

There was silence, and Nick wondered if he had asked an inappropriate question. Finally, a few individuals raised their hands as they looked around at the others.

"Nonsense. All of you should have raised your hands," Nick said, raising his. "Where there is frustration there are opportunities. It might be as simple as becoming more aware of the big picture and why we do the things we do. More importantly, it might mean that you know a different way to approach a task but feel the organization won't change, so you don't bother bringing it up. When you get like this, you join the ranks of the learned hopeless. You think management won't change, nobody will listen to your idea, and so you just keep doing things the same way, even though you know there's a better solution. You grow more and more frustrated with what you think are obvious things to fix."

There were a few smiles in the group, and several nodded.

"Here is a simple form you can fill out and leave outside my office." Nick waved a sheet of paper in the air. "I have a special tray set aside just for improvement ideas and recommendations."

Several weeks went by and no one had stopped by to recommend anyone for acknowledgment, and only a few suggestions had been received. Nick handed out a total of seven cards the first month, and none had come back to be redeemed.

Most of the suggestions submitted were of a personal nature: more cream for the coffee, more salad choices in the cafeteria, introduce casual Friday—that sort of thing.

The only work-related idea came from Cindy about standardizing how the company tracked project tasks. In her last job she had used simplified Gantt charts to track assignments, monitor responsibilities, establish measurable deliverables, and identify areas of impact. She also implemented a color-coding and prioritization system to help her stay organized. She wondered if the team would want to use the tools. Nick jumped on the idea and asked Cindy to make a presentation to everyone.

She explained her suggestion, and they loved it. Well, most of them did. There were a few who mumbled something about more bureaucracy. Nick started using the Gantt charts to assist in documenting expectations and planning future team activities.

Nick was beginning to demonstrate what Mrs. Hortensis had suggested—model the preferred behavior from the top.

Nick added new entries into his journal:

COMMITMENT REVIEW

Review each person in the group using the commitment model.

- *Establish consistent and up-to-date guidelines.*

- *Discuss interests and opportunities for growth.*

Acknowledgment – focus on going beyond negative reinforcement and become more aware of opportunities every day to give feedback to individuals.

*Develop an **acknowledgment card** as a way of acknowledging people and the work they do, especially when they do it well.*

- *an individual who is making things easier for our internal customers*

- *members who are going out of their way to create handshakes of interdependability*

Standardize the work guidelines, and determine who has the appropriate skill sets. Assign individuals to work together at certain jobs following the new guidelines.

MODEL THE PREFERRED BEHAVIOR

Managers may complain about not getting support from the top of the organization; however, those working for you see you as the top. Start with what you can control and impact, and begin to model the preferred behavior.

GROUP INPUT

Conduct focus group sessions designed to gather input regarding key upcoming work activities.

- Use brainstorming techniques.

- Develop a criteria list for prioritizing and making decisions.

During group interaction it is important to air different points of view and find a way to move forward. Using the facilitated process of interactive voting, if the majority does not change after hearing from those in opposition, then the group supports the decision. Before starting the process, there should be a clear agreement that members will support group decisions even if they don't always agree.

Where there is frustration there are opportunities for improvement. Frustrations can come from individuals who know a different way to approach a task but feel the organization won't change, so they don't bother to bring it up. When team members get like this, they join the ranks of the learned hopeless, and commitment suffers.

ALL THINGS NATURAL

"At the heart of all complex issues lie fundamental truths."

—Paul Allman

December 12

Time had passed quickly since Nick's last visit with Mrs. Hortensis. It was Saturday, and he had gone to the office to finish items needed for Monday's meeting. It was such a beautiful day that by noon Nick left the confines of his office to enjoy what remained of it. He had taken his bicycle and, with spur-of-the-moment spontaneity, cruised by Mrs. Hortensis's house with the hope of encountering her working about the yard.

Mrs. Hortensis was busy trimming her rose bushes, and it appeared she had been planting new bulbs. She didn't see Nick coming as he leaned the bicycle against the fence. Winter had come to the garden, and even though they lived in a mild climate, the lushness of the garden had disappeared. There were still a few flowers blooming and Nick thought, *This truly is a magical garden if flowers are still blooming in December.*

Nick called to her over the fence, "Looks like you're killing your bushes."

Mrs. Hortensis turned. "Nonsense, the roses just need a good pruning."

"Want some help?"

"Sure, I never pass up an invitation for help." She waved him over.

Nick joined her and began picking up some of the cut debris. "Ouch," he exclaimed. "Wow, those thorns are sharp."

"We can complain because rose bushes have thorns, or rejoice because thorn bushes have roses," Mrs. Hortensis quoted. "That was Abraham Lincoln." She pointed to a nearby wheelbarrow. "Help yourself to a pair of gloves over there."

"Ouch," Nick said again pulling a thorn from his hand as he put on the gloves. "Cleaning up this mess is like working with the people in my office. I get surprised by hidden *thorny* issues." Nick laughed, carrying the debris over to a black plastic bag.

"Such as?" Mrs. Hortensis asked, holding open the bag.

"There are still a few individuals in my group who are resistant to doing anything new." Nick became animated. "I used that commitment model on my group and it worked! We started cross-training, I did a couple of focus groups, and we created a visible acknowledgment system."

"Sounds like you've accomplished several good things in a short period of time," Mrs. Hortensis acknowledged. "Those who are not going along with the changes, are they resistant or reluctant?"

"What's the difference?"

"Well, when you implement change, individuals in a group go through some predictable stages, much like this garden. After winter, spring will come, then summer, and finally fall and a harvest. These phases will occur naturally. You have to plan accordingly to go through them. You may not particularly like summer, but it doesn't mean you can skip that season of the year."

Nick removed his gloves and retrieved a piece of paper and pencil from his back pocket. As he sat on the porch, he congratulated himself for putting both items there while he was at work, thinking he might need them if he stopped for a visit.

"I'm ready," Nick said proudly, showing his paper and pencil.

Mrs. Hortensis clapped her hands together as if applauding. "There is nothing that offers as much fascination as the process, problems, promises, and possibilities of major organizational change. William Pasmore, author of *Creating Strategic Change*, expressed it in melodramatic terms:

"'The process of change is mysterious if not miraculous, as dynamic an achievement as any mankind could hope to accomplish. The process is beautiful to behold, enchanting in its shifts between subtlety and storminess, no more predictable in its course than the cutting of a river through granite. Change in human systems remains as thrilling to experience as the wind in a thunderstorm.'"

"You just happened to have that quote in the forefront of your thoughts?" Nick asked, impressed.

"Since our last meeting I've been doing some brushing up." Mrs. Hortensis headed to the porch to sit down. "During the 1980s and 1990s, thousands of corporate hours were spent on reinventing organizations, and many of those change initiatives failed to achieve their objectives. It became clear by the mid-1990s that two-thirds of corporate restructuring efforts did not accomplish planned outcomes. During that time nothing really changed except our understanding of the change process."

Nick had already filled half the front side of the page and started writing smaller.

"What became clearer was that there are four fairly predictable stages to change: denial, resistance, exploration/acceptance, and integration. What stage is your group in now?" Mrs. Hortensis asked.

"I don't know. Are you sure there's not a *blame someone else* stage?" Nick joked.

Mrs. Hortensis laughed. "It is a form of denial. When you are moving individuals through the change process you must first get them out of denial. In the workplace denial is experienced as the willingness to leave things as they are. Individuals say things like 'It's that group's fault, not ours' or 'Things are fine just as they are, why do you want to ruin it?' Many times that's because they're not aware of the need for change. Sometimes the motive for change is difficult to see, especially if it arises from outside the organization, such as a shift in technology or new regulations. Whatever initiates the process during the denial stage, for change to be successful the organization must realize it has to adjust to survive. The awareness that adjustments are needed leads to the next and possibly the most critical stage of change: resistance. Once you lead a group out of denial, they will start focusing on why new ideas *won't* work."

"My group has a lot of that going on," Nick admitted.

Mrs. Hortensis acknowledged his openness with a nod. "One of the real problems with change is that people stubbornly resist it, particularly those who have to change the most. The resistance to change is so common and destructive that it became the main focus of experts, like James O'Toole in his book, *Leading Change*. He found that some of the reasons for resistance were the perceived negative outcomes: fear of more work, lack of communication, and the need to break comfortable but ineffective habits. One of the key lessons learned during this stage of change is how to let go of things that individuals have become comfortable doing. Learning to focus on confronting and adjusting to the new challenges is not an easy step for many people. I discovered that allowing individuals to brainstorm and participate in addressing the changes assisted in managing their initial fears. Marvin Weibord, author of *Discovering Common Ground*, suggested holding *strategic change events*, or as some refer to them, *future search conferences*. At these events you get the individuals impacted by change to discuss and plan the new initiative. People do not resist their own ideas."

"There are individuals in my group, like Bill, who will never change," Nick said, shaking his head.

"Maybe it is not clear to him that change is required. There are some necessary ingredients for successful change to occur. It is important for there to be a clear understanding of the need for change to increase the acceptance for change. There is an old formula for change. Nick, let me borrow your paper." Nick handed Mrs. Hortensis his paper and pencil.

She wrote:

$$C = D + E + S > X$$

C = the probability of *change* being successful
D = *dissatisfaction* with the status quo
E = a clear statement of the desired *end state* after the change
S = concrete first *steps* toward the goal
x = the cost/resistance of change

Mrs. Hortensis explained that people resist until they are convinced of the need for change and then can begin to accept the change efforts. "Noel Tichy, coauthor of *Control Your Destiny or Someone Else Will*, maintains that waking an organization to the need for change is the most emotionally wrenching and terrifying aspect of growth."

"I believe that." Nick picked up his paper and began writing again as Mrs. Hortensis continued explaining the change process.

"In group dynamics, once the majority of the group is able to move through resistance, the group begins moving toward the exploration/acceptance stage. At this point the group has moved through understanding the need for change and expressed their initial concerns with what will be new and what will be lost. This is an important step to reach because the degree of acceptance will determine if the change will stick or not. A buy-in from the majority is a must at this stage."

"Individuals are all over the place in my group," Nick lamented. "We are clearly not in any one particular stage."

"That's because at any given time some people will still be in denial, some will remain actively in resistance, and some will move toward acceptance. That is why organizational change can take so long. Depending on the size of the organization, it can take between three to five years to move the majority through the key stages. Once you reach critical mass, usually around 65 percent, you will experience the tipping point, which begins the movement toward the final stage."

"Five years ... that long?" Nick turned the page over. "There are people in our company who have left because they didn't like our culture. They felt that it could never change."

"Well, then it is time to start." Mrs. Hortensis slowly got up to continue working. "Approach it like you are learning to walk, not like it is a specific race with a finish line. Change at the organizational level is never easy. It depends on the state of the organization, levels of trust, and how effectively the new culture is reinforced and modeled from the top."

"Well, there you go. Those at the top in our company will never change," Nick said adamantly.

"The challenge is to work through each stage until you reach critical mass as a group. In a perfect world, it would be nice to get support from the top of the organization, but you may not get that until you first achieve some measurable results within your group. That doesn't really occur until the final stage. During this stage the initial change efforts become the new fabric of the way things are done, the new culture of the organization."

"That sure would be nice, but it will never happen where I work." Nick was unmoved in his conviction.

"In order to accomplish that final stage your group needs support from above. And, Nick, you are the top! You have to create a clear, compelling vision that demonstrates how individuals' lives will be better. Without an appropriate vision, a transformation effort can easily dissolve into a list of confusing, time-consuming projects. You have to believe that change can take place, find true performance results, and create early wins as you lead the group toward the final stage, even if you don't get the support you want. The final stage of integration is where individuals begin to incorporate the change elements into all aspects of the way they work. They no longer question the new procedures or techniques and openly demonstrate the new way. It is easy to determine if you were successful in achieving this stage, because new employees entering the organization will perform according to the new direction. Why? Because that's the way things are done. They are demonstrating the new culture."

Nick woefully said, "This sure sounds like a lot of effort on my part."

"You are right, it takes a lot of effort through direction and modeling of behavior from the top to make it work. This is where you need to demonstrate leadership. There will be plenty of challenging decisions to be made from the top. For example, implementing new changes may initially slow down output. There will be a great deal of pressure to do things the way they have always been done just to meet an immediate deadline. Like I said, it takes up to five years, if you are lucky."

"Sounds like a lot of work," Nick said again with a heavy sigh.

"Well," Mrs. Hortensis replied, "to put it in gardening language, poor drainage or lack of top soil requires major effort to correct. In a few years, when you see the new flowers, you won't believe you started it all with barren soil."

"But I need some immediate results," Nick pleaded. "I had to go into work today, a Saturday, just to catch up. I feel the majority of the group is starting to move in the right direction. It's just that some of them, like Bill, will never get it."

"He may take longer, but give it time. Look at change using the gardening metaphor. A plant needs time to be truly established. Plants must develop deep roots and become firmly integrated with the soil. Until they complete this process, they are very susceptible to disease and changes in weather conditions. Don't fool yourself that just because a healthy plant is placed in the ground, it will take hold. It needs to be nurtured before it can stand on its own. Have you ever seen those newly planted trees with stakes holding them in place?"

"Yeah, but I don't know—" Nick still wasn't convinced as Mrs. Hortensis cut him off.

"Coincidentally, it seems to take about three years to establish a natural garden. It takes several seasons for the foundation plants to set in before you can finally begin to focus on accent areas. Landscapers can create a garden more quickly, but it is not quite the same. It doesn't look natural."

"I guess my group is somewhere in between the resistance stage and acceptance stage. Or maybe stuck in the weed stage of spring." Nick was able to laugh. "There are some who will never get out of denial. Some are really excited about the changes, and others are clearly against them all. Why is that?"

"It's what I call the 10–20–70 rule of change."

"What?" Nick shot back.

"When you implement change in any work group, 10 percent will immediately embrace the new idea. You might hear them say, 'Why didn't we try this before?' At the same time there are 20 percent who say, 'No way, absolutely not. Things have been just fine the way they are. Why change now?' Nearly twice as many are openly against the change as are for it in the beginning."

"So where's the 70 percent?" Nick asked.

"On the fence waiting to see who wins. The challenge at the beginning is to keep the enthusiastic 10 percent from burning out and to manage the 20 percent to minimize their impact. Focus on the 70 percent because as they shift, so does the culture. Once critical mass, or the tipping point, is reached—65 percent supporting the change efforts—watch how the change takes on a life of its own. If Vilfredo Pareto was right, there will be a certain percentage of your work group that will never become content with the change. Usually as the new process becomes established, they uproot and go elsewhere."

"Kind of like chasing a gopher from your yard to someone else's," Nick quipped, remembering a gopher he did that to on his grandparents' farm. "Who's that Vilfredo guy, again?"

"Pareto. His work is used quite extensively today in charting change and improvement efforts. You may have heard of a Pareto chart?"

"No, never heard of one."

"His theories led to understanding that 80 percent of an individual's work achievements are a result of only 20 percent of their productive effort. Improvement strategies are designed around reducing nonproductive activity."

"That I've heard before. I never knew what it actually meant. Let me see if I got all of this," Nick said, looking up as if about to go into deep thought. "There are four predictable seasons to change: denial, resistance, exploration/acceptance, and integration. It's like the seasons of a garden. Getting a group out of denial is like moving out of winter. Things have been dormant, slow, not much new going on. Then you enter spring, and with it come the unwanted weeds. Some plants do not survive the first few weeks. Then, the bugs come, and you sometimes wonder if it's worth it all. Finally, summer arrives and everything begins to fall in place and you enhance the new growth with additions to your garden. Eventually, you enjoy the fruits of your labor with some of the best vegetables you've ever had. The best part is that you know you created it. However, your work is not done because winter is just around the corner. It's always round the corner. And, before it arrives, you have to plan to make the next slow period the best that it can be, by looking into the future to start preparation for the next spring. Each year the garden gets stronger and stronger." Nick puffed up his chest as he said the last line.

"You are getting the hang of the gardening metaphor," Mrs. Hortensis said with pride.

"Thanks," Nick said, pumping his fist.

"You see," Mrs. Hortensis responded to Nick's excitement, "it doesn't take a great deal of effort to recognize those around you. Sometimes just a simple thank-you can go a long way. Remember, you don't need fancy tools or expensive supplies to grow a beautiful garden."

"You know," Nick said, "I can't believe all I've learned from you."

"We haven't even scratched the surface. I'm glad you have shown an interest. I have been lucky to experience so much, and I'm happy I can share it with someone in your position."

"Does that mean I can come by next week so we can talk more?"

"Next week isn't good for me." Mrs. Hortensis frowned. "I have to undergo some testing for health reasons. Then I have a trip planned to visit my daughter. Besides, there isn't that much going on in the garden. I should be back around the end of February. I could use your help then."

"What kind of tests?" Nick asked, surprised and concerned.

"Just the routine checkups. If you live as long as I have, you are glad they are routine."

"I hope everything turns out all right," Nick said, rushing over to help Mrs. Hortensis lift the bag containing the collected debris. "Let me take that."

"There is no need to worry about me. I'll be just fine. And I can lift the bag. I've been doing this since fifty years before you were born."

"I know, that's why I want to help." Nick gently took the bag out of her hands. "February works for me, but I could come earlier," Nick said, still concerned.

"February will be just fine."

Nick crossed over to a compost heap and emptied the bag. Mrs. Hortensis showed him how to trim the rose bushes, and after several hours Nick finally headed home.

"Good luck with the tests," Nick called out over his shoulder, not knowing what else to say as he left.

"Thanks," Mrs. Hortensis said, waving good-bye.

Once Nick got home he rewrote his notes in his journal as he thought about how he could identify what stage his team was truly in.

New entries in Nick's journal:

CHANGE MANAGEMENT

When you implement change, individuals in a group go through four predictable stages: denial, resistance, exploration/acceptance, and integration.

Denial. In the workplace denial is experienced as the willingness to leave things as they are. Whatever initiates change during the denial stage, for change to be successful, the organization must realize it has to adjust to survive.

Resistance. One of the real problems with change is that people stubbornly resist it, particularly those who have to change the most. Reasons for resistance are: perceived negative outcomes, fear of more work, lack of communication, and the need to break comfortable but ineffective habits. One of the key lessons learned during this stage of change is how to let go of things that individuals have become comfortable doing.

Exploration/Acceptance. At this point the group has moved through understanding the need for change and expressed their initial concerns with what will be new and what will be lost. Acceptance is an important step to reach because the degree of acceptance will determine if the change will stick or not. A buy-in from the majority is a must at this stage.

Integration. Individuals begin to incorporate the change elements into all aspects of the way they work. They no longer question the new procedures or techniques and openly demonstrate the new way. It is easy to determine if you were successful in achieving this stage, because new employees entering the organization will perform according to the new direction.

SIMPLE CHANGE FORMULA

It is important that there is a clear understanding of the need for change, to increase the acceptance for change.

A simple formula for that is: $C = D + E + S > X$
C = *the probability of change being successful*
D = <u>*dissatisfaction*</u> *with the status quo*
E = *a clear statement of the desired* <u>*end state*</u> *after the change*
S = *concrete first* <u>*steps*</u> *toward the goal*
X = *the cost/resistance of change*

10–20–70 RULE OF CHANGE

The hidden challenge is balancing the change effort. When you implement change, 10 percent will immediately embrace the new idea. You might hear them say, "Why didn't we try this before?" At the same time, there are 20 percent who say, "No way, absolutely not. Things have been just fine the way they are. Why change now?" Nearly twice as many are openly against the change as are for it in the beginning. The key is the 70 percent who are on the fence waiting to see who wins.

ASSIGNMENT

Find out what stage the group is in, and manage the group and individuals appropriately.
Develop a tool to identify, measure, and document the team's progress.

NURTURING THE GROWTH OF IDEAS

"You've got to go out on a limb sometimes because that's
where the fruit is."

—Will Rogers

January–February

Nick continued to bestow acknowledgment cards on his staff, and with each
one he sensed his increasing ability to identify opportunities to recognize
performance. The new focus on what was going right had created a more
optimistic perspective. Maybe things could change after all.

He had even presented a card to his boss and noticed the card displayed
on Mr. Morgan's desk, propped up against a pen and pencil set. During
the last two months Nick had disbursed thirty-five cards. In terms of
growth, that meant previously he had overlooked thirty-five chances to
demonstrate his appreciation for staff contributions.

Still, no one had requested to redeem any. Nick had asked several
individuals why. The response he received was that the cards were
gratifying to save. Individuals liked keeping the personalized recognition
comments with the signature on the back. Besides, when they had enough
for something really special they would turn them in.

A handful of individuals had submitted improvement suggestions, but
only a few were really focused on processes. Nick was a little disappointed
in the number and quality of suggestions but realized Mrs. Hortensis
was right. Some would want to make improvement efforts, while others
couldn't be bothered. Mrs. Hortensis had inspired Nick to do some reading
about change management, and he read John Kotter's book, *A Force For
Change: How Leadership Differs from Management*. Nick was aware that
part of the reluctance of being involved was the intuitive sense of how

daunting a simple change could be. Kotter used the following analogy in addressing the point:

> Imagine walking into an office to rearrange things. You move the chair, put a few books on the credenza, hang some pictures. Not much time is spent, since the task is relatively straightforward. Indeed, creating change in any system of independent parts is usually not difficult.
>
> Now imagine going into another office where a series of ropes, big rubber bands, and steel cables connect the objects to one another. First, you have trouble even walking into the room without getting tangled up. You try to move the chair, something you know you can do, but it doesn't budge. Straining harder you do move the chair a few inches, but notice a dozen books have been pulled off the shelf and the sofa moved in a direction you don't like. You slowly move the sofa back to the right spot, which turns out to be incredibly difficult. After a lot of hard work you succeed, but now a lamp is precariously hanging in midair, supported by cable going in one direction and a rope going in another.
>
> People understood the *interconnectivity* of work activities and choose to not start unraveling the process.

Nick knew his group was unwilling to start "moving things around," especially if it might mean more work. They needed to experience some change success. Nick combined several of the suggestions and formed a special team to resolve the issues. *If the group can experience some meaningful results, that might encourage more suggestions,* Nick thought.

The team consisted of the individuals who made the original suggestions and those directly impacted by the recommendations. Their focus would be how to improve the current processes and make tasks more effective and efficient. "Question everything—the rules, policies, customs, norms, management behaviors, and organizational structure. Find the missing handshakes," Nick had said to them.

Nick requested that the team submit a formal report at the conclusion of their efforts. The report needed to identify the current state of the process, future state of the process, specific recommendations, any cost savings, and how changes should be implemented.

As it turns out Cindy was the "improvement specialist" Nick's boss had said and was heavily involved in process change efforts in her previous company. They called it CI, continuous improvement, and she had done a lot of research in the field of quality. She had read many books by leading experts, like Deming, Feigenbaum, Crosby, Drucker, and several others. In her last organization she had been responsible for conducting training sessions and introducing others to some of the important tools of improvement efforts.

Nick wanted to give the new program a title and questioned Cindy, "Why did you call it continuous? Can't we call it PI, process improvement?"

Cindy responded with an analogy. "We all seem to put off cleaning our garages, but when we finally do, we find junk we don't really need. After we are done cleaning there is such a relief. Everything is orderly and in its proper place. We even make a promise to ourselves that we won't let things get that way again. But it doesn't take long before we start bringing things home because we have the extra room, and eventually the garage needs cleaning again. We realize it is inevitable to have a cluttered garage and plan ahead for another cleanup. Continuous improvement." She emphasized the last point. "All processes are bound to drift. Continuous improvement merely keeps the junk from accumulating."

"Okay, I get your point," Nick said, picturing his own garage. "But since it is important to understand that everything is a process, why not call it CPI, continuous process improvement?"

Cindy agreed.

She also recommended each team size be limited. She explained that as a group grows in size, overall participation changes. She had discovered that for maximum participation, and the ability of the group to adjust to absent members, between five and nine was the best number of team participants. To minimize conflict with normal work activities she also recommended that the group only meet for a fifty-minute session once a week. At the end of ten weeks the report Nick requested would be presented and the key people responsible for supporting the future improvement efforts would be invited to attend.

Nick and Cindy agreed to the ten-week format and notified participants when the program was to begin.

As expected there was some resistance to the idea. Most individuals invited felt they had too much to do and there was just no time in the day to waste on sitting around talking about improvement. Nick attended the first few meetings to make sure everyone showed up and even called people to remind them. He got responses like "That's today?" or "I can't make it, Bill is out sick." Nick reiterated the importance and reminded them that attendance at the meetings was part of the overall yearly performance review. By the third meeting Nick didn't have to do that anymore.

The first meeting was a six-hour orientation to the new CPI team process and covered the following topics:

- basic principles of CPI
- establishing a group name
- selecting a team leader
- establishing the essential roles to run effective meetings
- practice with process flowcharting
- working on the team's objective by beginning to flowchart the current state

Cindy volunteered to facilitate the first team. She asked Nick to work with her in drafting an objective statement to help the team stay focused. Nick thought they did a good job outlining the deliverables and overall scope of the effort.

He was surprised during the team's first meeting that they needed clarification about expectations. He remembered how Mrs. Hortensis had stressed that one of the most important tasks of a manager was clarifying expectations. That was something a manager could never spend too much time doing. It turned out that the challenge for the group was accepting that they could really recommend any solution, regardless of the costs. Nick made it clear any recommendation would be accepted. However, the team needed to justify the expenses.

The results of the first team turned out to be surprisingly beneficial and commendable. They recommended an upgrade for one of the central computer servers and the purchasing of a new, faster, more reliable printer. They documented the costs of the new equipment and justified the savings in productivity time. With a new server they could retire three old ones that had been pieced together. That would result in reduction to the annual equipment leasing costs. The new printer would alleviate the complaints and congestions resulting from jamming and individuals accusing each other of dominating the printer. The group had gone as far as to itemize savings on paper, ink, and repair time if the new equipment was purchased. It would mean an initial expense for the group, but within four months there would be a return on the investment.

For days after the presentation, staff members were talking about it, and some wondered if management would really follow through on the recommendations. Cindy had warned Nick that if the momentum was going to continue, it was imperative to visibly demonstrate support for the team's recommendations.

Nick's budget allowed for new capital assets, and surprisingly when he submitted the request, along with the justification itemized by the team, he received a note from his boss acknowledging the thorough analysis.

Nick also requested facilities to put up a bulletin board in the office area, and it became the improvement information space. He posted suggestions, the name and a photo of the first team, the name of team members, and their results. Cindy had helped the group create a team name using the same technique employed for the acknowledgment cards. The name of the first team was POWER—People Organized and Working toward Effective Results.

Nick decided to take personal responsibility for the follow-through with the first team and every week posted an implementation status. When the equipment finally arrived it created a real commotion. Members of the team were congratulated for "pulling off the impossible."

Nick decided that going forward all process teams, as he now dubbed them, would have an appointed sponsor to help with the follow-through. He would make team presentation meetings a special event for team members and order special acknowledgment gifts—special portfolios with the team name embossed on them and a nice pen and pencil set.

The number of suggestions almost doubled the week after the equipment arrived. Some of them were easy to fix, while others focused on missing handshakes and flaws in current processes. Nick and Cindy prioritized the suggestions.

They decided that easily fixed suggestions would be assigned to someone in management, who would resolve the issue and respond to the person making the request. They labeled these "management issues," assigned them, and established that they should be resolved in thirty days.

The other suggestions requiring work activity review, documentation, and changes to current processes were labeled "process issues." They prioritized the process issues and started planning how another process team could be launched. Nick wanted to take advantage of the escalating group interest in what everyone now called CPI, continuous process improvement.

Nick was eager to launch a new process team, but first he wanted to address concerns that came up during the first team's meetings. Cindy had shared with Nick that some of the team members complained about recommendations not being detailed enough. Others disliked the pace of the activities and frequently demanded, "Let's just get it done." Some were quiet and shared their concerns only with Cindy after the meeting and seldom talked during the team get-together. A few came late, volunteered to do tasks, and then promptly forgot about their commitments. They always had clever excuses.

It was all Cindy could do to keep the group together by guiding the team leader in the right direction. Several times Cindy tried to bolster the group by telling them, "Trust the process. It will come together in the end."

Nick asked Cindy if there was anything they could do to assist future teams in establishing more effective interaction. She mentioned training she had received on understanding interpersonal behavior. It had been invaluable for managing different personalities. She recommended that future teams receive training on behavioral styles.

Nick said he would think about it. The last two months had gone by fast. It was the end of February already, and this coming weekend he was helping Mrs. Hortensis with the garden. She might have information and suggestions about different behavioral styles and group dynamics.

Despite a few minor setbacks, things were progressing on the project and Nick was enjoying the visible changes taking place. He was looking forward to working outside in the garden and sharing with Mrs. Hortensis the group's new momentum.

I hope all her medical tests went well, Nick thought to himself as he closed the office door. It was late and he had finally finished his quarterly budget update. Maybe next week he might have time to start completing his overdue performance reviews.

New entries in Nick's journal:

EXPERIENCE SOME "CHANGE" SUCCESS

Suggestions

Develop teams of individuals to work on improvement suggestions.

Assign easily fixable suggestions to management, who will resolve the issue and respond to the person making the request. These are labeled "management issues" and should be resolved within thirty days.

Suggestions requiring work activity review, documentation, and changes to current processes are labeled "process issues." Process issues will be used to form a process team.

Key Challenge

If the momentum is going to continue, it is imperative to visibly demonstrate support for the team's recommendations.

In organizations that are lean in structure, allowing time for the strategic aspects of improvement can be difficult.

DEVELOP A CONTINUOUS PROCESS IMPROVEMENT (CPI) PROGRAM

Process Team Objective

The focus should be on how to improve the current processes and make tasks more effective and efficient. Question everything—the rules, policies, customs, norms, management behaviors, and organizational structure. Find the missing handshakes.

Process Team Structure

The team should consist of no more than nine individuals and include individuals who made the original suggestions and those directly impacted by the potential recommendations.

At the end of ten weeks, present a formal report identifying the current state of the process, the future state of the process, specific recommendations, any cost savings, and how changes should be implemented.

In the first meeting, a six-hour orientation will cover:

- *basic principles of CPI*

- *establishing a group identity*

- *selecting a team leader*

- *establishing the essential roles to run effective meetings*

- *practice with process flowcharting*

- *working on the team's objective by beginning to flowchart the current state*

PREPARATION: FOUNDATION OF A SUCCESSFUL HARVEST

"To forget how to dig the earth and to tend the soil is to forget ourselves."

—Mahatma Gandhi

February 27

It was a uniquely temperate day as Nick, with a jubilant spring in his step, strolled toward Mrs. Hortensis's house. He was looking forward to a day in the garden. Turning the corner, from a distance, he spotted Mrs. Hortensis gathering gardening supplies and organizing material.

She moved slower than usual, not with her normal endless energy, and Nick sensed a new tiredness. *I hope her lack of energy doesn't have anything to do with the medical testing,* he thought to himself.

"Hi, Mrs. Hortensis. I'm reporting for duty," Nick said as he sauntered up saluting.

Mrs. Hortensis turned and smiled. "You seem quite cheerful today."

Nick noticed a slight tremor in her regularly strong voice. "How did the tests go?" Nick had thought about her condition many times since their last meeting and hoped for good news.

"I'm as good as old gets," she said, turning to reflect her appreciation for his concern and then looked away.

Sensing she didn't what to talk about her situation in detail, Nick quickly changed the subject. "I've been looking forward to this all week."

"Well, so have I," Mrs. Hortensis replied, leaning against the front porch as she caught her breath. "I just can't lift the bags of mulch or dig up the ground the way I used to. As of late, I get tired doing just the simplest of things."

"Just tell me where to get started," Nick offered. "Are you sure you are okay?"

"Just fine. Let's get busy. We have a lot of work to do."

Nick carried bags of mulch to the backyard, and Mrs. Hortensis directed as he dug up an area approximately ten feet by twenty feet.

As they worked, Mrs. Hortensis explained why this spot was an ideal location for a vegetable garden. It was close to the back porch, the area drained well, and had a gentle slope facing the southeast. It received full sunshine throughout the day and was protected by shrubbery on the north and northwest. She had chosen the place because vegetables required all the sunshine they could get, a minimum of five to six hours of direct sunlight per day. "Oh how vegetables love their morning sunshine," she said with a song in her voice.

"It looks like you had a garden here before," Nick responded, recognizing the remnants of unharvested crops. "Why didn't you pick all the vegetables?"

"Just too much for me," Mrs. Hortensis explained. "There was a time when I couldn't grow enough. I've cut my garden to half the size of what I planted before. It used to be almost twenty feet by twenty feet. Did you know that the average backyard garden, typically twenty feet by twenty-five feet, could grow enough vegetables for a family of four or five? That would provide enough food for a year and still have some left over for freezing. Part of the current unnecessary carbon footprint is that we rely on food grown, packaged, and shipped when we could grow healthier, better-tasting produce in our own backyard. During World War II, victory gardens supplied as much as 40 percent of the produce Americans consumed. I wasn't even going to plant a vegetable garden this year, but you have inspired me, Nick. You can help me harvest the fresh vegetables so they won't go to waste. Would you like that?"

"You bet," Nick said. "That will be the best part."

Nick worked for several hours digging up the soil and mixing in mulch. At first, he only chipped away at the surface until Mrs. Hortensis pointed out he needed to dig at least a foot deep. "Like most things in life, you need to dig deep to prepare for growth," she said. Mrs. Hortensis instructed him to blend in a little fertilizer as he added the new mulch amendment to the soil.

Nick joked about how his poor digging technique resembled inappropriate management. "If you only do things on the surface and don't dig deep enough, you won't get to the root of your problems."

Mrs. Hortensis faintly smiled and added, "Yes, and adding fertilizer is like giving the sustenance of acknowledgment."

Nick asked if she could explain more about the amendments and deep digging. "Phosphorus must be worked in since it doesn't move down from the surface on its own. Digging deeply will also allow plenty of room for sturdy root development. *Roots* create the *fruits*. In other words, what you don't see under the ground creates what is seen above the ground."

"A solid foundation for development, just like good acknowledgment provides," Nick countered, thinking of his new acknowledgment cards.

"Just like an organization's culture, it is the invisible that creates the visible."

The numbers on the bag caught his eye. "What do these numbers signify?"

"In general any material added to the soil, which aids plant growth, is a fertilizer. The common use of the term refers to manufactured products that contain different amounts of the three key elements required for plant growth. The first number represents the percentage of nitrogen in the fertilizer, the second the percentage of phosphorus, and the third the percentage of potassium. Most fertilizers also contain trace elements of sulfur, iron, and boron required for healthy plant growth. A good all-purpose fertilizer labeled 5–10–5 contains 5 percent nitrogen, which promotes leaf and stem strength and stimulates growth; 10 percent phosphorus for roots, which encourages flowering and improves foliage and flower color; and 5 percent potassium, which wards off disease, stabilizes growth, and also intensifies color. The remaining 80 percent consists of chemicals, such as calcium, sulfur, and other fillers."

Mrs. Hortensis pointed out that "Good gardening begins with good soil preparation. The critical top few feet is where all things grow. It is this surface layer of earth that supports all plant life."

"What would be the management analogy for the percentages on the fertilizer bag?" Nick asked.

"Just like in preparing soil, it would depend on what needed to be improved. Using a standard all-purpose 5–10–5 fertilizer as an example, to improve performance add 5 percent 'directed purpose'—like nitrogen it stimulates growth. Next add 10 percent 'skill utilization and acquisition'—like phosphorus it improves roots and flowering or confidence and promotes success. Finally, add 5 percent 'measured and acknowledged results'—like potassium it wards off maladies of organizational life. Some work groups might need more amounts of each ingredient depending on the issues identified."

"And the remaining ingredients?" Nick asked, squinting one eye.

"They would be analogous to writing down expectations, documenting processes, planning work tasks, and analyzing work flow. Those activities represent the necessary foundation for efficient work to develop. Well-structured processes determine the quality of the topsoil in your organization."

Nick was surprised that she had given such a quick and thought-out response.

Mrs. Hortensis grabbed some soil and let it drift through her fingers. "If you do those things with continuous improvement in mind, new discoveries are made all the time to improve processes. The new discoveries are like adding organic amendments to the soil, which improves the structure."

"What kind of soil is this?" Nick asked, holding up a handful of dirt.

"Soil is usually classified according to its texture, meaning the size of the particles in it. We want good tilth, or soil that has a crumbly structure, dark sufficient humus, and drains well."

Nick crumbled the dirt in his hand and let it pour to the ground. "This soil seems sandy."

"That's why we used a combination of peat moss and sea weed to improve the soil's structure. Sandy soils require larger additions of humus and nutrients than heavy soils but can leach badly, so several light applications during the season give better results than one heavy application."

"There sure is a lot to learn about just putting plants in the ground," Nick said. "It's not as simple as it looks."

"Not unlike trying to manage others," Mrs. Hortensis said smiling. "It just takes understanding basic principles and following the appropriate steps. When you invest effectively in the beginning you won't believe the harvest in the end."

"And I thought dirt was just dirt," Nick quipped.

"Anyone can have dirt," Mrs. Hortensis responded. "Gardeners have soil."

"Maybe I should test the soil of my team and analyze the climate of my organization to better understand the appropriate amendments to add?" Nick laughed.

"Not a bad idea," Mrs. Hortensis said with a twinkle in her eye. "If soil hasn't been cultivated for a while, a good application of about four inches of organic material and superphosphate is needed. Superphosphate, usually pulverized phosphate rock or bonemeal, may not become available to the plants for a year or more. In management terms that means immediately apply a complete new layer of ideas and begin adding elements to the structure that may not be realized until sometime in the future."

Nick found out there was an exact science to the pH factor of soils. A reading of 7 indicated the neutral point, and numbers below pH 7 indicated the degree of acidity. Numbers above pH 7 indicated the degree of alkalinity. Vegetable gardens were grown most successfully in slightly acid soil, such as soil with a pH of 6 to 7.

"Vegetables must have good drainage," Mrs. Hortensis explained. "Many factors can impact the success of your harvest, but proper preparation of the ground is one of the most important. Since my soil is primarily sandy I don't dig it up in the fall. Winter washing by rains can deplete the nutrients in the soil. I typically wait a month before planting and then start preparing the garden."

Nick made a mental note that he was definitely going to test the team's soil, find out what they were missing, and discover what he could add to make the environment more productive.

Mrs. Hortensis asked Nick to apply about two to four inches of a thick mixture of organic materials by digging it in and under so the surface would be clear for planting. He wondered how she had managed to do all this work on her own.

As Nick worked, he shared with Mrs. Hortensis the new developments with his group during the last several months. He explained the concept and structure of the process improvement teams, and Mrs. Hortensis thought they were a fantastic undertaking.

She told Nick about her encounter during the 1950s with Dr. W. Edwards Deming. He had shared with her his approach for managing productivity and output. His concepts were new and there was initial resistance in corporate America to his techniques for measuring statistical process control. Ironically, the Japanese, struggling at the time to rebuild their industries, adapted his methodologies. The successes they achieved eventually convinced American industries to revisit Demming's concepts. Mrs. Hortensis recalled, after meeting Deming, the impact his systems thinking had on her and the realization that everything was a process.

Deming's approach clarified that using specific measurements made it easier to learn from mistakes and continually improve. Mrs. Hortensis shared that she had successfully applied the concept of continual improvement with her own team. The simple concepts were at the core of why her garden looked as it did today. "A gardener," she said, "learns more from mistakes than from their successes."

"Before, how did you do all this work by yourself?" Nick asked, leaning on the shovel and wiping the perspiration from his forehead.

"Well, my daughter and late husband helped quite a bit. It's been almost ten years now since my husband passed away, and my daughter moved up north quite some time ago. She plays violin in a philharmonic. In the last few years I've learned to spread the work out over several weeks. It has always been good exercise, but I certainly have … missed their help."

"I enjoy helping," Nick said quickly, trying to change the subject as he noticed a quiver in Mrs. Hortensis's voice. "Plus, I'm learning so much about how to do my job, and it's really good to be outside. It smells so fresh and so … earthy."

Mrs. Hortensis regained the strength in her voice. "Fortunately, I have been part of some fascinating experiences, and I am glad I have a chance to share them with you. I was wondering what would become of all the information I've collected."

"Are you sure there isn't something about the medical tests you aren't sharing?" Nick asked cautiously.

"You know enough about me by now that it's not my behavioral style to share that kind of information," Mrs. Hortensis said warmly.

"That reminds me. Do you know anything about different interactive styles?"

Mrs. Hortensis smiled. "You've come that far in your exploration of group dynamics that you are now interested in interactive styles?" Mrs. Hortensis exclaimed. "That subject was part of my undergraduate work. Have you read any of Dr. Carl Jung's work?" Mrs. Hortensis asked.

Nick shrugged, indicating he wasn't familiar with Dr. Jung. "That's a lot of psychobabble about people, isn't it?"

Mrs. Hortensis looked at Nick sternly. "It is a powerful tool for influencing team behavior and managing tensions. Conflict is inevitable in any organization and is the result of two factors. One factor is the clarity of the organization's processes. If processes are unclear, then it is easy for people to blame someone else for mistakes. Most people don't come to work wanting to perform poorly. When they do, it's usually because something in the work process was unclear, or responsibility was undocumented, vague, or sometimes redundant. People become frustrated and complain about the ridiculous way things are done but do nothing about it. Many have ideas for, if not solutions to, the unclear process issues, but the focus is usually on getting the work done, not on how to be more effective and efficient."

"I'm glad the new CPI process teams are starting to document our processes," Nick said, relieved. "I can see how a visible work structure reduces conflict."

Mrs. Hortensis nodded. "The second factor of conflict—and this is the one you just asked about—involves behavioral styles. If individuals with different styles are on a team, you have unlimited possibilities for insights and approaches. But you also have the possibility of strong differences of opinion. Some people want results now. Others want work done right. Still others want to interact without unnecessary tension and conflict. Some think work should be innovative, exciting, and as fun as possible. Those who want results put relationships second to the outcome, while those who want to maintain relationships do not like to confront individuals and pressure them with deadlines."

"We sure have both. We have several unusual characters in my group. There were interesting discussions when we started documenting unclear project activities. Bill comes late to every meeting, always with an excuse about something important to do. John has to discuss every point in detail. Celeste volunteers for things but doesn't follow through, and Mary just sits there. Cindy mentioned that Kathy, in her logical and open conversations, was a real contributor as far as mediating tensions."

"Welcome to the real source of conflict regarding interactive challenges in most organizations today—a combination of both unclear process and diverse personalities. Nick, your new program focuses on clarifying group processes, so now would be a good time to provide additional guidance to participants. Providing your team with a better understanding of how they can interact with and appreciate each other would be a rewarding investment."

"Yeah, there are definitely some people I would like to change!" Nick said with earnest. "There are people at work who really frustrate me, like Bill and Mary."

Mrs. Hortensis said with a soft smile, "Dr. Jung wrote, 'Everything that irritates us about others can lead us to an understanding of ourselves.' It is not so much about changing others, Nick, or changing who you are, as it's about managing strengths and weaknesses. I'll show you the basics now, and later I will look for material you can have for more in-depth reading."

"Great," Nick said, leaning the shovel against the porch railing as he pulled a neatly folded piece of paper from his back pocket.

Mrs. Hortensis and Nick walked over to the chairs on the porch and sat down. *These Adirondack chairs are actually comfortable,* Nick thought to himself as he spread his paper on its wide armrest.

"Let's start simply," Mrs. Hortensis said, waiting for Nick to unfold his piece of paper. "There are many different systems that provide insight into behavioral styles. The ones I feel work best focus on observable behavior. I developed an approach several years ago and used it with my teams, based on two different axes of observation."

"This is your system?" Nick asked.

"Not mine alone. Identifying personality styles dates back over two thousand years to the Greeks. My tool is loosely based on some of these earlier approaches but mostly on the original work of Dr. Jung outlined in his book, *The Archetypes of Personalities.* Archetypes are tools that help us think about interconnectedness in the world. Since his publication, there have been many behavioral topologies based on his findings, and despite minor variations there is a general agreement about the structure and content of interpersonal behavior. Ultimately, I drew from many sources."

"You certainly are full of surprises," Nick said.

Mrs. Hortensis continued without even looking up. "Interactive behavior is structured around two basic observable dimensions. On your piece of paper draw a giant plus sign (+) with each line about six inches long. At the far left end of the horizontal line write *more.* At the other end of the line write *less.* Under the line write the word *assertiveness.*"

"Here?" Nick asked, pointing at the paper.

"Yes, where the two lines meet. Individuals to the left of the vertical line, on the assertive line, are perceived as more assertive, and those to the right are perceived as less assertive."

Nick looked at his lines on the page and pointed to each side of the vertical line as she spoke.

"Now label the vertical line *responsiveness.* At the top of the line write *less* and at the bottom of the line write *more.* In general, individuals near the top of the scale interact less responsively, while those near the bottom interact more responsively. "

"Like this." Nick said showing her his diagram.

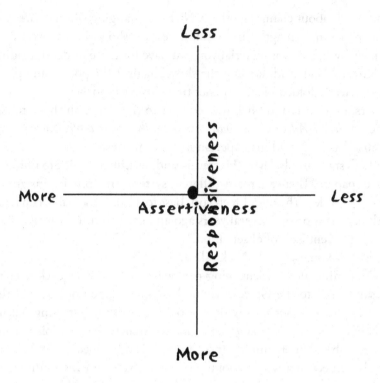

Mrs. Hortensis nodded.

Nick's interest was piqued. "Will this tool help me change the individuals I work with?"

"Nick, this is not about changing people, but being more aware. Let's take the horizontal line of ASSERTIVENESS. Assertiveness is a measure of the degree we tend to tell or ask as we interact with others. It is a reflection of how we see ourselves influencing others. If you are perceived as more assertive, you may state your opinions with assurance, confidence, and force. You make positive statements and declarations and attempt to direct the action of others. If you are perceived as less assertive, you tend to be more cautious and reserved about sharing opinions. You attempt to influence the thinking and actions of others in a more quiet, low-key, questioning manner. The key word here is perception."

"By 'assertive,' do you mean someone who is pushy and demanding?" Nick questioned.

"Yes, but think of pushy behavior in a less negative way. Think of someone who is willing to share opinions, demonstrate an urgency to act, uses gestures, is confident and outwardly direct during a challenge, makes requests, give directions, and in general is more tell-oriented. You might classify them as more demonstrative or outgoing. On the other end of the scale are those we perceive as less assertive. They may appear risk-aware and less impulsive, decide less quickly, speak softly, are less direct in their responses, prefer time to prepare and organize their thoughts, are less confrontational, and in general are more task-oriented."

"You mean the quiet ones?" Nick asked.

"Yes, but they may not always be quiet, and when they do speak, their words tend to be well selected. Remember, these are only tendencies and vary from person to person. Observations are based on our own perceptions, and those perceptions are filtered by our comfort zone and our own individual style. What may seem quiet to one person may not seem quiet to someone else. It is very important to stress that one behavior is not better than the other. It is just observable and based on perceptions."

"Well, there are certain things I've learned to count on from some people at work," Nick said quickly. "Kathy is really quiet in group settings, but when asked one-on-one, she has some interesting insights for someone as young as she is. She perceptively identifies who is comfortable and who is not during group interaction and seems quite aware of how others feel. I try to schedule some one-on-one time with her on a regular basis to hear her insights. Bill is always late to meetings and yet when challenged he says, 'I'm here now. Let's not waste time. Get on with it.' At times he is like a bull in a china shop."

"That's it. You now see how we perceive a person as being less or more assertive," Mrs. Hortensis said with excitement in her voice. "To make the subtleties of interaction more visible, focus on typical behaviors when a person is under tension. During calm moments during group dynamics it is easier to be flexible with your style and, therefore, more difficult to read. It is under moments of tension when interactive characteristics become exaggerated."

"What do you mean by 'tension'?" Nick asked.

"By tension, I mean engaging in something you are not comfortable doing, like confronting a coworker, asking your boss for a raise, firing someone, or putting together a detailed report full of facts and numbers at the last minute."

"This isn't simple stuff," Nick said, grinning slightly. "This is as complex as preparing the right garden soil."

Mrs. Hortensis nodded. "Interactive behavior is very complex. We have to be careful that we do not oversimplify it. As I said earlier, a system for understanding others can be a powerful tool for knowing how to adjust your style. It should be more about managing your behavior than managing others. Also, be careful about labeling individuals too quickly."

"You mean overgeneralizing?" Nick asked.

"Yes. There have been studies about the situational aspects of interaction. You should read some of Blanchard and Hersey's writing on situational leadership. Certain circumstances may demand that individuals demonstrate different behavior. For example, quiet people willing to support others instead of leading may find themselves in a situation where there is no one else to take charge. They uncharacteristically jump in and take the lead, provided they don't withdraw from the task. When a person of authority shows up, they are willing give up that leadership role. On the other hand, there are those who, even when others are willing to take charge, won't relinquish authority. For one individual it's taking control, and for the other it is giving up control. Both can be uncomfortable situations depending upon one's natural style."

"When you first mentioned someone who was more assertive, I thought of Bill," Nick reflected. "He will interrupt in the middle of a sentence and ask abruptly, 'So what's your point?'"

"Good. I think you get the idea of the assertiveness scale," Mrs. Hortensis said. "Now the other scale is more challenging. It's the scale of responsiveness. We seem to be more naturally aware of the degrees of assertiveness, but the degrees of responsiveness are more challenging. The vertical line on your paper represents responsiveness."

"Do you mean when you tell people to do something they respond immediately?"

"No. Responsiveness means how comfortable a person is expressing feelings under tension. It is a measure of the extent we tend to control, keeping feelings and emotions to ourselves, or how we emote, outwardly displaying our feelings and emotions with others. In part it is a measure of how we react to emotional influences, appeals, or displays. If we tend not to react, then it's more likely we focus on ideas, things, data, and tasks. If we do respond, we may be more comfortable expressing anger, joy, hurt, and other feelings. Under tension some are less responsive and others more responsive."

"You mean like having a poker face?"

"Yes. Some people are hard to read and give off no external sign as to what they are feeling. With others you can tell their moods by their outward expressions. They wear their feelings on their sleeve. For example, less responsive persons might appear more serious, focus more on facts, are more task-oriented and less interested in small talk, and demonstrate a more disciplined use of time. Whereas more responsive persons may have more facial expressiveness, appear friendly, focus on feelings, be interested in anecdotes and jokes, and demonstrate a more relaxed use of time."

"As a manager I've heard you shouldn't let your staff know what you are thinking. Keep them guessing and maintain the upper hand."

"Unfortunately, there are those who promote that belief. There are times when it is important to be able to rise above a crisis and not indicate you are affected by it. If you are naturally comfortable doing that, then you may find yourself thriving during a crisis and rather bored when there isn't one. That is one of the hidden reasons that some organizations continually find themselves involved in crisis management. Those in control create an environment that supports their natural style."

"They intentionally create a crisis?" Nick asked, doubting that was possible.

"No, not necessarily intentionally, but firefighters love to put out fires, and if none are burning, they create the sparks that ignite smoldering embers."

"So, those with the poker face are on the less responsive side because they control emotions?"

"Exactly," Mrs. Hortensis said.

"How about individuals on the *more* side of responsiveness? Are they fairly easy to read?"

"Don't be fooled. They can be just as hard to understand. They focus on the people side of issues. They are approachable and demonstrate sensitivity to individuals through interacting with respect, and by listening. Both of which are perceived as supportive behaviors."

"So they are concerned about how everyone is getting along and if anyone needs support?" Nick asked.

"Yes and no," Mrs. Hortensis replied. "Some may pledge the support but not follow through. Others may feel like it is more important to be agreeable and go along with the group than to have their own way."

"Sort of passive-aggressive?" Nick asked.

"Under certain circumstances, yes."

"You keep saying 'sometimes' and under 'certain circumstances.' What do you mean by that? I wish I knew more about my specific style."

"You go on into the kitchen and wait for me there," Mrs. Hortensis said, slowly getting up and heading toward the house. "I'll meet you there in a few minutes."

Nick's notes:

PERFORMANCE ENHANCEMENT

Only doing things on the surface (not digging deep enough) prevents you from getting to the root of your problems.

Just like the organization's culture, it is the invisible that creates the visible. Understanding the value of systems thinking leads to the realization that everything is a process.

Using standard, all-purpose 5-10-5 fertilizer as an analogy for improving performance, add:

- 5 percent directed purpose. Like nitrogen, it stimulates growth.

- 10 percent skill utilization and acquisition. Like phosphorus, it improves roots and flowering, or confidence, and promotes success.

- 5 percent measured and acknowledged results. Like potassium, it wards off maladies of organizational life. (Some work groups might need more amounts of each ingredient, depending on the issues identified.)

The remaining ingredients would include written expectations, documented processes, measurable work tasks, and a continual review of work flow. These activities represent the necessary foundation for efficient work to develop. Well-structured processes determine the quality of the "topsoil" in your organization.

INTERACTIVE BEHAVIOR

Understanding different interactive styles is a powerful tool for influencing team behavior and knowing how to adjust your style. Dr. Carl Jung wrote, "Everything that irritates us about others can lead us to an understanding of ourselves." These observations are based on our own perceptions, and those perceptions are filtered by our comfort zone and our own individual style. To improve, the focus should be on managing our behavior more than managing the behavior of others.

MANAGING CONFLICT

Two keys factors that influence the possibility of conflict are unclear processes and diverse personalities.

Clarity of the organization's processes. *If processes are unclear, then it is easy for people to blame someone else for mistakes. Most people don't come to work wanting to perform poorly. When they do, it's usually because something in the work process was unclear or responsibility was undocumented, vague, or sometimes redundant. People become frustrated and complain about the ridiculous way things are done but do nothing about it. Many have ideas for, if not solutions to, the unclear process issue, but the focus is usually on getting the work done, not on how to be more effective and efficient.*

Interactive behavior. *If individuals with different styles are on a team, there are unlimited possibilities for different insights and approaches. But you also have the possibility of strong differences of opinion.*

Some people want results now. Others want work done right. Still others want work done without unnecessary tension and conflict. Some think work should be innovative, exciting, and as fun as possible.

Those who want results put relationships second to the outcome, while those who want to maintain relationships do not like to confront and pressure others toward results with deadlines.

SELF-AWARENESS

"It is through meaningful observations that we finally see the hidden obvious."

—Paul Allman

February 27

It seemed to take a long time for Mrs. Hortensis to return. More than once Nick went to the kitchen doorway and loudly offered his assistance, but each time he got the same muffled response: "Just a few more minutes." In the distance, he could hear items being moved about and the occasional shuffling of feet across the upstairs floor. Finally, Mrs. Hortensis slowly appeared carrying a musty green booklet.

"I thought I might have one or two of these left. It's a questionnaire to help individuals identify their own behavioral style. It is fairly simple and by no means a complete diagnostic tool, but it may help you understand the application of the theory. Go ahead, Nick, fill it out."

"Now? Shouldn't I spend time really going over it?"

"No. You don't need to dwell on the answers. It's best to complete it with your initial feelings. It works well during group settings because there is always a competition among participants as to who will get it done first. That keeps individuals from spending too much time on their answers."

Nick took the test while Mrs. Hortensis went outside to collect some cuttings to make tea.

"Done," Nick said as Mrs. Hortensis returned, throwing his arms in the air as if he had just crossed a finish line.

"That was fast."

"You said it was a competition. How did I do?"

"You finished in about the same amount of time as most do," Mrs. Hortensis said, rolling her eyes and shaking her head. "Let's see what you did. Yes, you even transferred your answers to the grid on the last page—very good.

"Let's see. You have four points in box area 1, twelve points in box area 2, sixteen points in box area 3, and eight points in box area number 4. There were forty questions … so that should add up to forty points, and it does."

Nick was looking at a large box divided into four equal parts. A line running vertically divided the box in half, and a line running horizontally divided the box in half. The result was four small boxes, two boxes of equal size on the top and two on the bottom.

"What does it mean?" he asked impatiently.

"I found some handout material you can have that will help explain the questionnaire," Mrs. Hortensis said, putting a small booklet on the table. "I even have an extra blank questionnaire in case you want to give it to your team members."

"Thanks," Nick said, reaching for the booklet.

"Let me look up your results first," Mrs. Hortensis said, holding onto the booklet and thumbing through it. "Your numbers indicate you are a *controller* who wants action. You are also successful in situations that require creativity because you are a *promoter* as well. That means you use intuition and new ideas when faced with challenges. You need to concentrate on staying focused on the task at hand and improving interpersonal relationships."

"I guess I got the answers right. That's an insightful description of me," Nick said, taking the booklet as Mrs. Hortensis handed it to him. "Now I know what to change."

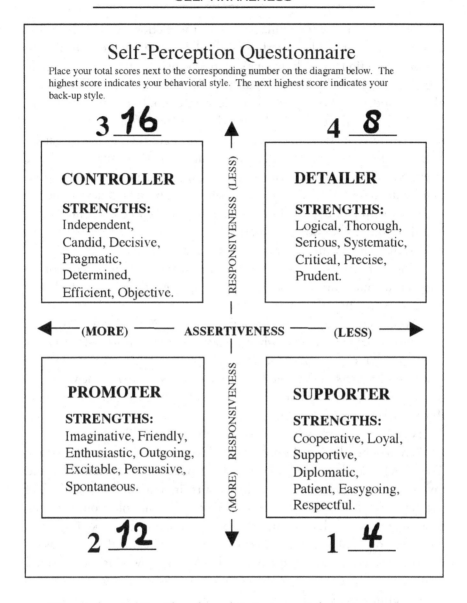

Self-Perception Questionnaire

Place your total scores next to the corresponding number on the diagram below. The highest score indicates your behavioral style. The next highest score indicates your back-up style.

3 **16**   4 **8**

CONTROLLER

STRENGTHS:
Independent,
Candid, Decisive,
Pragmatic,
Determined,
Efficient, Objective.

DETAILER

STRENGTHS:
Logical, Thorough,
Serious, Systematic,
Critical, Precise,
Prudent.

RESPONSIVENESS (LESS)

◀——(MORE) ——— ASSERTIVENESS ——— (LESS) ——▶

PROMOTER

STRENGTHS:
Imaginative, Friendly,
Enthusiastic, Outgoing,
Excitable, Persuasive,
Spontaneous.

SUPPORTER

STRENGTHS:
Cooperative, Loyal,
Supportive,
Diplomatic,
Patient, Easygoing,
Respectful.

(MORE) RESPONSIVENESS

2 **12**   1 **4**

"Remember, as I said earlier, there are no right or wrong answers. The key is not to focus on how you can change, or change other people, but how you can better manage yourself and perceptions. As you manage your behaviors others may perceive you differently and adjust their style. The strategy under tension is to move your perceived behavior toward the comfort zone of those you wish to interact with and influence."

"That sounds like manipulation to me," Nick said frowning.

103

"Well, it is. Look manipulation up in the dictionary. The definition is 'to handle, treat, or do something skillfully.' Certainly it can also mean 'to use a situation unfairly to one's own advantage.' That's the typically negative image attached to manipulation. But to determine if it's negative, we must understand the intention of the interaction. If it's win-win–based, then the manipulation is similar to what we enjoy from a good coach, parent, or teacher. If it's win-lose … well, you get the picture, negative. Manipulation, the act of skillfully handling a situation, isn't bad; it's the intention behind the act that determines if it is a positive interaction. Being able to flex or manipulate your behavior can, in fact, determine the success of your communication. It's the intention behind communication that determines if it's honest or not.

"Well, that's a different way to look at manipulation," Nick said.

"There are situations where we need to manipulate our behavior, to step outside our comfort zone. If, in so doing, we are able to send a better message, is that negative manipulation?

"Well, I guess not if the intentions are good," Nick said quietly.

"It is amazing that, even when it makes sense for us to shift, we can't move from our comfort zone. It is like a boss who has given an assignment that was misunderstood. Some bosses will give it again the same way, only the second time with much less patience and blame the person receiving the message instead of adjusting it."

Nick knew exactly what she meant. His boss was like that.

"I remember the time I was living in Africa. I visited the coastal area of Tiwi Beach outside of Mombasa, far away from any tourist traffic. I found myself in a situation where I was lost. I was tired and hungry, and I had left my phrase book back at the hotel. There was a nice old woman sitting by a small fruit stand, and I approached and asked if she spoke English. I got no response. In fact, she looked away and motioned with her hands for me to do the same. I asked again, only louder and slower, as if that would help. I even began waving my hands to emphasize my point."

"It sounds like you were making the situation very uncomfortable for her," Nick said.

"You're right. English is *my* comfort zone, and even though this person didn't understand it, I kept speaking English. Trying over and over, waving my hands, only made her more uncomfortable. I eventually asked in broken Swahili where the road to Mombasa was. '*Barbara Mombasa ili wapi?*' I asked, feeling very uncomfortable."

"What happened?" Nicked asked.

104

"I got a somewhat puzzled look, but she pointed in a direction. I was on my way. '*Asante*,' I said thanking her, to which she responded, '*hakuna matata*.' I felt uncomfortable speaking a foreign language. You see I was outside my comfort zone. But amazingly she understood because I was in hers."

"You mean interactive behavior is like speaking a foreign language?" Nick asked, confused.

"Yes, very much so. As you learn a foreign language, you feel uncomfortable at first, but as you practice, you become less inhibited. Most people speaking a foreign language will usually have an accent. You might sense they are not speaking their primary language, but that doesn't make a difference because they are making an effort to flex and communicate with you in your comfort zone. They adjust so you can understand."

"Like you did with the woman alongside the road."

"Yes, exactly. Interpersonal interaction is the same. The individual willing to speak to someone else in that person's behavioral language, or comfort zone, is the one able to more effectively communicate his message. Essentially there are two behavioral languages and four dialects to be aware of."

"And they are …?" Nick wondered.

"We talked about them months ago. I can review them as I look at your numbers on the questionnaire," Mrs. Hortensis said, pulling Nick's survey closer to her.

"There were forty total points, and if evenly distributed, you would have ten in each box."

"That would be perfect, right?" Nick asked.

"No, and it doesn't happen very often at all. It indicates a lack of a 'home' comfort zone. If you score five points or below in any box then that is, under tension, essentially a foreign language for you. A score of ten or higher indicates an ability to recognize a different language, but depending on the situation, you may not adjust easily. Sixteen points or higher indicates a comfort zone. This is your 'home' base under tension; you go there first," Mrs. Hortensis said, pointing at box number three on the paper.

"If you score twenty points or higher in any area, that would indicate an unmanaged comfort zone. People may use this style even when they are aware they shouldn't. You scored highest in the 'controller' box and second highest in 'promoter' box."

"What does that mean?" Nick asked.

Mrs. Hortensis picked up the other booklet she brought, and they spent some time going through the information. She reviewed the characteristics of each style and what Nick's numbers meant. He was amazed. It was as if she really knew his behavior. Not everything was exactly right, but much of it was. Mrs. Hortensis explained that she was describing general groups of behavior and that individual behavior was much more complex.

Nick and Mrs. Hortensis talked about earlier conversations regarding the two languages spoken in any group—*task* and *people* language. She pointed out that some individuals speak task language more assertively, some less, while some individuals speak people language more assertively and others less. Those were the four different dialects. She shared that Nick spoke task language assertively but was also able to speak people language assertively under certain circumstances.

Nick knew he needed to work on nonassertive "people language" skills, like listening, patience, and in general the perception of supportive behavior. Nick argued that he thought he was building positive relationships, but Mrs. Hortensis explained that what Nick perceived his behavior to be might be different from those who actually experienced it.

Nick began to think of people at work and where they might fall on the scales. Bill was maybe a controller, but John was definitely a detailer. And Mary was probably a supporter. Interestingly Nick thought that she was so difficult to understand and that was the area he scored the least. Cindy was maybe a combination of supporter/detailer, and you could not have described Celeste any better than the description of a promoter. "I'm still not sure if you can fit everyone into just four groupings," Nick said. "There is more variety in people than four categories can explain."

"Let us go outside in the garden," Mrs. Hortensis said.

They walked through the garden to the farside near a hilly slope covered in sun and no shade nearby.

"Do you see all of the different succulents, primarily the different cactus near the top where it's the brightest?"

"Yes," Nick said. "But they're not all cactus, are they?"

"Sure they are. Some are the typical ones with the thick leaves and prickly spines. See those that look like living stones—lithops—and those that have bright red heart-shaped leaves? They are all cacti."

"Is there a difference between cacti and succulents?"

"Nearly all cacti are succulents, but not all succulents are cacti. Cacti are lumped together with other succulents because of their ability to survive. The word 'succulent' is derived from the Latin *succos*, meaning juicy, and is used to describe some ten thousand plants that adapt to store and conserve water and thereby survive drought. You would be surprised that cacti, geraniums, and even orchids are all succulents."

"You're kidding!" Nick exclaimed. Even I know that a cactus and an orchid are completely different types of plants. They're like night and day!"

"Many succulents live in semi-arid or arid regions; you might be familiar with some, like the yucca, sagebrush, and mesquite, which actually prefer the hardship of prolonged dry spells. These are called xerophytes, the Greek word for dry plants. More surprisingly, some succulents are epiphytic, living on trees or rocks in South American forests. They don't need soil at all."

"That sounds pretty special. I would like to see some of those."

"You have, Nick. They are the bromeliads in the covered side yard."

"Oh, I need to look closer next time."

"A simple cactus is quite special. Of the succulents, cacti have made quantum biological leaps in the struggle to survive. Found almost entirely in the Western Hemisphere, the cactus has found niches for itself in one unique form or another, at every altitude, and in a surprising range of habitats. As exasperate as the spines of the cactus are to would-be admirers, they are one of the most versatile and effective design features in the plant world."

"Do you mean the cactus plants we see growing everywhere?"

"Yes, there are over 1,300 known species and 3 major subdivisions of cactus. However, there are some basic characteristics that group them all together. For example, you wouldn't plant a typical cactus or succulent next to a water-dependent plant. They have completely different needs."

"So what's your point?" Nick said in disbelief as he looked closer at the plants that looked like small stones, when they were actually cacti.

"Behavioral style is the same. There are so many factors that determine how we interact with others. Yet, there are certain basic characteristics that we can use to group similar individuals together. Grouping them together doesn't mean they aren't still unique in their own way. Just like the cactus, some have really long prickly spines and others, sharp fuzzy hair. But they conform under pressure—like lack of water for the succulents—basically the same way."

"I think I understand," Nick said. "The general characteristics apply to a broad group of people."

"Yes, and within any group there can be many different types of subcharacteristics, which is why effective interactive behavior is so complex and difficult at times."

As they walked back to the kitchen, Mrs. Hortensis shared with Nick the importance of perception. "It is how individuals perceive you, certainly under tension, that can provide incredible insight into how behavior can be adjusted. If you have a strong opinionated interactive style, a subtle shift into a more supportive listening style can signal to an individual under tension that it is okay to continue exchanging information. At times going to where you are uncomfortable so that the message sent is more comfortable to receive is the challenge.

As they headed back to the house, Mrs. Hortensis pointed out it was easier said than done.

They sat down at the table and Mrs. Hortensis picked up the questionnaire. "Actually, in a group setting where individuals are working at making it easier to receive a message, the communication efforts are heading here, toward the center." She pointed to the middle of the page where all the boxes met.

"Here?" Nick pointed to the center as well.

"Yes, this is where communication synergism takes place. It occurs because others are sensitive to the message that is being exchanged, but not necessarily spoken. When that message is managed, the results become a more effective and open communication. Understanding the basic behavioral groupings provides a starting place for influencing the communication results you're trying to achieve."

"So would you say this is a scientific approach to communication?"

"Nick, by no means is what I am sharing a perfect science. It is simply a tool to help you manage your own influential behavior. Your ability to flex your style strengthens clearer communication in different situations. It is very simple to learn a few words in a foreign language, but it takes practice to communicate effectively. The more languages you learn, the wider the range you can travel and still comfortably communicate. Once you learn the first foreign language, a second or third becomes easier to grasp."

"I hear that in Europe you can get by just fine with English," Nick said. "You really don't need a second language."

"Nonsense! That is a lazy way to approach the true excitement of discovering different cultures. If you always want to be dependent on someone else's translation, perhaps you are right. Maybe you don't mind always being the tourist, but as the person in charge of your group, you should be their travel guide. They are hoping you can provide a translation when they can't."

Nick didn't respond, but he got her point.

"You don't need to continually adjust your message. Just become more aware of when you should, like when you have been coaching someone and he isn't getting it, or your boss starts arguing with you and you have not even made your point yet."

Mrs. Hortensis picked up the small booklet and placed it in front of Nick. "Read this booklet. In the back there are some reference materials listed if you would like to learn more."

"What style are you, Mrs. Hortensis?"

Mrs. Hortensis just smiled. "Go home and read through the booklet. The next time we meet you can tell me. For your style, Nick, here's the key: Because you can do something doesn't mean you should. And for those working around you, because they say they can't doesn't mean that they shouldn't."

When Nick arrived home, he did as he had done after previous visits with Mrs. Hortensis. He took the time to review and rewrite the information Mrs. Hortensis shared with him in his journal.

Nick and Mrs. Hortensis agreed to meet the first weekend in April. Nick was excited. They were going to plant a new vegetable garden, and the work he just finished was an important step in preparing the ground ahead of time. Mrs. Hortensis said a month was needed before planting to allow for a partial decay of the new amendments.

Nick had never planted a vegetable garden before, and he was looking forward to a new experience.

He had taken the notes from his journal and started a binder with inserted tabs dividing the information from each visit. He had already referred to the information a number of times when issues came up at work.

Nick titled the binder "Essential Skills of Management and Leadership" and added the additional information to the binder.

BASIC BEHAVIORAL STYLE RECOGNITION

Effective communication is the foundation of corporate life. Individuals willing to adjust their behavioral language or comfort zone are able to more effectively communicate their message. Essentially, there are two behavioral languages and four "dialects" to be aware of. There is no right or wrong style. It is about adjusting your perceived behavior to make others more comfortable in receiving your message. In order to do that, you need to identify your own basic style, as perceived by others, and determine the additional styles you need to flex. Some individuals speak task language more assertively, some less, while some individuals speak people language more assertively and some less.

Task language includes:

Planning, budgets, schedules, deadlines, policies, procedures, departmental structure, reports, measurements, goals, rules, regulations, urgency, decisions, and controls.

Those who are more assertive under tension look for action. Those who are less assertive under tension look for documentation.

People language includes:

Support, ability to listen, mentoring, counseling, relationships, trust, respect, coaching, guiding, representing, innovation, participation, and competency.

Those who are more assertive under tension look for credit.

Those who are less assertive under tension seek ways to support.

How individuals perceive you under tension provides incredible insight into how behavior can be adjusted. If you have a strong opinionated interactive style, a subtle shift into a more supportive listening style can signal another individual under tension that it is okay to continue exchanging information. Going to where you are uncomfortable so that the message sent is received more comfortably is the challenge we all face at times.

CAN EVERYONE FIT INTO JUST FOUR GROUPINGS?

There are many factors that determine how we interact with others. However, there are certain basic characteristics that we can use to group similar individuals together. Grouping them together doesn't mean they aren't still unique in their own way.

Understanding the basic behavioral groupings provides a starting place for influencing the communication results you are trying to achieve. It is simply a tool to help you manage your own influential behavior. Your ability to flex your style strengthens your ability to communicate clearly in a variety of situations.

You do not need to continually adjust your message. Instead become more aware of when you should (i.e., when you have been coaching someone and he isn't getting it, or your boss starts arguing with you and you have not even made your point yet).

Two basic perspectives:

Just because you can do something doesn't mean you should.

Just because you feel you can't do something doesn't mean you shouldn't.

ASSIGNMENTS:

Read more about your style and then practice flexing during challenging situations. Identify individuals from the different basic styles to practice with.

Try to identify those you need to flex with the most.

DISCOVERING VARIETY IN THE FAMILIAR

"Study nature, love nature, stay close to nature. It will never fail you."

—Frank Lloyd Wright

March

Process enhancement was becoming a consistent part of the team's undertaking. Nick was receiving ten written suggestions per month. One or two were saved as potential process team issues, while the majority were assigned as management's responsibility. He was mindful that process improvement initiatives were beginning to take root and germinating a new focus for the team.

Nick, and the select few handing out acknowledgment cards, were issuing close to forty-five a month. He enjoyed discovering ways to surprise staff members with recognition, and it was clear they appreciated receiving the praise. Some displayed acquired cards taped to bookshelves over desks; others kept a neat rubber-banded stack in a front desk drawer clearly displayed for all to see.

So far, Sally was the only one who had redeemed any. She had been saving for something special but was being transferred to the east coast and reluctantly handed in three acknowledgment cards with a receipt for a new CD.

Nick was concerned that if people weren't going to turn the cards in, they might become complacent and content with the few they already had. The challenge was how to get individuals to cash them in and want to earn more.

A few days earlier Nick had purchased a ticket for the local high school's annual Education Foundation benefit raffle. Using that idea, Nick decided to offer a raffle where staff could use their acknowledgment cards as a way to participate.

As a promotion item, one of Nick's vendors had given him a new handheld Garmin nüvi 350 Personal Travel Assistant and auto GPS system. It came with voice-prompted navigation, a full-featured MP3 player, a 3.5" touch screen, and preloaded street-level maps of the entire United States. Nick already had a GPS system in his car so he offered it as a raffle item and acknowledged the vendor as the contributor. He also convinced his boss to reserve one of the parking spots closest to the main entrance as a special CPI spot. Whoever won that could park there until the next raffle.

Nick hoped that the drawing would give additional visibility to the CPI efforts and posted the information on the CPI bulletin board with a large sign in colored letters advertising the special event. The notification of the raffle welcomed everyone and explained the rules. Staff could only enter by using an acknowledgement card and could put in as many cards as they wanted. Cards would be voided after the drawing and could only be used once. If anyone chose to, they could pick up the voided cards after the drawing as a keepsake of the original recognition.

Nick was amazed at the excitement the raffle generated. Fifty-seven cards were entered, and he calculated that was close to one-half the cards in circulation.

Kevin won the GPS system and was ecstatic. He proudly wore his new designation as Mr. Lucky because he submitted only one card. Celeste had submitted five cards, didn't win anything, and the morning after the drawing Nick received two new suggestions from her. One of them was very innovative, and Nick immediately followed up on it.

Phyllis won the parking spot and proudly pulled into her new space the very next morning. Since then, she has been asked often to drive to lunch because she was the only one privileged enough to have a guaranteed spot when she returned. She enjoys the newfound status.

With the raffle success, Nick began to make arrangements with vendors on how he could obtain items so that he could hold a raffle at least every quarter.

News of the raffle spread, and several people outside of Nick's group asked how they could participate. Nick explained the process improvement program and the rules of the raffle but that it was currently limited to his group. They thought it was a great idea and wondered if Nick would talk to their management about launching a CPI program in their area. Nick met with several other managers to explain the CPI concept.

After seeing the interest other departments had in the CPI efforts, Nick began to contemplate how he could use acknowledgment cards as a tool for recognizing individuals outside of his immediate staff. He imagined the impact CPI would have, and the issues that could be resolved, if different work groups from all over the organization participated on CPI teams.

The team had become quite efficient over the last several months and were acknowledged at a special luncheon for their hard work and assiduity.

Nick's boss had even authorized improvements to the work area. The walls had been painted, beautiful motivational pictures with nature scenes added, and new lighting and a new air-venting system eliminated the need for a fan. Tensions in the group had reduced drastically, and their main project was ahead of schedule for the first time. Nick's diligent efforts had not gone unnoticed by management, and he was assigned even more responsibility. With the growth of his team, Nick was asked to promote someone to a supervisory position to assist in managing all the projects.

Nick immediately thought of Cindy. She had been a main contributor in the CPI efforts and was well liked by members of the team. She was always available to lend a listening ear. Unlike Mary, Nick felt Cindy focused more on helping individuals understand the challenge, instead of just sympathizing with the complainer.

Cindy was his opposite. She was detailed and precise, yet approachable and always looked out for those taken advantage of. On occasion, Cindy could be slow to change and asked "why" when approached to try something new, but she had incredible patience and was one of the best listeners on his team. She always seemed to understand the people side of issues.

When Nick asked Cindy to take the supervisor's role, he was surprised at her response. Cindy wasn't sure she wanted to accept the position, and Nick remembered what Mrs. Hortensis had shared. "Because they think they can't doesn't mean they shouldn't."

"How about Kathy?" Cindy offered.

"She would be good, but she doesn't have the process improvement background you have. What are you afraid of?" Nick pushed, trying to encourage her to accept it.

"I'm not afraid of anything," Cindy replied. "Truthfully, I'm not sure how well we would work together," she said, not looking at him directly.

"We work great together now!" Nick exclaimed, surprised by her comment.

"Well … this will be different," Cindy continued hesitatingly. "I would need you to stop undermining my authority. If you want me to lead effectively, then we will have to make decisions together. That's not your style, Nick. You are creative. You make decisions on your own, based on intuition. The few times you asked my opinion, you became impatient when I didn't respond at your pace."

"So what's wrong with that? We still get things done, don't we?" Nick was growing visibly agitated by the conversation.

"Nothing … if you're the only boss," Cindy said, tightening her lips and shifting her position. "I want people to accept me as their boss, and in order for that to occur, you have to empower me."

"Okay, you're empowered," Nick, said with a smile.

"If it were only that simple." Cindy frowned as she took a deep breath. "This is serious, and I don't think it's funny. There are two essential elements to an empowered environment, Nick. First, you need to give me the responsibility. Secondly, you need to give me the authority to make my own decisions. We need to spend time up front clarifying the end results, and then you need to let me guide the team as I see fit."

"Okay, so you don't need any support," Nick said, looking serious and throwing his hands up in the air.

"No," Cindy said. "Why is it always black or white with you? I need your support, but I also need you to understand and accept my style. Sometimes slow down a little, and let go."

Nick remembered what Mrs. Hortensis had said about his style. "Because you can doesn't mean you should."

"Okay, I'll do that," Nick said, trying to exercise Mrs. Hortensis's comment about flexing his behavior. "Do you remember the interactive training we talked about for the process teams? Maybe it would help if we offered a training session for the whole group explaining behavioral styles. I just started learning about how I can flex my style. We could see where everyone fits and encourage support for our differences. I would like to learn how I could better interact with the new supervisor in *our* team," Nick said with a cautious smile.

Cindy nodded slowly.

Nick gave Cindy a stack of acknowledgment cards and asked her to hand them out whenever she saw an opportunity. "Look for individuals who are correcting missing handshakes. You can even identify people outside our immediate group and recognize them as well."

He also asked Cindy to find an organization that could provide training on behavioral style awareness. Nick shared with Cindy his discussions with Mrs. Hortensis and showed her the test he had taken. Cindy said it was similar to one she had completed. She recognized the basic concepts, but the names were different for the behavioral groupings.

"In the training I went through," Cindy said, "you would be a driver/driver." In an attempt to flex his style, Nick thanked Cindy for her observation without arguing or challenging what it meant.

Nick wasn't quite sure where Cindy would fall in Mrs. Hortensis's system. He was surprised that Cindy didn't think they worked well together. They always got results. Maybe it was his lack of people skills during interaction that Mrs. Hortensis had mentioned.

Both Cindy and Nick agreed that it would be interesting to discover how they could work better together.

After several calls, Cindy found a company called PTS-Professional Training Services and scheduled a meeting to discuss what the training should cover.

During the meeting, Nick explained what he hoped to achieve. "I want people to become aware of how they are perceived by others and conscious of how they can take responsibility for communication."

Cindy chimed in, "I hope people also realize that they are not the only ones who have certain feelings. We need to learn not to take things personally and understand that there are strategies we can use to improve our workplace. As uncomfortable as it might be at times, confront issues and stand up for ourselves."

Over the next several weeks, the consultant from PTS developed an outline for the proposed session. The material was similar to the system Mrs. Hortensis and Nick had discussed, but with a more in-depth focus on how to apply the information.

"Once you are aware of the different styles, the true challenge becomes how to manage behavior appropriately," the consultant said. "The session should be conducted in a room set up in a U shape so everyone can face each other. It may be uncomfortable for some, but we want an environment where people can't hide."

"It will be hard to get everyone free at the same time, but we will find a way to make it work," Nick confided. "I think I understand the four basic style differences and the labeling for each. Have you ever associated the style groups with different types of plants?" Nick asked the consultant from PTS.

"No, I've never had that request before," the consultant replied curiously. "Some systems use colors, some use animals, and ours is number-based. Let me do some research and see what we can come up with."

A training date was set.

New information added to Nick's "Essential Skills of Management and Leadership" binder:

ACKNOWLEDGMENT

Issuing close to forty-five acknowledgment cards a month, Nick was discovering missed opportunities to acknowledge individuals who were correcting missing handshakes.

Conducted first raffle:

- *Create visibility for the CPI program.*

- *Encourage more suggestions.*

EMPOWERMENT

There are two essential elements to an empowered environment:

First: *Clearly define goals and give individuals specific responsibilities.*

Second: *Clearly define objectives and give individuals authority to make their own decisions.*

Stop undermining the authority of those individuals around you, and encourage them to make decisions on their own. Focus more attention on establishing clear expectations and what the end/measured results will be.

PREPARING FOR THE FUTURE

"Knowledge held is a seed. Knowledge shared is a flower."

—Paul Allman

March

The awaited behavioral-style training event took place in the executive boardroom. Nick had worked hard to reserve that particular space because the PTS consultant mentioned training was better received if presented as something important. The executive boardroom did just that.

It turned out harder than Nick had imagined getting everyone to postpone pressing issues and attend the training. Some came willingly, but Bill was reluctant and vocal about what a waste of time it was going to be. Despite some resistance, overall the training was an impressive success.

Not only had the training been entertaining, it provided the group with insightful concepts on how to understand and respond to each other during tension. The majority of the group continued to discuss the information after the session and reflected on ways they could improve interaction.

There were those like Jim and Bill. Nick referred to them as the clueless 20 percent who complained that all they got out of the training was being labeled and put in a box. Nick heard comments like "You just can't simplify people that way," "I refuse to be labeled," and "I don't want to be stereotyped."

Nick tried to explain that the information was only a tool to assist in improving communication. It wasn't the training but their own behavior that was putting them in a box. However, a few still resisted. Ironically, their reaction to being labeled only emphasized the prediction of their behavioral style.

Nick scored about the same as on the questionnaire Mrs. Hortensis had given him. He was identified as a Quadrant 3–2, which meant his main interactive style was action-based, but he could also relate as an expressive. The names of the labels were different, but the concepts were the same. Nick learned that his number combination indicated his comfort zones, which were:

OPTIMISTIC (highest scores in boxes 2 and 3):
Action and expressive tendencies are both high in this personal style pattern. The individual is energetic, confident, and willing to explore new ways of improving things. There is a need to work on balancing his result orientation with more consideration for human relations.

PRODUCTIVE (high scores in boxes 2, 3, and 4):
A dynamic balance between the rational and intuitive tendencies characterizes this productive pattern. There is a keen insistence on quality results, but also a searching sensitivity regarding new perspectives and the unexpected. This pattern is characterized by intensity, consistency on creative quality, and results all at the same time.

OVERALL
This individual uses thinking to run as much of the world as may be theirs to run. He organizes facts and operations well in advance, defines objectives, and makes a systematic drive to reach these objectives on schedule. He enjoys being an executive, deciding what ought to be done, and giving the necessary orders. He has little patience with confusion, inefficiency, halfway measures, or anything aimless and ineffective, and he knows how to be tough when the situation calls for toughness.

This style lives according to a definite formula that embodies a basic judgment about the world. Adjustments in their ways require a deliberate change in the formula. Need to stop and listen to the other person's side of the matter, especially with people who are not in a position to talk back. Need to make some conscious use of feelings, preferably in appreciation of other people's merits. Should mention what is done well, not merely what needs correcting, as part of their formula. Tends to choose like-minded associates and needs someone to keep them from overlooking relevant facts and important details.

Mainly interested in seeing the possibilities beyond what is present, obvious, or known. Have curiosity for new ideas, tolerance for theory, taste for complex problems, insight, vision, and concern for long-range consequences.

The PTS instructor used numbers when referring to the different styles, because when added together all the style numbers—1,2,3,4—equal a perfect ten. That reinforced the point that all styles are needed for a team to be successful. It was amazing how evenly distributed the group was among the different styles.

During the session certain people epitomized typical representations of a specific style. Nick was surprised that he and Bill ended up primarily with the same behavioral characteristics. They both had high numbers in quadrant 3, Action. Nick could see some similarities, but he knew Bill as someone who could be very opinionated, direct, and demanding. If they were the same, why was it that team members complained about Bill but not about him? Nick did agree that they both focused on getting results. He could give Bill a task and count on it being completed.

John turned out to be the highest in the group in quadrant 4, Analytical. Nick assumed that was why he was so successful building those complex floats. Celeste, who was the center of fun for the group, was the highest scoring in quadrant 2, Expressive. No wonder she seemed to have fresh and creative spins on new challenges.

Cindy ended up being, as anticipated, Nick's opposite. She scored high in both quadrant 1, Harmony, and quadrant 4, Analytical. Nick learned the most when the consultant discussed the differences between his style and Cindy's. They both agreed that the information covered would be useful in preventing potential tensions or clashes between them in the future.

PTS-Professional Training Services had classified the behavioral styles, as Nick had requested, in terms of plants. Nick had fallen under the classification of succulent /conifer. His best guess was that Mrs.

Hortensis would be classified as a shrub/vegetable. He planned to share the information with her at their next meeting.

After the training, some people posted the results of their style questionnaire on their office doors, as if to say, "Come on in, this is who you will be dealing with!" Linda, who typically sat in the back area by herself, had become a real supporter of the CPI efforts. In the last several weeks she could be found encouraging people to submit ideas for improvement. She organized the making of behavioral style signs and handed them out for those who wanted to post something more formal in their office. They read:

> *Quiet*—QUADRANT 4: *Working, make an appointment.*
> *Beware*—QUADRANT 3: *Enter at your own risk and know your results.*
> *Smile*—QUADRANT 2: *Willing to discuss all ideas and challenges; creativity expected.*
> *Relax*—QUADRANT 1: *The journey is just as important as the destination.*

During the class the instructor mentioned how different motivators are associated with each behavioral style. These motivational comfort zones could be used to understand individual initiative toward challenges.

This was an area Nick felt could really have an impact on team members and asked the instructor for a good source of information about motivational theory. The instructor mentioned that PTS was offering a public seminar on motivation at the main hotel near downtown in two weeks. There were openings, and Nick signed up.

The course offered interesting insights for Nick. He had always assumed responsibility for motivating individuals but found out you don't really motivate people. The instructor in the class had emphasized that people motivate themselves and that true motivational force is intrinsic. A manager's focus shouldn't be on motivating individuals but on creating an environment where motivation can take place.

Nick had also believed that some individuals were naturally self-motivated and only needed basic guidance. However, he learned that everyone needed the right environment to reinforce motivation.

The course revealed that, just as Mrs. Hortensis had pointed out several months earlier, there are intrinsic and extrinsic motivators. Extrinsic motivational force, primarily through fear and reward, came from outside the person. To be effective these forces needed to be reapplied and intensified to get the same results on an ongoing basis.

Nick also learned that managers fall into traps believing that employees remember motivational efforts. Extrinsic efforts last about as long as it takes to deliver them. That meant that extrinsic motivators needed to be continual and varied to maintain a motivational environment.

The extrinsic force of fear can make people compliant. But what happens when that force is not there? Will they still do the same job in the same way?

The other major extrinsic force was rewards, playfully labeled by the instructor as "the trinkets and trash" side of motivation. You can offer small tokens of your appreciation, but how many times can someone receive the same coffee mug, with the company logo on it, before they say, "Thanks but I already have three of these" The first time the "trinket" hits a motivational nerve, but the second and third time it no longer provides the same excitement. That isn't to say that extrinsic motivational forces aren't important. Appropriate recognition and acknowledgment, earned promotions, and discipline have a place in motivating individuals.

However, true motivational force comes from within. It is intrinsic, a sense of pride, purpose, contribution, and belonging. The real management challenge is to create an environment where motivation occurs on its own.

Nick discovered how the information learned during the behavioral styles session could be applied to understanding individual needs, goals, and objectives. Nick laughed to himself during the class as he recalled Mrs. Hortensis's comment: "Get to know your plants, create the right environment for them, and they will thrive." He smiled as he realized how right she was. Maybe there was something to the gardening metaphor after all.

In order to create a motivational environment, Nick learned that the focus of management should be to create an environment of desired objectives. This can be challenging, the instructor pointed out, because you must deal with an individual's internal thought processes, or self-talk.

A majority of self-talk is negative and an original component of a survival strategy. When our early ancestors were discovering the new and unfamiliar, they reacted in a cautionary way. They were skeptical of items outside their comfort zone, until they discovered the positive or negative consequences.

This negative perspective is part of the internal voice, which focuses on potential risks around us. If the majority of our inner voice is skeptical and cautious, the instructor pointed out, "then the secret to motivational force is to make the positive voice stronger than the negative."

Help the positive voice by reinforcing the value of taking risks and exploring the uncomfortable. You don't support the positive voice by reminding individuals of what they are doing wrong and discourage them from exploring new challenges. The more present the negative voice in the work environment, the more likely individuals will perform within safe boundaries. Don't encourage people to make mistakes, but instead find value in setbacks. Learn from them without paralyzing individuals with the fear of failure. In other words, fail forward.

Participants were asked to take a minute and reflect on their own work groups. At the end of each day, which voice was reinforced and resonated louder and stronger in staff—their positive voice or their negative voice? Instead of reinforcing the negative voice, the focus should be on what people are doing right and encourage them to do more of it. Work toward making statements in the positive. For example, instead of saying you are against people who show up late, say you are for those who are punctual.

The instructor reminded participants that there certainly was a need for extrinsic motivators. It was important to reinforce deadlines, challenge individuals, and discipline or terminate those unwilling to adjust or comply with the needs of their work. But if basic fear and reward were the primary means of motivational force, then the real forces of motivation were yet to be tapped.

Motivational environments consisted primarily of clearly defined goals, awareness of intrinsic and extrinsic motivators, simplified reinforcers through visible feedback, and realistic visioning. For a manager, it meant creating an environment where a common purpose was understood, good behavior was demonstrated and reinforced, and coaching skills and performance feedback were applied appropriately. Nick discovered that a motivational environment consisted of good communication skills, strategic employee development, and meaningful performance conversations.

To further enhance his skills for building a motivational environment, Nick enrolled in two more classes, Coaching Skills and Managing Performance, which included effective discipline, giving feedback, and having performance conversations.

After the training, Nick began immediately to complete his delinquent performance reviews. In the process he asked his boss if he could complete them differently. By now Mr. Morgan was getting used to Nick's unusual approaches and gave him the okay, as long as HR was satisfied with what he completed. Nick worked with the HR department on how he wanted to do the reviews.

"For high performance to occur, an environment must be established with three key components: opportunity, ability, and willingness. Salary increases should reflect the performance of the group," Nick shared with the HR manager.

He wanted to remove expectations that there would be a salary increase regardless of team results. He developed a "critical incident" log that he would use in capturing information throughout the year. He suggested that performance conversations should be focused more on the quality of the feedback and lessons learned than on a form that was filled out or a potential pay increase.

Conversations should be a meaningful dialogue about the completion of established goals. To be an effective motivator the feedback must be: (1) fair and goal-focused, (2) include performance-based criteria, (3) appeal to employee values, and (4) provide feedback regarding specific performance factors, such as quality, quantity, and timeliness. Individuals who meet their established goals receive a percentage of their annual salary—around 2 percent. If the department or organization also accomplishes its goals, then a matching percentage is given—another 2 percent. An employee has the opportunity to receive a 4 percent increase based on total performance, both theirs and the organizations. He knew some in his group would not be happy with this approach because they expected to get an increase regardless of their performance.

The difficulty would be in establishing measurable goals and standards. Nick used the categories provided by HR but worked with his team to design a method to establish fair standards for measuring performance and goal completion.

For some performances, no goal existed. For example, an employee demonstrated exceptional skills in handling a crisis, took on extra work during a transition period, or took the initiative to improve the organization beyond his normal scope of responsibilities. Individuals who stood out were offered opportunities to choose assignments and were given promotions and incentives other than pay.

"Incentives should be given for some reason, and the perception should be because of meaningful contributive performance. Employees should understand through performance conversations how they supported the goals and expectations."

HR was very supportive of Nick's efforts. They were struggling with the existing performance review system and were willing to try something new. It was a constant battle between HR and management to get reviews done on time.

Nick added the information from the classes to the "Essential Skills of Management and Leadership" binder. He made a copy of the different styles and plants references to share with Mrs. Hortensis.

He wondered how motivational theory applied to the garden metaphor. It would be interesting to hear Mrs. Hortensis's thoughts on gardening and motivation when he visited her on Saturday. They were going to plant a vegetable garden.

Notes taken during the classes and added to binder:

ALL STYLES NEEDED ON A TEAM

A perfect 10 is: 1-2-3-4. All styles contribute toward a successful team.

Interactive style signs that can be posted in work areas:

Relax—QUADRANT 1: The journey is just as important as the destination.

Smile—QUADRANT 2: Willing to discuss all ideas and challenges; creativity expected.

Beware—QUADRANT 3: Enter at your own risk and know your results.

Quiet—QUADRANT 4: Working, make an appointment.

MOTIVATIONAL ENVIRONMENTS

Motivational environments consist primarily of:

- *clearly defined goals and expectations.*
- *visible efforts at flexing interactive communication style.*
- *awareness of intrinsic and extrinsic motivators.*
- *opportunities to grow and contribute.*
- *simplified reinforcers through visible feedback and realistic visioning.*

It means creating an environment where:

- *a common purpose is understood.*
- *good behavior is demonstrated and reinforced.*
- *coaching skills and performance feedback are applied appropriately.*

A motivational environment consists of good communication skills, strategic employee development, and meaningful performance conversations.

Extrinsic Motivational Force

These come primarily from outside the person and are achieved through fear and reward. To be effective, these forces needed to be reapplied and intensified to get the same results on an ongoing basis.

Fear can cause compliance as individuals respond to the demands of the workload. What happens when that force is not there? Will they still do the same job in the same way?

Rewards are playfully labeled the "trinkets and trash" side of motivation. Like fear, rewards can be overused with diminished effect.

There is a need for extrinsic motivators. It is important to reinforce deadlines, challenge individuals, and discipline or terminate those unwilling to adjust or comply with the needs of their work. If basic fear and reward are the primary means of motivational force, then the real forces of motivation are yet to be tapped.

Intrinsic Motivational Force

This is the true motivational source, and it comes from within an individual. It captures a sense of pride, purpose, contribution, and belonging.

The focus of management should be to create an environment of desired objectives and reinforce an individual's positive voice by acknowledging the value of taking risks and exploring the uncomfortable.

MANAGING PERFORMANCE

A high-performance environment includes:

- opportunity
- ability
- willingness

Performance Conversations

Planned meetings with those on the team should focus on discussing growth opportunities, ways to increase capability, and acknowledge willingness. These conversations should be more about the quality of the feedback and lessons learned than on a form that must be filled out. Information captured and shared throughout the year should be used to provide the feedback. There should be a process to assist managers in having a meaningful dialogue about the completion of established goals. To be an effective motivator, the feedback must:

- be fair and goal-focused.
- include performance-based criteria with agreed-upon standards.
- appeal to employee values.
- provide feedback regarding specific performance factors, such as quality, quantity, and timeliness.

For some tasks, the difficulty may be in establishing measurable goals and standards—for example, an employee demonstrating exceptional skills in handling a crisis, taking on extra work during a transition period, or taking the initiative to improve the organization beyond his normal scope of responsibilities.

ASSIGNMENT

Review which "voice" is reinforced and resonates louder and stronger in staff—their positive voice or their negative voice?

Instead of reinforcing the negative voice, the focus should be on what people are doing right and encouraging them to do more of it.

PLANTING THE SEEDS OF GROWTH

"Planting seeds of inspiration in well-prepared soil ensures
a bountiful harvest of fruitful thought"

—Paul Allman

April 3

It was somewhat overcast and foggy as Nick closed his front door. The
weatherman predicted morning fog until around noon, with a slight chance
of rain, but the cloud cover was expected to burn off by late in the day.

As Nick headed up the street he knew he was going to be early. They
had agreed to meet around 10:00 AM, but Nick was eager to share with
Mrs. Hortensis the new realizations he had unearthed during the last
several weeks. Also, with enthusiastic expectations, he anticipated working
in the garden. *I never knew that playing in the dirt could be so much fun*, he
thought to himself and laughed.

As he walked briskly, Nick's nose caught the smell of fresh soil, leaves,
and the invigorating moist air surrounding him. Mrs. Hortensis had said,
"Gardening was about enjoying the smell of things growing, getting dirty
without feeling guilty, and generally taking the time to soak up a little
peace and serenity." Nick was beginning to realize how true this was.

Today, for the first time, Nick was going to plant a vegetable garden.
He had heard that fresh tomatoes from the garden tasted better than ones
purchased from a store and hoped they would plant some.

He wondered why he hadn't planted a vegetable garden before. Sure, it
was challenging exercise, with the digging and hauling, but it was also an
extremely creative process resulting in healthy and delicious food.

Nick always thought that a large plot of land was needed; however,
he had recently read about growing crops using containers. It didn't

require much space, and in some inner city environments gardens were grown on rooftops and window planter boxes. Chicago currently had the greenest roofs in the United States, amounting to two million square feet. Utilization of space included the top of marquee signs and unused trash containers. He made a mental note to ask Mrs. Hortensis about container gardening.

When Nick arrived, Mrs. Hortensis was already in the yard. "Hi, Mrs. Hortensis," Nick said. "Kind of a bad day for planting. It's so overcast."

"Nonsense! The plants love it. It is like fresh air and water misting all at once. As long as we only have a few days it will be beneficial. However, more can encourage mildew on the tomatoes. This is just perfect weather for planting the vegetable garden. It's not too hot in the sun, and the plants love the moisture in the air."

"So we are going to plant tomatoes!" Nick said with excitement. "Is there ever a bad day for you?" Nick asked smiling, noticing that Mrs. Hortensis had more energy today than the last time he was there.

"Not as long as I get to make a choice," Mrs. Hortensis fired back. "We all have choices about whether to make it a good or bad day, and as long as I get to choose, I choose a good one. Lincoln said, "'We are as happy as we make up our minds to be.'" Happiness is a state of mind. Your mind is a garden, your thoughts are the seeds, and the harvest can be either flowers or weeds."

In preparation, Mrs. Hortensis had laid several small potted plants in rows on the ground, and she had arranged a variety of seed packages on the porch. Nick noticed she was holding a diagram of the area.

"Come over here, Nick. Let me show you our plan. The act of planting is one of the most exciting and hopeful moments in gardening," Mrs. Hortensis said, pointing at the piece of paper. "The key, like most things in life, is preparation. Years ago they used to say, 'Put a one-dollar plant into a ten-dollar hole.'"

"That's catchy."

"The preparation we did over a month ago has set the stage for a bountiful crop this year," Mrs. Hortensis explained, pointing toward the old vegetable garden that Nick previously tilled. "We will stagger the plants and only insert one-third of them in each row. Every other week we will add new plants. That will allow us to extend the harvesting season instead of everything coming up at once. We will also follow some crops with plants that benefit from the ones before. For example, snap beans will follow the radishes. It's called succession planting."

The plan included six tomato plants—two determinants and the rest indeterminate, several rows containing string beans, onions, radishes, Swiss chard, carrots, beets, cabbage, squash, leaf lettuce, white endive, muskmelon, and corn.

"I want these to be the best-tasting tomatoes I've ever had. Ones that melt my taste buds," Nick exclaimed.

"For flavor you can't go wrong with heirloom tomatoes," Mrs. Hortensis responded. "We're planting Gardener's Delight, an heirloom cherry tomato. It will have clusters of golf ball-sized, crack-resistant fruit. This indeterminate vine is one of the parents of the old standard Sweet 100."

"What do you mean by an indeterminate vine?"

"Indeterminate tomato vines have an undetermined growth pattern and ramble about bearing fruit until the weather conditions change. Determinate vines have a more compact and bushlike growth with heavy fruiting all at once. Both will give us some great-tasting tomatoes."

"Sounds good for salads," Nick said, smacking his lips.

Mrs. Hortensis smiled. "For a larger fruit, we're planting Brandywine, the Amish heirloom tomato first recorded in 1885. It has strong flavor and is intense and rich. Also," she said, pointing at two small plants near them, "Champion VFNT and Early Girl VFF. Since the summers along the coast can be foggier than expected, like today, we'll plant Oregon Spring V and Glacier. These varieties have the ability to produce fruit even in cool weather. They can sometimes even grow late into the season. These are my selections, Nick, but there are over three thousand varieties to choose from."

"Why is everything with nature so vast and complex? Why can't a tomato just be a simple tomato?"

"The 'simple' tomato has a varied and complex history," Mrs. Hortensis answered pedantically. "Originating in the Andes mountains of Peru, it was grown in Europe primarily for its unique-looking fruit. Because it was a member of the suspicious deadly nightshade, it was considered dangerous. Some of the nightshade plants were poisonous enough to kill even a wolf. As a result, the tomato was originally called 'lycopersicon,' or 'wolf peach.' The first edible reassurance came from Italy, where tomatoes became known as *poma amoris*, or love apples. By the early 1800s, tomatoes had become a main component of the American garden with a new reputation as a ripe aphrodisiac."

"How do you know when they are ripe?" Nick asked.

"A ripening tomato is simply a magical thing, the touch of nature's wand that rewards all that fussing and fretting in the garden from spring through summer. Tomato fruit needs forty to sixty days of good weather to ripen. When they ripen depends partly upon the variety, partly on the weather. The same type of plant may ripen in Georgia in May, in Virginia in June, in Delaware in July, and in New Jersey in August. A certain amount of heat is required to do the work. So temperature is important. Tomatoes do not do well when the temperature is cooler than 50°F or hotter than about 86°F. Ripening and flavor then depends on variety, weather, soil, and other influences. The United States Department of Agriculture (USDA) found that the key components of tomato flavor were three to ten times more abundant in tomatoes ripened on the vine than those off the vine."

"I always wondered about that."

"If you want tomatoes to ripen indoors, there is less chance of spoilage if you wash them in a solution of one part household bleach to four parts water, rinse in tap water, and dry. They shouldn't be stored cooler than 40 degrees. Cooler temperatures murder the tomato flavor. It is much better to let them ripen on the kitchen counter."

One area in the garden space was dedicated to herbs, and Mrs. Hortensis had selected different types of basil, two kinds of parsley, cilantro, several types of thyme, rosemary, sage, oregano, tarragon, and comfrey.

She had already laid string on the ground to indicate rows and asked Nick to run furrows between the strings. This created raised mounds under each string.

There were two large old oak wine barrel planters at the far end of the twenty-foot plot where Mrs. Hortensis had placed a collection of mint plants. "Placing the mint plants in the barrels will keep them from taking over and crowding out the other plants," Mrs. Hortensis said.

After reviewing the plan, Mrs. Hortensis sat on the porch and rested nearby as Nick worked. "I had a company come in and facilitate a meeting with the team about behavior styles. The questionnaire they gave us to fill out was similar to yours, and my results were about the same."

"What did it reveal?" Mrs. Hortensis asked.

"I was labeled an *action* person, one who expects results, measures others through achievements, makes decisions, puts out fires, is a bad listener under tension, and also tends to be impatient. I also had the ability to be *expressive* or *analytical* depending on the situation. To make it interesting, I asked the company to identify the different styles using plants."

"That is an interesting approach. Did they?"

"Yes. The *action* group I belonged to was labeled 'succulents and conifers.' This group can handle the tough situations, like drought, and can focus on just the essential items during a crisis. They will do whatever it takes to survive. This can give the perception of being tough-skinned and uncaring. They are also seen as the trees in the group. Imposing individuals who unintentionally look down on others, creating shady, protective areas where those not seeking the spotlight can thrive and sometimes hide."

"I like it," Mrs. Hortensis said as she looked over at one of the tall trees.

"They classified my opposite, the *harmony* group, as 'bulbs and ground covers.' They establish a link to other parts of the garden, through color and open spaces. Their reliable ground cover provides a space where interaction can take place, and from their open perspective you can observe everything. Like bulbs, sometimes their skills may be hidden, but given the right attention they can produce some of the most miraculous flowers. They just need to be tended to, or weeds might set in. Once established they are one of the more reliable, hard-working parts of the garden."

"Interesting," Mrs. Hortensis said, letting the word draw out. "So what style did you determine I might be?"

"Well, it is through observations over time and how individuals behave under tension that lead to insight on behavioral styles. I haven't seen you under any real tension."

"Oh, really," Mrs. Hortensis said, tilting her head to the side.

"No, I don't think I have. It must be all the gardening you do and the serenity and peace you say you find there."

Mrs. Hortensis looked at him and shook her head.

Nick put down his shovel, walked over to the porch, and sat down. He looked at Mrs. Hortensis, propped his chin in his hands, and thought for a moment. "I would say you are … an *analytical/harmony* person. However, you have learned to be direct and to the point when you need to be."

"Very good, Nick. On the green survey I gave you, I actually tested highest as an analytical. I also had high numbers in what you are calling the *action* and *harmony* styles as well. Somewhat an opposite to your style. What type of plant would that make me?"

"You defy classification," Nick quipped. "But the instructor classified the analyticals as *shrubs* and *vegetables*. Shrubs because they become the framework of the garden and many times create a protective boundary or windbreak. Vegetables because they provide the food for nutrients that keep us going and, like the analyticals, provide the procedures, guidelines, and structure for group dynamics. To be successful with a good harvest, you need to follow the rules and do things within a planned structure. That is what being an analytical is all about. I guess with your high score in the *action* and *harmony* styles as well, you would be at times a tall shrub or vegetables from a bulb."

They both laughed.

"You were right," Nick said, "about some people resisting the concept. Some felt like they were being prejudged or put in a box. Just like you did, the class emphasized it was only a tool to help understand and manage perceptions. Most people can exhibit a wide range of natural behaviors, putting them at times in all the different styles. The key is understanding what you can do when there is conflict or tension in communication. Even if the tension is content-based, you can manage the message by adjusting the paralinguistic aspects of communication. The secret to effective communication is simply a willingness to adjust, make it more comfortable for the other person to receive the message."

"That training was a good source of information, Nick. I like the way you tried to tie it together with the garden metaphor."

"I shared with the team how you can make tea using plants from the backyard. How the first time I tried it, all I saw was a bunch of leaves, but with a little understanding I became aware of the unique differences each one contributed. I found the behavior styles training the same. It provided me with a tool to be more aware of subtle differences and the essential ability to recognize unnecessary tensions. Flex my style. If the message was important to be understood, then shift the way the message is sent."

"It's also important to remember that it's not always easy to be flexible." Mrs. Hortensis added.

"Yes, and just because I flex my style doesn't guarantee success. It's only another tool used to help manage things, like expectations, group tension, and coaching situations. But if it works, why wouldn't I use it?"

"There are still many who don't," Mrs. Hortensis said. "They feel they don't have responsibility, and that poor communication is the fault of the receiver."

"If nothing else, I have exposed several people to a tool they can use. The majority of the group really enjoyed the session. I hear them kidding each other from time to time, saying things like 'You're just way too much of 3 for me right now.' Or 'The 2 is coming out in you!' Some even created signs to place on desks to let people know their tendencies. One of the 2s in the group even had a personalized license plate made for his car, which read SUCHA2."

"Don't let them clutter up their desks too much, Nick. They still have work to do."

Nick thought to himself, *That's what a quadrant 4/analytical style would say.* "The instructor talked about how the characteristics of the different groups also indicate needs and desires. So I signed up for a seminar on motivation to add to my awareness of motivational forces. In that class I received even more information to help me focus on creating better motivational environments."

"What do you mean?"

"Environments where people can tap into their intrinsic motivators. The same characteristics that group individuals together can also give you general insight into how to better shape a motivational environment for them."

"Give me an example."

"Okay, for example, the style I fall into likes being in control and in charge. A motivational environment for me might be one where decisions need to be made rapidly, issues confronted directly, and there must be a general sense of urgency to produce results. Certain manufacturing environments fit the bill perfectly. Other environments or work tasks may not be as interesting to me. That doesn't mean I can't do them, but it does mean they may not tap the same motivational force as the other. In the class we reviewed 'Vroom's Expectancy Theory (Valence x Expectancy = Motivational Force). Valence is what is important to the individual, and expectancy is the belief that important needs will be met."

"That is good stuff. Remember when we talked about motivation several weeks ago? Did the instructor talk about the three R's?"

"He taught us that we need to have SMART—Specific, Measurable, Agreed upon/Attainable, Realistic/Relevant, Time-bound—goals and a strategy to support them," Nick answered.

"Yes, that's basically it. For a successful environment of motivation to develop, you have to address the three R's of motivation."

"What are the three R's again?

"Realistic, relevant, and reinforced," Mrs. Hortensis said. "First, goals need to be realistic, challenging yet doable. This can be difficult because many factors can affect the original goals: changes in economy, business climate, management, and immediate employees. Periodically the goals need to be adjusted to provide a sense of success. If it is a major, long-term goal, then it should be divided into smaller logical milestones where completion can be visible."

"To give people a sense of accomplishment," Nick added.

"Yes. Second, the goals need to be relevant or relatable. In other words, the individual or group must feel some attachment to the goals. If they are allowed to negotiate and periodically modify the goals, they are more likely to take ownership of the outcomes. They also need to feel capable in performing to the required expectations."

"That sounds like the influence part of your commitment model."

"Commitment and motivation are closely related. Thirdly, the goals need to be reinforced. Specific measurement for success, periodic review, and acknowledgment can go a long way here. Sometimes just a simple phrase placed visibly throughout the organization can be enough to reinforce some fairly complex objectives. The garden stones I placed throughout the yard are an example of that."

"What stones?"

"Since we're almost finished here and you need a break, come on and I'll show you."

Mrs. Hortensis got up from her chair slowly and motioned Nick to follow her toward the back part of the garden.

Nick folded the paper he was writing on and quickly offered to help her up.

Nick's notes:

MOTIVATIONAL ENVIRONMENTS

Establish an environment where people can tap into their intrinsic motivators to produce the most long-term results. The same characteristics that allow us to group individuals together using interactive style can also give us general insight into how we could better shape a motivational environment for them.

SMART GOALS: *Specific, Measurable, Attainable, Realistic, and Timely*

FIRST: *To implement SMART goals, make sure they are realistic and challenging, yet doable.*

SECOND: *Goals need to be relevant or relatable. Individuals or groups must feel some attachment to the goals. If they are allowed to negotiate and periodically modify the goals, they are more likely to take ownership of the outcomes. They also need to feel capable to perform to the required expectations.*

THIRD: *Goals need to be reinforced. Specific measurements for success, periodic review, and acknowledgment can go a long way. Sometimes, just a simple phrase displayed visibly throughout the organization can be enough to reinforce some fairly complex objectives.*

THE STEPPING STONES OF MOTIVATION

"Even the most resistant and reluctant person may stumble upon a motivational truth."

—Paul Allman

April 3

Mrs. Hortensis and Nick meandered to the back part of the garden along a path Nick had never taken before. The bushes along the path had been trained to grow into an arch creating a tunnel effect. It was like walking through a giant bush of greenery. As they exited the farside of the tunnel, Nick found himself walking on the main path he had always taken. He stopped for a brief moment and turned around. *I never noticed that path before. Mrs. Hortensis sure has used every square inch of her yard.*

"There." Mrs. Hortensis pointed at the ground. "The stepping stone next to the bench. Can you see it?"

Nick had walked through this garden many times and had never noticed it before. There was a small stone in the pathway, about five inches by eight inches that looked like a stepping-stone. On it was: *The earth laughs in flowers. —Ralph Waldo Emerson.*

"I never looked at flowers that way, but he's right." Nick grinned. "Are there any more?"

"Some aren't that easy to spot unless you know where to look. It's in the same manner we create a motivational environment. To be effective, motivational strategies should blend in and become a part of the environment. Too much emphasis can make them an end objective and take away from the actual work at hand. Just like air, it should be there, essential but not visible. You know what visible air, better known as smog, can be like."

They laughed together, and Nick grabbed his neck to make a choking gesture.

"Look over there." Mrs. Hortensis pointed to some stones nestled in a bed of ivy and flowers.

Nick read them to himself.

> *The wind whispers my memories*
> *The sun warms my heart*
> *The earth reflects my being*
> *As nature owns my soul.*
>
> —PGA

> *May all of your weeds be wild flowers.*
>
> —Anonymous

> *How lovely is the silence of growing things.*
>
> —Anonymous

"Those sayings make you stop and think. I wonder if that's why there are signs on the wall at work with sayings, like 'Quality First,' 'Do it right the first time,' and 'The customer is always right.'"

Mrs. Hortensis smiled and nodded her head. "There are some more over here."

> *Cultivate the garden within.*
>
> —Anonymous

> *More grows in the garden than the gardener sows.*
>
> —Old Spanish proverb

> *As the gardener, such is the garden.*
>
> —Hebrew proverb

A flower is an educated weed.

—Anonymous

As a gardener you can always put PLANT MANAGER on your résumé.

"Wow! There are a lot of them. I think I'll post some signs in the office to reinforce our group's goals. Sayings that would support a more positive environment."

"Nick, let's sit down over here on the bench," Mrs. Hortensis said, catching her breath.

Once they were settled, Mrs. Hortensis, said, "It is even better if you work with the team. The process of developing them together can be very effective."

"You mean like I did with the group's purpose statement?"

"Yes."

"I'll try that … Okay, Mrs. Hortensis, I have a challenge for you. How does motivational theory fit with the gardening metaphor for management?" Nick grinned as he asked the question.

Mrs. Hortensis thought for a moment. "If you don't replace the nutrients in the soil, over time the soil becomes depleted. By periodically replacing those nutrients you create an environment where healthy plants can grow. But too much fertilizer and you can kill them."

"That's a good one."

"Now it's your turn, Nick. Apply a gardening concept to your work group."

"Like what?"

"For instance, fertilizers are essential during transplantation," Mrs. Hortensis said. "Synthetic or artificial fertilizers don't last as long as natural ones. How would those apply to management?"

"I guess …" Nick said, hesitating, "that when you are moving people from one job to another, you need to focus initially on acknowledging their performance in the new area, and in some cases additional incentives will help?"

"There you have it."

"That came to mind because I'm thinking about moving some people around at work."

"Sometimes putting a person in a new job can rejuvenate the individual. That is the basic principle behind rotating crops. Herzberg discusses the pros and cons of moving people around in his classic *Harvard Business Review* article, 'One More Time.' That's where Herzberg created the term 'job enrichment.' Sound familiar? Like when we dig up and add nutrients to the soil, we are enriching the soil."

"Yeah, it does."

"However, just like certain plants, some people don't need to be rotated. Herzberg pointed out that not everyone wants or needs an enriched job. Some plants actually grow better not being disturbed, and some actually thrive in poor soil."

Nick jumped in. "I have another one. Artificial fertilizers are like motivation from outside the person and aren't as powerful as motivation from within," Nick said proudly.

"Yes, you've got it. Those points are reinforced in the stones over there."

A good gardener takes responsibility for poorly producing plants.

—Anonymous

Your mind is a garden, your thoughts are the seeds, the harvest can be either flowers or weeds.

—Anonymous

"So that's where you came up with that phrase a while ago," Nick said, recognizing he had heard the saying before. "There is one thing I struggled with during the class on motivation. How does motivational theory address holding people accountable?"

"Holding individuals accountable can be challenging. Have you read Maslow's theories?"

"After the class," Nick shared, "I read about Maslow's hierarchy of needs, the ultimate level being self-actualization, a self-driven sense of fulfillment. In our work group some are really far from that. They won't follow through at all."

"Just because you are creating a motivational environment," Mrs. Hortensis said, "doesn't mean that you won't need to hold people accountable. Some people are at a more actualized state than others. They are at a stage where they can react and learn from their experience. Like

Mark Twain said, 'Experience leads to good judgment, so where does experience come from? Bad judgment.'

"Most individuals don't achieve a high level of self-actualization. As their leader, you need to provide your staff with guidance toward that fulfillment. Managers set themselves up for disappointment if they don't have clear guidelines with built-in measurements for individual and group performance. That's what holds individuals accountable."

"We are working on that," Nick said.

"It is nothing more than making it clear who is responsible and that they have authority to proceed. If the goals are realistic, the individual is capable, and the environment supportive, accountability is pretty simple. All you need is planned periodic measurements to keep things on track."

"Is that the ownership you talked about a while ago?"

"That sense of ownership is what McClelland and Burnham referred to when they said that power is the great motivator. Getting individuals to realize they have power over outcomes can be one of the most challenging aspects of holding people accountable. Most individuals don't know how to prioritize tasks and, if they do, may not prioritize them the same way the organization expects. The key is to discover which items are important and not yet urgent."

"I don't worry about items that aren't urgent. I have enough pressing items to occupy my time. If I worked on those kind of things, I would never get anything done."

"Nick, you should never worry about getting something done. Instead, worry about getting it started. I wrote a paper on identifying which activities are important and urgent. Once you identify them, the discipline becomes protecting your time to address items that are not urgent but important and require a problem-solving focus."

"So, it's all about knowing how to work smarter, not harder. There are people in my group that I wish I could just get to work, let alone work smarter."

"Work is not always easy, and sometimes it might be important to remind individuals about consequences."

"You mean write them up and put documentation in their personnel file," Nick said with conviction in his voice.

"No, that's nonsense. There is a time when you should focus on the punitive and take appropriate action. But there are a lot of steps to go through before you get there. Remember, punishment doesn't teach how to do something. The focus should be on coaching, not disciplining.

Nick, you need to attend a class on effective discipline," Mrs. Hortensis suggested, rolling her eyes.

"Funny you should say that. I signed up to take one in two weeks," Nick replied, as if to say, "So there."

"Good. Effective discipline is not about reminding people you are the boss and that you carry the biggest two-by-four. It's about redirecting behavior. As Thomas F. Gilbert said in his book, *Human Competence: Engineering Worthy Performance*, 'If managing and motivating people is about anything, it is about finding ways for people to be competent and perform at their full potential.' It's about building people up, Nick, not about tearing them down."

"Yeah, but you have to hold people accountable."

"Nick, holding individuals accountable means they understand the consequences at stake for the organization, what the stakeholder needs, and what the expectations are. What will happen if something is not completed or accomplished as planned."

"Does that mean I need to focus on the big picture and away from the person?"

"Actually, on both," Mrs. Hortensis said. "But it is easy to forget about the bigger picture when someone has missed a deadline. That's one of the reasons you developed your purpose statement, to provide a reminder of what a team member's focus should be. During the 1970s, it was popular to use the techniques of performance management. Later, many of those concepts were incorporated into the quality improvement and reengineering efforts of the late 1980s and early 1990s."

"What do you mean by 'performance management'?"

"The focus of performance management is that business is behavior. All management ultimately comes down to managing behavior, since it is through the behavior of people that all things are accomplished. Antecedents get behavior started, but consequences keep behavior going or make it stop."

"So I was right when I said a manager needs to be heavy-handed at times." Nick smiled slightly.

"Consequences are not always negative. They are simply the result of an action or condition. There are positive consequences, such as group recognitions, certificates of achievement, and of course promotions."

"Why would I reward someone who wasn't accountable?" Nick asked, puzzled.

"You wouldn't. But sometimes accountability can be improved by just making it clear who is responsible and making the consequences visible. Implement simple strategies and avoid several individuals with the same accountability for key project responsibilities, such as specific planning activities, key group decisions, and deliverables. Do this consistently for a period of time, and a team based on trust will develop.

"I'm learning there are some people in my group I cannot trust to get things done. How do I regain lost trust?"

"Trust is the key component in holding people accountable. If individuals lose trust in their management or the organization, they become less and less accountable. They let things go because they feel things have not been fair to them."

"That makes sense. You have to be fair and consistent. I know that." Nick stood up to stretch.

"At the center of any successful work group is the concept of trust. At the most basic level, employees trust that if they show up to work and perform satisfactorily, they will receive an agreed-upon wage. Employees also trust that what they signed up to do is what they will be asked to do. For example, if they signed on as an executive assistant but only answer the phones all day, it is not what they agreed to. Of course, that's part of the job, but they were led to believe there was more. Employers also trust that employees will show up and perform satisfactorily. Those basic trust principles lie at the foundation of McGregor's Theory X and Theory Y approach to managing people."

"If I trust someone to do a job, is that supporting accountability?"

"Yes, to a point. A relationship needs to be there to support trust when work becomes difficult."

"How do I build that trust and those relationships?"

"Several scholars have addressed this topic, even as far back as Socrates and Aristotle in the fourth century BC. The concept of trust building was debated. Aristotle wrote in *Rhetoric* that 'ethos, the trust of a speaker by the listener, was based on the listener's perception of three characteristics of the speaker:

1. the *intelligence* of the speaker—correctness of opinions, or competence
2. the *character* of the speaker—reliability (a competence factor) and honesty (a measure of intentions)

3. the *goodwill* of the speaker—favorable intentions toward the listener

"It hasn't changed much. Essentially you need to make meaningful contributions to the belief systems of the individuals you share mutual dependencies with."

"That sounds complex."

"No, it isn't really. It primarily requires a conscious effort. It means following through on your commitments, making sure your words align with your actions, and building up an account with the individuals you may want to withdraw trust from."

"Like a checking account?" Nick asked.

"Something like that, only this account is more like a savings account, better left untouched and allowed to collect interest. Once the account has reached a certain amount—some people require only minimal deposits, some more than is possible to fulfill—then the investments in trust begin to work. It is a very fragile thing. One can gamble and lose everything in an account with a person. Usually when that happens, it takes more in the account the next time to reach the same level of security. Sometimes an account is closed and can't be reopened. I coauthored a paper on trust I think you might like," Mrs. Hortensis said. "I'll share a copy with you."

"Thanks."

"Using our gardening metaphor, it's the same with plants. You can tell plants you are going to water them, but if you don't they will die. You won't hear a word or a whimper. They'll just die. Building trust is the same. Your actions are more important than your words. Indeed, it is through visible action that the foundations of trust are built."

"Maybe I haven't been the best role model. I know I've done things that if someone did them to me ..." Nick didn't finish.

"Some employees, even though their trust has been broken, continue coming to work. They show up physically but never really arrive. They go about the motions, but they are really somewhere else."

Nick just nodded. "I wonder if that's why Jim won't do even the simplest of assignments without some type of problem. He does his work only partway, never really completing anything. I know he's more capable than the work he delivers. Maybe I've closed the account."

"Maybe," Mrs. Hortensis continued. "There have been some very fascinating studies conducted on trust. I still receive several scientific journals, and I remember last year a review by the National Institutes of

Health (NIH) of a study done by the Swiss. The Swiss discovered that oxytocin, a brain chemical, increased trust in humans by reducing activity and weakening connections in fear-processing circuitry. The hormone oxytocin's effect on human brain function revealed that it quelled the brain's fear hub, amygdala, and brainstem relay stations in response to fearful stimuli."

"That's interesting," Nick said, but he was still thinking about Jim.

"Studies have shown that oxytocin plays a key role in complex emotional and social behaviors, and British researchers have linked increased amygdala activity to a decrease in trustworthiness."

"Is that information contained in the paper you have for me on trust building?" Nick asked, still somewhat distracted.

"No." Mrs. Hortensis smiled. "My paper was written a long time ago. I guess I'm getting off the point. The point is, once you have established trust, then the group can begin to slowly shift from the status of being a group to that of a team."

"We have talked about that before. You have called those I work with a group. How was it again we become a team?"

"Remember, a team has a common purpose—awareness of interdependency, sense of contribution, willingness to continually improve, and understanding of team processes. Teams are the foundation of high-performance organizations. There are all kinds of teams: process teams, work teams, management teams, and self-directing teams."

"I guess my group would be a combination of a work team and a process team. So how do I know if they are a team?"

"Back in the early 1950s, there was something called a 'sociotechnical' approach to workplace design. It has been described as one of the most 'highly relevant, least understood, and rarely applied perspectives' on management and organizational design. Under this system, individuals were multiskilled instead of only performing specific tasks. The approach placed emphasis on learning, support for innovation and risk taking, job design, role of management, teamwork, and sociotechnical balance. People and technology are treated as having equal importance."

Nick pursued his original question. "But how do you know when a group is a team?"

"The traditional roles and responsibilities shift when you change from the concept of a group to a team. To accomplish the transition, focus is on technical skills, administrative skills, interpersonal skills, decision-making skills, problem-solving skills, and leadership skills. Team members take on more responsibility for the day-to-day management of team operations. The shift is in the incongruence between the needs of individuals and the requirements of a formal organization."

"Are there factors that determine the extent of the incongruence?" Nick asked with concern in his voice. "Can you explain that?"

"First, the lower the employee is positioned in the hierarchy, the less control they have over their working conditions and the less they are able to exercise all their capabilities. Secondly, the more there is directive leadership of an individual, the more dependent the employee. Finally, the more unilateral the managerial controls, the more dependent the employee will feel."

"So it's the lack of power?"

"It's the dependency on top-down authority. You want to replace it with team-driven control and acknowledgment. In order to establish that, trust has to become a key component of work life."

"How do I lead my group to become a team?" Nick asked again, feeling he was getting nowhere.

"You've already started taking important steps toward that goal. There are some predictable stages that a group goes through in it's journey to become a team. Bruce W. Tuckman labeled them 'forming, storming, norming and performing.' Once you *form* a team, conflict is inevitable. That conflict leads to the *storming* stage. To resolve this stage, the group agrees upon *norms*—like how to compromise or move forward during conflict. Then *performance* begins. Periodically, the group can address performance-related issues and existing norms by going back to the storming stage. Properly facilitated, it is called brainstorming."

"If I get my group together and we discuss how we can become a team, will that be enough? How about developing the trust you were talking about?"

"Ultimately, trust becomes an established belief. At the lowest level, individuals must believe they have the capability to perform. We addressed that basic belief in the commitment model. Also, the role of a manager moves to addressing external relationships and removing obstacles to team performance and development."

"So I must focus on working with my management," Nick said, rubbing his chin.

"Effective team leaders become viewed as those responsible for managing the team's relationship with the rest of the organization."

Nick sat silently for a moment and then added, "Instead of just taking credit for team success, team leaders are expected to help team members grow and develop. Everyone on the team, including the team leader, is expected to perform 'real' work."

"Yes. It also means team leaders don't delegate the unpleasant jobs to others just because they can."

"This sounds like another five-year journey," Nick said with disappointment in his voice.

"The transition from being a group to becoming a team can take time and commitment. There are many factors that can impact how long it takes, including: amount of interdependence among members, size of team, functional diversity of members, amount of change required, expertise of members, organizational culture, and geographical locations. It takes time, Nick, and dedication toward developing group members. I found that I needed to free up about 10 percent of my members' time for training each year."

"So if there are approximately fifty-two weeks in a year, that's about five weeks a year on training?" Nick asked. "That represents a great deal of money!"

"Yes, organizations like IBM, McDonnell Douglas, Boeing, and Xerox spend around 3.5 percent of sales on training."

"Is training more important than selecting the right person for the right job?"

"The selection of the right person is very important. Putting someone in the right job because of their capability and desire is more powerful than training someone to do a job."

"Like my mom always said, you can't make a silk purse out of a sow's ear." Nick laughed out loud.

"Something like that," Mrs. Hortensis said. "Effective teams then should be made up of competent individuals who complement one another. That doesn't mean some members on the team won't have to flex more than others or that team diversity won't lead to conflict."

"Building a team is about managing the mix you have. I think I get it."

Mrs. Hortensis hesitated a minute. "Let's use a gardening metaphor called *companion planting*. *Symbiotic* is the scientific term for this association. Perhaps the best historical example of companion planting is the 'Three Sisters' in which corn, beans, and squash are planted together in one garden. Native Americans developed this system to provide food for a balanced diet from a single plot of land. Each of the crops is compatible with the others in some way. The tall corn stalks provide a support structure for the climbing beans. The beans do not compete strongly with the corn for nutrients since, as legumes, they can supply their own nitrogen. Squash provides a dense ground cover that shades out many weeds that otherwise would compete with the corn and beans."

"Oh, that's why we planted the beans next to the corn."

"Yes. Another example, maple trees can move groundwater from their lower roots to the upper roots, where the water is exuded into the soil. Herbaceous plants can use this groundwater when conditions are dry. Because of this, shade-tolerant plants often grow better under maple trees than away from them. The list goes on: Leaf lettuce grows well in shade provided by taller crops. Rhododendrons and azaleas thrive under pine trees. Corn growers often seed clover between rows so it will germinate after the corn is established. The clover grows throughout the fall and winter after the corn is harvested, increasing soil nitrogen when it decomposes the following spring. Grasses often are planted between rows of perennial crops, such as fruit trees. The grass alleys cool the soil, prevent erosion, improve water penetration, exclude weeds, and harbor beneficial insects.

"When planning a garden, remember that companion plants, though diverse in their characteristics, share the same requirements for good growing conditions. Unless you recognize and provide for these requirements, your plants will not succeed."

"I assume the same is true for organizational teams."

"Yes," Mrs. Hortensis said with conviction. "The transitional journey for building a team is learning skills to lead and develop a team. Manage the tasks at hand, of course, but also manage the perceptions of communication, establish motivational environments, invest in trust, document objectives, and identify essential performance measurements. With those conditions, and putting the right members together, you can take any group to the next level."

Nick and Mrs. Hortensis continued to talk until she finally indicated it was time to rest. It had been a long day. She complimented Nick again on his eagerness to learn and for allowing her to ramble on about her opinions and ideas.

He expressed his gratefulness and told her the privilege was all his.

Nick had avoided asking her directly about her doctor visits, but as they sat on the bench, he finally did. "Can you tell me more about the medical testing you are going through?" he asked cautiously. "If you're not comfortable discussing it, I understand, but I am worried about you," Nick said, putting his hand gently on her shoulder.

Mrs. Hortensis turned slowly toward Nick and took a long pause.

"They are not sure. It seems I have cancer in my lymph nodes, and it has been slowly spreading. They say it's too late to operate and, at my age, not really an option. The doctors have recommended medications and diet, and I am feeling the effects of their efforts. Not necessarily better," she sighed.

"Is there anything I can do?" Nick quickly offered.

"Nick, you don't know how much you are doing for me. As I review some of the management concepts with you, I am reliving my past. I am so lucky that we met when we did and that you have become so excited about both gardening and the information I have to share."

"You're lucky? I'm the one who is lucky. I've never been so excited about learning new information."

Mrs. Hortensis smiled. "I guess we are good for each other. Let's look at your notes."

"Just let me know if there is anything I can do. Promise?"

"I will, Nick," Mrs. Hortensis said gently.

They reviewed his notes, and Mrs. Hortensis filled in some of the important information he had missed. Finally, they walked into the house to find the papers Mrs. Hortensis had copied for him.

He offered to help Mrs. Hortensis as they walked down the path, but she said if she couldn't do it on her own, she had no business walking anyway.

As Nick was leaving the garden, he noticed a sign near the steps leading to the back porch: *A garden is a grand teacher. It teaches patience and careful watchfulness. It teaches industry, thrift, and above all it teaches entire trust.*

As they entered the kitchen, Mrs. Hortensis again mentioned a book she had looked everywhere for but couldn't find. It contained information she had collected over the years. She kept coming across a few of the pages, but there was a master book that must have been misplaced.

Nick asked Mrs. Hortensis about container gardening. She promised she would try and dig out some information about it, if she could only find her missing book of notes.

She said she would be traveling again to see her daughter, and they agreed to get together the following month.

Notes from the April meeting:

MOTIVATIONAL STRATEGIES

To be effective, motivational strategies should blend in and become a part of the environment. If there is too much emphasis on motivational strategies, it can take away from the actual work at hand and become an end unto itself. Just like air, it should be there, essential, but not visible.

The focus of motivation is to engineer a positive change in attitudes, to provide a simple way to focus a group's energy, especially under certain challenges.

Create a process for developing affirmations as a group, and post the results.

HOLDING INDIVIDUALS ACCOUNTABLE

Just because there is effort toward creating a motivational environment doesn't mean individuals won't need to be held accountable.

Managers set themselves up for disappointment if they don't have clear guidelines with built-in measurements for individual and group performance. That's what holds individuals accountable. Make it clear who is responsible and that they have the authority to proceed. If the goals are realistic, the individual is capable, and if the environment is supportive, accountability is fairly simple. All that is needed are planned periodic measurements to keep things on track.

Getting individuals to realize they have power over outcomes can be one of the most challenging aspects of holding people accountable. Most individuals don't know how to prioritize tasks, and if they do, they may not prioritize them the way the organization expects. The key is to discover which items are important but not yet urgent.

Holding individuals accountable means they understand the stakeholder needs and expectations and the consequences at stake for the organization. They understand what will happen if something is not completed or accomplished as planned.

Never worry about getting something done. Instead, worry about getting it started.

COACHING AND DISCIPLINE

Punishment doesn't teach how to do something. The focus should be on coaching, not disciplining.

At the heart of performance management is the realization that business is a behavior. All management ultimately comes down to managing behaviour, since it is through the behavior of people that all things are accomplished. Antecedents get behavior started, but consequences keep behavior going or make it stop.

TRUST

Trust is the key component in holding people accountable. If individuals lose trust in their management or the organization, they become less and less accountable. They let things go because they feel they have not been treated fairly.

At the center of any successful work group is the concept of trust.

How is trust built? By:

- *following through on commitments*

- *making sure words align with action*

- *establishing a "trust" account with individuals, an account where issues are addressed that are meaningful to them.*

Some employees, even though their trust has been broken, continue coming to work. They show up physically but never really arrive. They go about the daily motions, but they are somewhere else.

MORE THAN A GROUP—BUILD A TEAM

The transitional journey for building a team is learning skills to lead and develop a team. Manage the tasks at hand, but also lead toward a strategic future.

A team has:

- *a common purpose.*
- *an awareness of interdependency.*
- *a sense of contribution.*
- *a willingness to continually improve.*
- *an understanding of team processes.*

Teams are the foundation of high-performance organizations. There are all kinds of teams: process teams, work teams, management teams, and self-directing teams.

It is important to replace dependency on top-down authority with team-driven control and acknowledgment. In order to establish that, trust has to become a key component of work life.

The role of a manager is to address external issues and remove obstacles to team performance and development. Effective team leaders are viewed as those responsible for managing the team's relationship with the rest of the organization.

To establish a motivational environment, invest in trust, document objectives, and identify essential performance measurements. With those conditions and putting the right members together, any group can reach the next level. The selection of the right person is very important. Putting someone in the right job because of his capability and desire is more powerful than training someone to do a job.

DEVELOPING ROOTS

"What is a weed? A weed is a plant whose virtues have not yet been discovered."

—Ralph Waldo Emerson

May

CPI-Continuous Process Improvement concepts were beginning to spread, and several managers requested that Nick present an overview of CPI to their groups.

Cindy and Nick formed what they termed a resource team to lead the CPI efforts. Nick read in William Pasmore's book, *Creating Strategic Change: Designing the Flexible High-Performance Organization*, that for change to be successful you need to build a strong, committed coalition, including top management to lead the efforts. The resource team was just such a coalition, made up of senior individuals who owned resources—people's time, budgets—or had decision authority. Cindy recommended that the resource team, just like the process teams, be limited to nine individuals, and Nick agreed. There were several informal process teams developing and the new resource team would facilitate these as well. The informal teams consisted of individuals who had already participated on a process team, learned the tools, and wanted to initiate their own improvement effort. The new resource team would keep things consistent and organized.

So far, only one other group had initiated a resource team but as of yet hadn't launched any process teams. Ed had helped Nick in spreading the value of CPI to other areas. There were rumors that the CPI concepts might be utilized across the whole organization, but Nick hadn't really seen any evidence of that occurring.

However, Nick had been asked to make a presentation to senior management about CPI. He thought it might be remotely related to a recent meeting he had with his boss. During that meeting Nick highlighted a documented $280,000 his team had saved the company in just five months. Nick had developed a very simple cost benefit analysis tool that compared cost saving associated with improved process flow. Using both soft and hard dollars and expenditures for implementation, Nick projected the savings on a yearly basis.

At the senior management meeting there appeared to be some interest in CPI, but Nick had learned that at this high level individuals would appear to support just about anything until they really had to make it work. This was especially true if the president invited the idea. Nick remembered Mrs. Hortensis's comment about the 70 percent who waited to see which "side wins" before making any commitments toward implementing change.

One day Nick noticed that someone had earned an acknowledgment card from another resource team. He smiled to himself. *If we implement more of these resource teams, there could eventually be a competition to see who collects a complete set of acknowledgment cards.*

Nick read through the information Mrs. Hortensis gave him on trust, team building, and time management, and thought about sharing it with other managers. He also wanted to share the gardening metaphor but wondered if only he found it useful because of his new interest.

Finally, Nick mentioned the information during a lunchroom conversation, and to his surprise several other managers asked for copies. Nick duplicated and distributed them. Soon there was talk about getting together once a month to discuss the material and exploring how the concepts could be used.

The organization was about to enter the busiest time of the year, so a discussion time hadn't been scheduled, but they agreed to set something up in the near future.

Nick finally shared the gardening metaphor during the usual lunchtime get-together. The group found the idea interesting and christened the concept "corporate gardening." They had fun identifying references to gardening in everyday work language and came up with things like: *budding interest, planting* the seeds of ideas, *branching* out, *blossoming* individuals, *harvesting* time investments, and *germinating* change.

During some of the kidding one of the managers asked, "Okay, so how does your garden grow?" The phrase stuck. This interactive fun reminded Nick of the idea for designing a soil-testing kit for team performance.

The goal would be to determine the current state of a team and culture by analyzing how their garden grew. It could be a way to discover what needed to be added to improve the nature of a group's soil so it could nourish a team.

During one lunch discussion several managers were complaining about the finger pointing and blaming that was occurring in their groups. One of them quoted a Texan proverb: "When you throw dirt, you lose ground." Everyone laughed as they agreed that was another gardening metaphor.

During his last visit with Mrs. Hortensis, Nick found the idea of placing motivational phrases around the garden inspirational. He realized how they could make a person reflect on current efforts and refocus. Nick met with Cindy and discussed the posting of motivational phrases around their work area. She agreed it would be good as long as they weren't too "cheesy." Nick suggested then that the team, with Cindy's assistance, come up with some signs. So far only a few had been posted:

- *If on the weekends I want to be free, then right now it is up to me.*
- *Good ideas must be heard to ensure good results.*
- *Procrastination: the art of inappropriate delegation and of making everything late.*
- *Customers are everywhere!*

Nick wasn't exactly thrilled about the content of some of the signs, but they seemed to give the group something to talk about.

Cindy suggested rotating the signs once a quarter, and the CPI resource team was given the task of coordinating the effort. One of their members was assigned to manage the CPI bulletin board area and post current pictures of process teams, their objectives, the status of team recommendations, the status of employee suggestions, motivational signs, and the schedule of team skill development sessions.

Even though things were really busy, Nick made time to attend the coaching and performance management sessions he had signed up for. Performance management included effective discipline and, just like Mrs. Hortensis had explained, the focus of discipline should be on managing behavior and not on reminding people who has authority. Along with effective discipline, the sessions covered performance conversations, and the two together made up what the instructor called "effective performance management."

Nick discovered that coaching was actually one of the key components in creating a motivational environment. The coaching session subdivided on two key components: career coaching and performance coaching. The instructor had focused on career coaching first because all too often coaching wasn't done until there was a performance issue. If done appropriately, many of the performance coaching situations would disappear if efforts were placed on developing the necessary skills up front.

Nick learned that in career coaching, a manager takes responsibility for the personal growth of team members. Individuals should take the initiative to grow, but it is the manager who provides opportunities to develop skills based on a strategic focus.

The perception that managers should only use the skills individuals already possessed, without any planned growth, had always bothered Nick. He understood the reasons behind it; the pressure of work deadlines and a streamlined workforce didn't leave much time to develop people.

In many organizations being in the moment and getting things done "right now" was the main focus. That led to forgetting about looking into the future and planning personnel development efforts. There were also old beliefs that if you develop skills in employees they would only ask for more money or, once trained, go somewhere to be compensated.

The strategic development of employees was relegated to something to be avoided or only done when there wasn't a crisis. The trouble was there weren't many times when there wasn't a crisis, and when a lull occurred, it became comfortable to just relax and catch a breath before the next whirlwind began.

The instructor presented several key steps to successful career coaching:

1. Determine where the organization is going and where it needs to be. This would provide strategic information on what skill sets would be important to develop for the future.
2. Evaluate the current demands on the work group and determine what the group's skill levels are in meeting the demands.
3. Identify the specific interests of the individuals, and align them with future strategies.

The instructor pointed out that career coaching should become an essential part of the long-term skill development focus of a manager. He asked how many in the group had developed a spreadsheet of team talent.

Almost no one in the class raised their hand. He gave an explanation of how simple one was to develop. Across the top of a sheet of paper, list the key skills needed to successfully perform a job, both current and strategic. Then, along the side of the paper list the names of the people in the work group. Next, identify group skill levels by placing an X in the areas individuals were capable of performing and an O in the areas they were not prepared to handle. The evaluation of capability was determined through discussions with team members and upon existing task measurements.

Finally, a plan would be developed for each individual on how to turn the Os into Xs. The list should include both hard and soft skills. Hard skills, he explained, were those that were technical to the job—for example, running a specific piece of machinery or following a step-by-step manufacturing procedure. Soft skills, on the other hand, didn't follow specific steps but were governed by certain principles. They were described as ones that create the fabric of group interaction: communication skills, problem-solving skills, and teamwork. Soft skills didn't mean they were easier to do, just that they were guided more by concepts than specific linear action.

The instructor emphasized that skill development was probably the most important activity a manager does. He shared that since most were so caught up in completing the tasks at hand, they didn't see a real crisis coming until they were in it. That crisis occurred when key individuals left and no one was prepared to take over their responsibilities.

This made Nick recall when Fred left. Nick's boss knew Fred was thinking about leaving. Fred had even complained to Nick about his disappointments working in the organization. Yet, no one thought about what would happen if Fred actually left. When Fred finally announced he was leaving, there was a scramble to train someone else to perform the work that only he could do.

Nick remembered how he felt at the time. *If I was in Fred's shoes, what would be my motivation for training my replacement?* He had just signed on with another company and was not happy in the current organization. That's why he was leaving. What kind of commitment did he have to want to make his replacement successful?

The instructor indicated there was a question just as important as who would take over for a key person who might be leaving. *Who is going to take over your job when you want to move up in the organization?*

He pointed out that organizations are full of supervisors and managers who complain about being passed over for promotions. Yet, no organization is going to remove an individual from a successful work group and leave a big performance hole behind. In many cases, the lack of promotion is because no one was developed to take over for them.

The instructor pointed out that there was a dangerous double-edged-sword approach to how some individuals view their jobs. Some hold onto the secrets of their work and justify doing so because it is a means of job security. There are certainly those who do it because they are insecure in their abilities, but ultimately it is a form of security. You may become so secure in your job that you are unable to move on to the next one!

Nick found out that a great deal of key skill information in organizations was handled as closely guarded secrets.

The instructor had asked a poignant question, "How many of you earned better grades in school because you cheated?"

Everyone in the class looked at one another as if to say, "Are you kidding?" Some laughed, and one guy raised his hand and then quickly dropped it after looking around the room.

The instructor explained that most people were competing to get the top grade in a class and they learned at a very young age that knowledge was the answer to getting it. Individuals covered their answers during tests, and teachers looked for and punished those who might be caught exchanging information.

Eventually people move into the business world and some even into the role of managing others. They retain the belief that exchanging information is wrong, that it may be cheating, or somehow it will keep them from being at the top of the class. So people do not share information.

The instructor made it clear that successful organizations view the exchange of information as not only important, but critical to their competitive existence. Good managers encourage the sharing of information and the desire that the whole team should be at the head of the class. They create an environment where people feel comfortable in an open exchange of knowledge.

The instructor stressed that it begins with the manager of the group, and within acceptable limitations, they share the information available to them.

"Career coaching is easy to overlook and put off until the time is right. But without planning to make time for it, the right time seldom comes. Career coaching is about mentoring group members with an eye on the future," the instructor insisted. "Performance coaching, on the other hand, is more immediate. It's about dealing with the ongoing, day-to-day responsibility of managing the performance of individuals through counseling and tutoring."

A handout from the class explained:

As a performance *counselor* one should:

- assist in the accurate description of problems and their causes.
- develop technical and organizational insight.
- facilitate the venting of strong feelings.
- encourage commitment to self-sufficiency.
- provide objective insight into an individual's behavior and others' perceptions.

As a performance *tutor* one should:

- increase technical competence.
- increase breadth of technical understanding and problem solving.
- plan guidance to become a recognized expert.
- establish commitment to continued learning.

One of the most challenging aspects of performance coaching is confronting individuals about their performance. Another handout explained a performance coach's role when confronting an employee:

- Provide clarification of performance expectations.
- Identify specific performance deficits.
- Establish acceptance of the difficult and challenging tasks.
- Establish commitment toward continued improvement.

During the class Nick and the other participants role-played confronting performance. It was not easy to focus on constructive coaching without criticizing.

Ultimately, a coach establishes an environment where individuals understand their strengths and weaknesses. Through appropriate support and guidance, individuals learn to address tensions, conflicts, and concerns.

After the seminar Nick, along with Cindy, created a matrix of the essential skills needed in each work area. Three different job titles were identified, and a team talent/skill matrix was developed for each one.

Nick met with each individual in his group and together they filled in the Xs and Os of performance. Nick had decided to keep the evaluation criteria fairly loose. He based the criteria primarily on discussions of capability. In the future, he would adjust the ratings based on customer feedback.

Everyone was notified that Nick would be conducting "performance conversations" at least every month. He made it clear that the objective was to increase the number of Xs and decrease the number of Os. He also wanted to discuss future goals and determine what direction team members were interested in pursuing.

Things were so busy at work that Nick wasn't sure he was going to have time to meet with Mrs. Hortensis. It had been only a month since their last discussion, but it seemed like ages ago.

Being responsible really takes a lot of your time, Nick said to himself one day.

The weather was a lot warmer now, and the approaching summer was starting to show its presence. Nick found himself noticing different plants and flowers for the first time. Maybe that was what was meant by the phrase "Don't forget to stop and smell the roses."

It feels good to become more aware of everyday items and occurrences, he thought. Paradoxically they were there all the time but never noticed. *Awareness of those subtle things present but overlooked*, he reminded himself, *is such an important part of being a good leader*.

Before the recent crisis at work, Nick had made a couple of special weekend trips. One trip was to see the desert in full bloom after a series of spring showers, and the other was to view fields of tulips in a town several hours to the south.

It was not that long ago when he would not have made the time for things like that. *Stop and smell the roses*, he said again to himself.

LEADING IMPROVEMENT EFFORTS

Establish a resource team to lead the CPI efforts. It is a coalition made up of senior individuals who own resources (budgets and people's time) or have decision-making authority. Teams meet monthly to prioritize suggestions, assign and review management issues, and select and launch process teams.

The improvement teams utilize a cost-benefit analysis tool that compares cost savings associated with improved process flow. Using both soft and hard dollars, and expenditures for implementation, savings are projected on a yearly basis.

A member is assigned to manage the CPI bulletin board area and post current pictures of process teams, their objectives, the status of team recommendations, the status of employee suggestions, motivational signs, and the schedule of team skill development sessions.

Attend a performance management class that includes effective discipline.

CAREER COACHING AND PERFORMANCE COACHING

Career Coaching

This is easy to overlook and usually put off until the time is "right." Without planning to make time for it, the "right" time seldom comes. Career coaching is about mentoring group members with an eye on the future. A manager takes responsibility for the personal growth of all team members. Individuals should take the initiative to grow, but it is the manager who provides opportunities to develop skills based on a strategic focus.

Develop a spreadsheet of team talent. This prevents a crisis from occurring when key individuals leave and no one is prepared to take over their responsibilities. Cross-training can be challenging because some individuals hold onto the "secrets" of their work and justify doing so because they equate it with job security. There are certainly those who do it because they are insecure in their abilities, but ultimately, it is a form of security. Individuals may become so secure in their job that they are unable to move on to the next one.

Performance Coaching

This is typically focused on the immediate situation. It's about dealing with the ongoing, day-to-day responsibility of managing the performance of individuals through counseling and tutoring.

One of the most challenging aspects of performance coaching is confronting individuals about their performance.

Ultimately, a coach establishes an environment where individuals understand their strengths and weaknesses. Through appropriate support and guidance, individuals learn to address tensions, conflicts, and concerns

ASSIGNMENT

Review how information is being shared within the group. How does information flow from top down and bottom up?

OBSTACLES AND CHALLENGES

"When gardening stops, weeds begin."

—Unknown

May 17

When Nick arrived at Mrs. Hortensis's house, he could barely see her as she knelt down in the vegetable garden. Nick let himself in the front gate and briskly strolled over. Next to Mrs. Hortensis was a considerable mound of fresh green plants she had extracted from the ground.

"Did we plant them in the wrong place?" Nick asked as he approached.

"Nonsense," Mrs. Hortensis uttered, barely looking up. "Just clearing out the new weeds and thinning some of the vegetables. That will make more room for the ones left behind to develop and grow."

"It's good to see your energy is back. The new treatment must be working?" Nick asked, hoping Mrs. Hortensis would provide him with more insight into how she felt.

But that wasn't Mrs. Hortensis's way, and she just nodded.

"How can I help?" Nick asked, wanting to do something.

"Well, I'm already down here, so I can work for a while longer. Sit over there," Mrs. Hortensis said, pointing at the bench near the back porch, "and tell me about your month at work."

Nick sat on the bench, made himself comfortable, and took out a piece of paper from his back pocket. Since meeting with Mrs. Hortensis, he had become better at taking notes as well as listening to people at work. He found that if he captured on paper the message people were trying to send, he was less likely to interrupt. He could focus on the intent of their message instead of feeling the need to have an answer.

Still, with some individuals, he just powered through their conversations. He recognized that in many ways they were very much like him. With those who reported to him, he would have them write down what they discussed. At first some weren't happy taking notes, but it had prevented potential disagreements.

"I read through your articles," Nick said. "I really enjoyed the one on prioritizing work. I have set aside 10:00 AM to 11:00 AM every Tuesday and Thursday to work on priority A1 items. Did you come up with that system yourself?"

Mrs. Hortensis nodded. "It was a combination of several different sources. Some of it based on Benjamin Franklin's writing about making time for the thirteen virtues, and some from books on the ABC's of time management. I found that in the typical A task there was something missing. I felt I needed to focus more on strategic time, so I created the system. Ironically, strategic items turned out to be the ones most easily put off."

"Well, it works for me," Nick said. "I haven't fully introduced the concepts to my team. Cindy, our newly appointed supervisor, has started using it. She really likes the idea of having several hours a week where I agreed not to interrupt her. You know, in some ways she reminds me a lot of you."

Mrs. Hortensis smiled. "I'm sure that's a compliment."

"In many ways," Nick let the words hang in the air a few moments, "I showed several of my comanagers the articles on trust and managing priorities, and they asked for copies. I hope that is okay?"

"Yes, absolutely."

"Several of us are even planning on getting together and brainstorming how we could use the information with our groups."

"I am glad some of that old stuff is being put to use again," Mrs. Hortensis said. "You spend your whole life learning and collecting information, but when the end is in sight, you wonder what you should do with it all."

"I'm glad the chance arose for you to share it with me."

"Well, I think the timing was right for both of us. Nick, tell me about the class on discipline."

"You remembered," Nick said, surprised it was important enough for her to recall.

Mrs. Hortensis was already gazing at Nick when he glanced her way to give a response. "The instructor described performance management and how coaching and discipline are related. 'You need to coach and coach and coach, and then discipline,'" Nick said, allowing his voice to rise with each word.

"That's a good way to put it," Mrs. Hortensis said.

"Before you discipline someone, you must be able to demonstrate a coaching plan." Nick explained the new career coaching matrix he had created and how he was meeting with his team members periodically. He had developed a specific plan for those whose performance didn't improve through coaching: performance improvement plan (PIP).

"As you shared last time, discipline is about managing behavior. There are basically two types of situations that may require discipline. One involves compliance issues. If certain rules are broken (which were clearly part of the organization's culture and everyone was informed), then consequential action is appropriate and should be immediate. This is especially true if individual or group safety is involved."

"Compliance issues are usually well documented," Mrs. Hortensis added.

"Yes, usually identified in the organization's employee handbook and mirror what is inappropriate in society. For example: selling drugs, intentionally damaging equipment, falsifying information, or different types of harassment. The instructor referred to this as compliance discipline.

"He also explained performance discipline. Basically, if there are no established or clear procedures on performance, then prolong the coaching before disciplining. For example, you may have certain expectations about how loud individuals can talk during meetings or the quality of certain reports, but if there is no written procedure, then extend the coaching."

"Did the instructor say how long to coach?" Mrs. Hortensis asked.

"Well, you are looking for movement by the individual to adjust behavior. A coaching plan is developed to identify specific agreements and designed in a way that can give immediate feedback on the individual's willingness to adjust. The instructor spoke about a 'will' and a 'won't' as well as a 'can' and a 'can't' in most situations. When an individual demonstrates willingness but lacks ability, then coaching should be the focus. However, if the person demonstrates a *won't* attitude and the request is part of the job requirement, recognition of consequences and appropriate discipline may be called for."

"If they won't take responsibility for improvement, then the activities in the coaching plan are reviewed," Mrs. Hortensis offered.

"Yes, a coaching plan is designed in a way that future tasks can be documented if they lead to broken commitments. One just needs to simply keep track of broken commitments, and eventually the level of discipline required can be honestly justified."

"Good, Nick. You actually focus on behavior changes."

"Yes, the instructor described behavioral change with regard to individual habits. He said for most of us to integrate specific changes into our lives we must actively pursue supporting activities for a minimum of twenty-one days. After that a new habit is developing to support the change. Consequentially, if you need a coaching timetable, establish a performance improvement plan that focuses on the next thirty days. Look for and compliment progress. If there is no movement, start the process of discipline. There are several factors that affect the level of performance discipline: degree of egregious behavior, length of time with the organization, and past record."

"Nick, we called that progressive discipline," Mrs. Hortensis shared. "We realized that discipline would not succeed if we didn't gain the employee's commitment to change. Our strategy was to focus on improving future performance rather than punishing for past misdeeds. The process went through certain stages, such as verbal counseling or a warning, then a written warning, suspension or probation, and finally termination. We also tried to follow the golden rules of discipline: demonstrate respect for the individual, maintain a positive attitude, and ultimately, based on the employees actions, provide a second chance."

"I guess when it comes to disciplining people, things haven't changed that much," Nick said.

"Well, maybe the documentation part has changed. I remember when input from the manager was enough. No one really challenged the decisions made thirty years ago regarding poor performance. I would imagine now that there is a great deal more concern about being able to justify disciplinary decisions."

Nick nodded. "Inappropriate discipline is a hot topic in today's organization. Disgruntled employees are suing companies left and right for unfair treatment. Sometimes they are justified. The instructor reviewed with us an analysis guide to help make decisions justifiable. There were six key questions that covered everything from process-related issues, skill-based issues, quality standards, and existing policies."

"That sounds like a good checklist," Mrs. Hortensis said.

"There were two additional key questions that needed to be answered: What was the behavior you modeled? And what were the things you allowed? The instructor indicated that the issues surrounding the behavior you model were fairly obvious. Were you disciplining someone for behavior you were doing yourself? If so, to obtain better compliance, simply start demonstrating the appropriate behavior. If you were engaged in the inappropriate behavior for a while, then go out of your way to demonstrate the new behavior. Openly compliment those doing it correctly and acknowledge that you were doing it incorrectly. If you have been allowing certain behavior to occur then the focus should be on not permitting individuals to continue to behave inappropriately. Confront individuals and start reinforcing proper behavior by directing individuals to meet the agreed upon performance. In the class we had to role-play confronting individuals directly."

"I'll bet that wasn't easy to do it," Mrs. Hortensis said. "It took me a long time to get comfortable with directly confronting people. It takes skill to confront an individual in a way they don't feel attacked. Finally, I realized that the longer I put things like that off, the worse they usually got."

"You're right, it's not easy," Nick said. "The instructor talked about DJA. During any coaching session you can easily be sidetracked by denial, justification, and accusation. We learned some great strategies for staying on track. The instructor also had another way of looking at things you allow. Have you allowed the person to take charge and be responsible for his actions?"

"That is an interesting way to look at what you allow," Mrs. Hortensis agreed.

"If you successfully answered all of the questions, then it is appropriate to immediately begin the disciplinary process."

"Nick, these classes have really shaped your understanding of the role of managing others. Many people don't really appreciate what an honor it is to guide the development of a group or an individual. They only focus on the results of the team and forget their responsibility to improve team members. You have honestly taken on that responsibility and have really grown over the last several months."

"Not as much as some of your plants," Nick said, trying to make a joke and pointing at the vegetable garden. "I wonder how coaching and discipline fit into your gardening metaphor for management."

Mrs. Hortensis shook her head and began to get up slowly. "Well, it's time for you to take over now," she said as she pushed off the ground near the vegetables.

Nick jumped up, rushed over to help her up, and then took over the weeding.

Mrs. Hortensis sat down slowly on the bench and said, "We prepared the soil and planted the seeds in a situation where they could succeed. We are providing discipline now by removing those that don't comply. It can be a difficult decision and hard work, but by removing a few that don't belong, we create a better space for others to grow in."

Nick smiled. She could find a gardening analogy for just about anything.

They continued to talk about performance management issues. Nick asked Mrs. Hortensis if she had ever thought about developing a training class where plants were used as the instrument for learning basic management skills. She said she hadn't but thought it was an interesting idea.

That day over lunch they outlined what it might look like. The first part of training would review some of the key skills needed to successfully manage others. Nick shared with Mrs. Hortensis that he had started developing a notebook he called "Essential Skills of Management and Leadership," which contained the information from the classes and what she had shared with him. They could use some of that information.

Then they would have class participants work together in teams to grow different plants. The teams would be arranged, based on results of the behavioral style survey, with the objective to keep the team as diverse as possible.

The class would review leadership, mentoring, and communication skills and discuss the challenges of understanding group dynamics using soil preparation as a metaphor. Then the class would literally plant seeds and nurture them for ten weeks. During that time they would discuss motivational theory, coaching, discipline, time management, trust building, and problem solving.

Mrs. Hortensis mentioned how the National Gardening Association aimed to put a garden in every public school. Currently in three thousand California schools, children are learning how food gets on the table. Children who hated vegetables in the past have become avid gardeners and consume the fruits of their labor. Research has shown that children change their eating habits as a result of tending a garden. Maybe managers would change some of their concepts about guiding people through a gardening exercise.

Nick had read that some cities, with public parks of five acres or more, were carving out spaces for community gardens to encourage people to grow their own food. He suggested at the end of the class that the group could eat a salad using the output from the class.

Mrs. Hortensis wasn't so sure that eating a salad at the end of the class was a good idea because of potential liabilities, but they kept the idea as a possibility.

Nick shared how he wanted to create a learning organization, a work setting that would provide an opportunity to extend the utilization of the information he was discovering. Important learning occurs on the job or in situations of application, and not in a classroom. The most effective learning is social and active, not individual and passive. And the most important things for people to learn aren't the explicit rules, procedures, and policies of the workplace, but the tacit stuff found in intuition, judgment, and common sense that are embedded in the chaos of every day activity. One article by Daniel Kim, *The Link Between Individual and Organizational Learning*, pointed out that the organization's unrecorded wisdom is more valuable than its captured knowledge. These assets should be developed and enhanced by social exchanges.

Nick had reflected on his process teams and understood they were a great venue for harnessing this knowledge.

Early writings from Chris Argyris, Peter Senge, and Donald Schön supported Nick's opinion of the process teams. They agreed that effective learning organizations help people recognize and share with others the mental models that influence their actions. Without clear processes people make assumptions. Chris Argyris called this predisposition for jumping to conclusions "climbing the ladder of inference." Our mental models misrepresent reality, and as a result, we attack the symptoms of our problems rather than identifying and correcting the underlying causes of them. These ineffective mental models arise from incompleteness and internal contradictions.

Edgar Schein, one of the chief proponents of learning cultures, defined organizational cultures as "the accumulation of prior learning based on prior success, a pattern of assumptions ... invented, discovered, or developed by a given group ... as it learns to cope with its problems." That is what Nick had hoped the process teams would do, review the assumption and through group interaction develop a culture of continual learning.

Schein proposed creating psychologically safe havens in organizations to encourage learning. If the training class envisioned by Nick were implemented, the participants would have safe opportunities to practice, with support and encouragement to overcome the fear associated with making errors. At the same time managers could provide coaching for efforts in the right direction and develop norms to reward innovative thinking.

Nick had taken good notes and was looking forward to designing something he could put in place.

After lunch, Mrs. Hortensis showed Nick how to take cuttings to start new plants. This was the prefect time of the year to do so. As they trimmed some of the plants, they potted the cuttings to start new ones. Mrs. Hortensis pointed out that the principles used in making cuttings could be applied in the business world. It could be a metaphor for when a business begins to expand and create branch offices. As they talked, Mrs. Hortensis as usual threw out some amazing quotes. Nick wrote down as many as he could:

> *An old shrub can be rejuvenated by removing its dead stems and trimming the strongest ones that remain.* —Unknown

> *When planning for a year, plant corn. When planning for a decade, plant trees. When planning for life, train and educate people.* —Chinese proverb

> *Plant trees. They give us two of the most crucial elements for our survival: oxygen and books.* —A. Whitney Brown

Toward the end of their day together, Mrs. Hortensis showed Nick how to plant new vegetables in the incomplete rows started the month before. He didn't need much coaching.

Nick talked about work and explained that things were busier than any time before, but more interesting and exciting than ever. He shared that he almost didn't make it this weekend. A couple of issues came up that could have caused him to work on Saturday, but at the last moment they had been resolved.

Mrs. Hortensis shared that she was thankful he had made it because her energy came in spurts and some days weren't as good as others. Today, she felt good. She explained that new treatments were scheduled in the next few weeks and she was sure she would be back to her old self by June.

Nick took the opportunity to inquire more about how she was really feeling. He reminded her of her promise to let him know if there was anything he could do. She shared with Nick that whatever the results were, she had led a complete life. She had been given the chance to achieve so much and was okay to move on. Those who fear death, she expressed, were the ones burdened with regret in that they had not undertaken the things they really wanted to do, creating a sense that more time was needed to pursue what had been put off.

In contrast, she had been fortunate to be involved with the things she enjoyed her whole life. Nature and the garden had provided such a unifying thread. She felt that if you lived long enough, there is a point in one's life when you feel you're reliving experiences. As exciting as spring is, there becomes a time when winter seems to last longer. She compared it to rewatching your favorite movie. It was still enjoyable but the surprises were gone.

"Besides," she said with a smile, "one of the measures of a fulfilled life is knowing you will continue to live on in the minds of those you have given to. As you share, so have you distributed your existence into the future."

Mrs. Hortensis reminisced how her uncle introduced her to gardening as a young girl. She always loved going to his house and discovering the secret gardens he had hidden around his property, utilizing every space available to delight the senses.

Nick was still concerned about the new treatments and again asked politely if there was anything he could assist with. She assured him that if there was anything he could do, she would let him know, and they agreed to get together again in June after her next series of treatments.

Mrs. Hortensis warned Nick to look forward to more weeding and trimming. "By that time," she said, "our garden will be in full bloom. Nick smiled at the "our" garden part.

She gave Nick a few more handouts to look over and mentioned again about that "master" book she was still unable to locate. Nick noticed a tone of disappointment in her voice.

Meeting notes, May 17:

DISCIPLINE

A good performance manager understands the difference between coaching and discipline. You need to coach, coach, and coach, and then discipline.

Before you discipline someone, you must be able to demonstrate a coaching plan. Develop a specific plan for those whose performance doesn't improve through coaching, and transition your efforts to a performance improvement plan (PIP).

Two types of situations, which may require discipline, are:

> *compliance discipline*
> *performance discipline*

Compliance Discipline

If certain rules are broken that were clearly documented as part of the organization's culture and everyone is informed about them, then consequential action is appropriate and should be immediate. This is especially true if individual or group safety is involved. Compliance issues are usually well documented in the organization's employee handbook or workplace procedures and many times mirror what is inappropriate in society—for example, selling drugs, intentionally damaging equipment, falsifying information, or various types of harassment.

Performance Discipline

If there are no established or clear procedures on performance, then prolong the coaching before disciplining. For example, you may have certain expectations about how loud individuals can talk during meetings or about the quality of certain reports, but if there is no written procedure then extend the coaching. Spend time clarifying your expectations instead of confronting the individual and threatening consequences of poor performance.

- Develop a coaching plan that identifies specific agreements, designed in a way so that you can give immediate feedback on the individual. Schedule frequent planned interactions over the next thirty days, with measurable goals. Focus on positive reinforcement.

- Look for movement by the individual in an attempt to adjust their behavior. When an individual demonstrates willingness but lacks ability, then coaching should be the focus. However, if the person demonstrates a won't attitude and the request is part of the job requirement, recognition of consequences and appropriate discipline may be called for.

REACHING AGREEMENT

A coaching plan is designed in a way so that future tasks can be measured and documented. If they lead to broken commitments, just simply keep track of broken commitments, and eventually the level of discipline required can be honestly justified.

It is important to focus on improving future performance rather than punishing for past misdeeds. Follow the golden rules of discipline:

- *Demonstrate respect for the individual.*

- *Maintain a positive attitude.*

- *Ultimately, based on the employee's actions, provide a second chance.*

There are two key questions that need to be asked when reviewing performance:

- *What was the behavior you as the leader modeled?*

- *What were the things you as the manager allowed?*

CREATING SKILL DEVELOPMENT OPPORTUNITIES

Many people don't really appreciate what an honor it is to guide the development of a group or an individual. They only focus on the results of the team and forget their responsibility to improve team members.

Process teams are a great venue for harnessing the knowledge of the organization's unrecorded wisdom. These assets are developed and enhanced by the opportunity to learn from each other and plan social exchanges.

Develop training to create psychologically safe havens to encourage learning. And establish a learning culture.

Solo Flight

"When one tugs at a single thing in nature, he finds it attached to the rest of the world."

—John Muir

June

Nick launched a new management training series at work using planting seeds as part of the learning model. The concept was to link participants' success in growing plants to the essential skills needed for leading and managing others. Nick obtained management approval for the training because of the progress his team had achieved in such a short period. He remembered Mrs. Hortensis's advice. Support from the top will develop if one can show documented results. "Focus on what you can control and change, instead of worrying about what others should do to facilitate situations."

To Nick's dismay there weren't that many people who volunteered to attend. Mrs. Hortensis had warned Nick that if people were busy it would be easy to rationalize not having time for training.

Nick contacted PTS-Professional Training Services to do some of the classroom instruction. PTS had developed a ten-module program covering the necessary skills needed for effective management. In fact, they used Nick's suggestion for a program title. They called the training Essential Skills of Management and Leadership. The topics included: role of management and leadership, communication skills, leadership style, career development, performance management, coaching, problem solving and decision making, motivation environments, time management, continuous improvement, and team building.

Nick liked the mixture of presentation techniques PTS used. They created a learning environment, which encouraged participation, the sharing of experience, and comfortable personal growth. He was always amazed at how fast time went by during each session.

Once participants completed the classroom activities, individuals were selected to work together on teams and apply the principles learned. Everyone had to participate an hour a week for one month, but interaction could go longer if team members wanted.

During the month, the teams would meet to review and discuss the material from the class. PTS had developed a guide to help facilitate discussions and reinforce key points. The teams were challenged to grow selected plants and re-experience the principles learned during the training.

Nick found an old vacant laboratory room and received permission to use it. The space was perfect, out of the way, with north-facing windows and existing fixtures to hang growing lights. At first, Nick's boss questioned what they might be growing, but Nick assured him that everything was aboveboard, and his boss gave approval.

Nick felt Mr. Morgan agreed because of his firsthand experience with the training. He attended the session on communication and admitted he found it quite informative. Nick even noticed changes in the way they interacted since his attendance.

During the "growing plants" stage, participants would be evaluated for their level of support and contribution. Nick created a criteria list for reviewing the results, and resource team members volunteered to be the judges.

It went better than Nick had anticipated. The groups were having fun with what they called "nontraditional" learning. They all agreed it was very valuable to get together and revisit the material from the sessions.

As the plants grew, everyone could immediately see results. Nick hoped that if nothing else, during this part of the training, participants would become more aware of how to better observe measurable outcomes because the ability to nurture and grow team members was such a crucial part of successful management.

In the training room, someone had posted a sign near the growing plants: "No Chia Pets allowed."

Today was the first time Nick had not been punctual since he began meeting with Mrs. Hortensis. He arrived late from a research trip to

Chicago because the flight had been delayed several times due to weather, and at one point Nick thought the flight might be cancelled.

The company sent him to Chicago to learn more about process improvement techniques. Through contacts from his boss, Nick had arranged a meeting with one of the giants in his industry. Nick hoped to acquire insights on best practices and other ways to improve efficiencies. He also planned to find out what type of management development programs they currently utilized.

Nick was running at a fast pace as he approached Mrs. Hortensis's house. He noticed she was not in the front yard as he opened the gate. *She is probably in the back and started working without me,* Nick thought to himself. *By now she has dug up the whole garden and started over again. I know she will have something to say about me being late.*

Mrs. Hortensis seemed very persnickety about schedules and keeping commitments. Nick smiled to himself because he couldn't imagine her being late for anything.

Nick closed the front gate and with quick strides headed toward the back of the house by way of the shortcut through the tunnel of greenery on the side yard. Once he had discovered this path, he took it whenever he could.

He still marveled at the way this space was developed. The bushes had grown to twenty feet tall with the tops pulled across the space and tied to form connecting arches. Over time, the branches had intertwined and formed a wonderful natural arch. A beautiful collection of bromeliads lined the walkway, protected all day from direct sunlight. In the trees several different types of Tillandsias were growing.

Mrs. Hortensis had said this was a perfect environment for bromeliads because they were epiphytic and used their roots primarily as an anchor to whatever they choose to live on. They got their moisture not from the roots, but from scales on the leaves. If the scales were present in sufficient numbers, they gave a silvery cast to the leaves. Mrs. Hortensis had shared that sometimes their distribution gave the appearance of silver bands. Several of the bromeliads were in bloom with single long spikes capped with bright red seed tops, arising from the center of a rosette. The plants ranged in size from six inches tall to clusters that were two feet around. The dark green long-leaf brackets were pointed on the end, and when Nick brushed against them they jabbed him as if to say, "Look, but don't touch."

They are exotic and impressive-looking, Nick thought. *That these beautiful flowers came from a plant that doesn't have its roots in soil, or follow the conventional behavior of most plants, there must be some management lesson in that. Maybe that's the definition of a consultant.*

Nick had told Mrs. Hortensis that he was unfamiliar with bromeliads, and she reminded him that a pineapple was one of the better-known varieties.

Nick emerged into the backyard and joined the main path as he called out to Mrs. Hortensis. She did not answer. As he wandered through the garden searching for her, he was still amazed each time how his eyes were drawn to something new. Nick called for Mrs. Hortensis several times, with no response. Finally, he retraced his steps to the house from the farside of the garden.

That's strange, he said to himself, approaching the back porch. *If Mrs. Hortensis is not already working in the garden, maybe she's making us tea.* Approaching the back door, Nick noticed a note neatly pinned to the screen.

He sprinted over and grabbed the note. With incredible handwriting Mrs. Hortensis had written she would have to miss their meeting. She would be at a special facility up north, and the next several weeks looked unpredictable as well.

At first, Nick didn't really absorb the message because he was so impressed with the penmanship. *This is the way everyone should write. It has flair and is perfectly aligned, a flowery style almost like calligraphy.*

The note suggested they get together next month and wondered if July 17 would work. Nick mentally reviewed his calendar. He couldn't remember anything conflicting with the date. The note continued and invited Nick to look in on the garden while he was there, pick some vegetables, and if he had time during the next few weeks, to stop by once in a while to keep the weeds from taking over.

Mrs. Hortensis also had uncovered several pages of information in her search for the master book she couldn't locate and had left them on the kitchen table.

"Make yourself at home," she wrote. "I left a key under the pot of gardenias to the left of the back door. Go in the kitchen and fix yourself some tea!"

Nick let himself in and walked over to the kitchen table as his mind began wondering what might be happening with Mrs. Hortensis. She indicated last time that things were getting better. *Maybe her new treatments just created a scheduling conflict and that's why she couldn't make it,* Nick said to himself, trying to manage his negative voice. *She said she would let me know if I could do anything, and she has. I will keep this garden in tip-top shape waiting for her return.* He noticed the articles she had promised him laying on the table along with scrap paper and pencils.

He wrote a note to Mrs. Hortensis conveying his disappointment that they couldn't meet. He expressed his concern and hoped everything was all right. He was looking forward to July, and the seventeenth would be fine.

Nick quickly thumbed through the neatly stacked pile of papers on the table. *This could take some time,* he thought to himself. *I should make some tea first.*

Taking a pair of scissors from the cabinet drawer, Nick headed back out into the garden.

"It smells so fresh," Nick said as he lingered, heading toward where the mint plants were located. He picked several different mints and noticed a flowering jasmine bush as he returned to the kitchen. Mrs. Hortensis had mentioned that jasmine sambac was the flower used for making jasmine tea and said it would be blooming soon. Nick decided to add some flowers to his tea.

As Nick stepped up on the back porch, he noticed all the weeds in the vegetable garden. "Where did all those come from, and so quickly?" he exclaimed out loud. "I'll drink some tea, read a few of the papers from the pile, and then I'll confront the weeds."

Nick prepared the tea leaves as he had seen Mrs. Hortensis do so many times. Then he went to the table and began going through the information. There was a note on the top of the pile that read: "I bet there are a lot of weeds everywhere! Here is some good reading material for you."

"Mrs. Hortensis is right about that. I can't believe all the weeds that have appeared in just a few weeks," Nick said out loud to an empty house.

He quickly sorted through the information. There were articles on giving feedback, measuring group quality progress, how to preserve and can vegetables, and of course container gardening.

The first two articles were clipped together. One was titled "Typical Weeds of the Backyard Garden," and the other was titled "Corporate Weeding: Identifying Roadblocks to Group Success." On the cover page of the article about backyard weeds, Mrs. Hortensis had left Nick a note.

"This might help you identify which plants to pull. The other article is about the challenges of managing team issues."

There sure are some weeds in our organization, he thought to himself. *It would be nice if everyone knew how to spot and identify them better so we could pull them out.* As Nick read, he made notes to himself:

Typical weeds
Getting to know your weeds is the first step in controlling them.
People who don't know how to weed shouldn't do it.
People who know how to weed are gardeners.

Typical weeds in the organization:
- apathy
- hopelessness
- overextended
- misdirected
- egoist/nonteam player
- unmeasured and unmaintained
- difficult people (a review of the different types)

Weeds can look just like a regular plant. However, like many unplanned guests, they consume resources with little contribution.

After completing several articles, Nick returned to the garden to begin work. It wasn't long before he realized there were more weeds than he possibly had time to pull.

He commenced with the vegetable area and then moved toward the back part of the garden. There were only a few types of weeds he had to worry about and, with practice, soon became proficient at spotting them.

He made sure to not just tug at the surface, but to get the roots out as well. He never realized how stubborn and difficult weeds were. They were everywhere and so invasive. As Nick pulled weeds he wondered if there was an equivalent management concept for their removal. He worked for hours and filled three giant black plastic garden bags.

As he was weeding and moving around the garden, Nick discovered new entertaining and enchanting stones with phrases on them:

187

There is no other occupation like gardening in which, if you were to creep up behind someone at work, you would find them smiling. —Anonymous

How fair is a garden amid the trials and passions of existence. —Benjamin Disraeli

I have never had so many good ideas day after day as when I worked in the garden. —John Erskine

I perhaps owe having become a painter to flowers and my garden. —Claude Monet

While weeding, Nick also noticed that some of the plant leaves were being chewed. Some had only the veins of the leaves left, giving them the appearance of fine lace. He returned to the kitchen table, located an article on pests in the garden, and began reading. The quiet of the house and the hours of hard work gently reminded Nick of how tired he was. He had accomplished a lot for one day and decided to go home and finish reading the articles. He could return at a later time.

After reading the article on pests, Nick thought about purchasing some pesticides but decided to consult with Mrs. Hortensis first. In the meantime he used the other techniques recommended and trimmed away the infested areas, washing the plants with an insecticidal soap solution. One of the recommendations using a garlic infusion was fascinating:

Garlic pesticide spray: Soak three to four ounces of chopped garlic bulbs in two tablespoons of mineral oil for one day. Dissolve one teaspoon of fish emulsion in a pint of water and add it to your solution. Stir. Strain liquid and store in a glass container—not metal! Dilute one part solution to every twenty parts of water. Kills aphids, mosquitoes, and onion flies.

He added the information Mrs. Hortensis left him in his binder, "Essential Skills of Management and Leadership." It was starting to become a considerable reference source.

The garden clearly missed Mrs. Hortensis, as did Nick. During the next several weeks, Nick spent time weeding and maintaining the garden.

As he worked surrounded by the calming nature of the plants, he reflected on what an important person Mrs. Hortensis had become in his life. She had literally opened Nick's eyes and taken him down a pathway of new discoveries, becoming more aware of things previously unnoticed. They had always been there but were transparent to his understanding. The ability now to recognize and comprehend the subtle differences between what before were just plants had spilled over into his work environment, and he had become very perceptive at listening to the unspoken messages around him. He was appreciative and mindful of his newfound insights and the wonderful gift Mrs. Hortensis had given him—the gift of awareness.

He hoped the treatments she was receiving were effective and only a little more time was needed before things would be back to normal. But deep inside he realized the possibilities. He knew she was a stoic person and would not confide in him if things were getting worse. That was Mrs. Hortensis. Nick realized that was what he admired about her—her ability to treasure each moment for what it was and not become consumed with what it could have been or should be.

He hoped he had expressed enough his indebtedness and respect for what she had shared with him. His small gift to her would be to maintain the garden so that when she returned it would greet her as the well-dressed friend he knew she missed.

Mrs. Hortensis had been in Nick's thoughts, and by July he was really looking forward to spending time with her again.

SUPPORT FROM THE TOP

Focus on what you can control and change, instead of worrying about what others should do to facilitate the situation. Support from the top will develop if you can show documented results. Stop blaming the management above you. To those below you, you are the top.

ESSENTIAL SKILLS OF MANAGEMENT AND LEADERSHIP PROGRAM

Nick's planned program included the following topics:

- *role of management and leadership*
- *communication skills*
- *career development*
- *performance management*
- *coaching*
- *problem solving and decision making*
- *motivation environments*
- *time management and planning*
- *team building.*

A key element in a training program is developing a learning environment, which encourages participation, sharing of experience, and comfortable personal growth.

The ability to nurture and grow team members is a crucial part of successful management and leadership.

ARTICLES FROM MRS. HORTENSIS

One of the articles, "Corporate Weeding: Identifying Roadblocks to Group Success," gave Nick the idea to review his group and post signs warning about inappropriate team behavior. Typical weeds in the organization:

- apathy
- hopelessness
- overextension
- misdirection
- egoist/nonteam player
- unmeasured and unmaintained goals
- difficult people (a review of the different types)

PROGRESS UNMEASURED IS UNRECOGNIZED

"The wise gardener anticipates July in January."

—Unknown

July 17

Using the information from the articles Mrs. Hortensis furnished him, Nick began to ferret out the weeds and pests in his group and throughout the organization.

Nick and Cindy posted signs on the different types of pests and weeds typically found in business, along with strategies for dealing with what they called "difficult people."

The signs sparked plenty of reaction from a few workers. Someone had marked up one of the posters and under the word "weed" wrote "cannabis rules." Most of the resistance came from people outside Nick's area, but a few were from his group. Ironically, those concerned were the same individuals complaining during the behavioral-style training.

Nick and Cindy had to facilitate several group sessions to clarify what the posters meant. In the end, everyone agreed in principle with the message that certain behaviors were inappropriate in healthy work environments.

Nick had been practically counting the days until he could meet with Mrs. Hortensis. When the day finally arrived, he woke early and jogged toward her house. He sprinted up the walkway to the front door and knocked. No one answered. *I wonder if I'm too early*, Nick thought to himself. He quickly darted around to the back looking for Mrs. Hortensis, calling out to her several times as he strolled through the garden. She was nowhere to be found.

Maybe she couldn't make it this month either, Nick thought, outwardly worried and fearful, his mind contemplating the worse. He rushed to the back door looking for a note, but none was there. He knocked again, this time waiting. Finally, he heard a faint shuffling noise slowly approaching the door.

Gingerly, the back door opened. "What's your hurry?" Mrs. Hortensis asked in a slow, weak voice. "First you make me go to the front door, and by the time I get there, I hear you knocking on the back door. I guess this qualifies for my exercise today."

"Sorry," Nick said, taking a deep breath to suppress his worst fears. "I've been worried about you. With all the medical test and treatments."

"Thanks, Nick. Not to worry, they are what they are. This old body has done me good for a long time, but it is finally running down."

"Nonsense," Nick said, attempting to express positive hope. "You've got plenty of years left. A person who is in her seventies shouldn't talk like that."

"Thanks for the compliment, but I turned ninety-one several months ago. Age is a question of mind over matter. If you don't mind, it doesn't matter." Mrs. Hortensis grinned faintly. "It's all about good maintenance. Speaking of that, I noticed you did a great job maintaining the garden. It is like I was never gone."

"Ninety-one! I can't believe you are that ..." Nick stopped himself from saying the obvious.

"Yes," Mrs. Hortensis said. "A long time ago, I was born to be a gardener and didn't know it. I was born in May, the month named for the Roman goddess Maia, who oversaw the growth of plants."

Nick put his things down and helped Mrs. Hortensis over to a chair next to the kitchen table. "How ever long ago it was, you haven't lost your quickness of thought."

She smiled. "Aging brains are more finely tuned than younger ones, the biological basis for what is called wisdom. Scientists now say that older minds are more balanced after spending decades 'upgrading' themselves, a process that isn't completed until midlife. Thanks, Nick," Mrs. Hortensis said as she sat down with his support.

"So I have something to look forward to," Nick said with a smirk as he sat down in the chair next to her. Sensing Mrs. Hortensis's wish not to talk about her treatments, he focused the conversation on the garden. "You were right about the weeds. They were everywhere! I also noticed various plants being consumed by pests," Nick said as he continued to look at Mrs.

Hortensis, still amazed at her age. "I purchased assorted products to spray, but I wanted to talk to you first."

"You have to be careful about spraying chemicals. They work, and you will kill bugs. The trouble is you will eliminate the beneficial insects as well. It's like making changes in an organization. You do not want to do things that will destroy the good going on just to squelch the bad. What did you do in the garden?"

Nick thought for a brief moment about the posters he and Cindy had hung notifying everyone about pests in their group. Maybe he could have handled that differently. "I trimmed the damaged parts of the plants and washed the plants I could with soap and water."

"That's what I've done for years, and it has worked just fine. Sometimes a consistent application of a less harsh technique will get the job done without the unwanted side effects. I hope you followed the basic rule I showed you: *tuck, and then trim*. Try and tuck the foliage in before you cut it off. Once it's gone you can't replace it."

"I did. Trim and prune in accordance with a plant's natural shape," Nick said confidently.

"You are getting the hang of the gardening world and starting to think independently. Sometimes being left alone to use your own intuition can be constructive. That's a good lesson to remember when managing others."

Nick moved his head up and down slowly. "I'm working on that," he admitted. "First, I want to be sure the pests aren't going to cause any permanent damage to the organization."

Mrs. Hortensis smiled.

Nick continued his confession. "I tried to apply what I learned about garden pests to organizational pests, but it wasn't received very well. I posted signs indicating the type of pests that can harm a work group, and some people found it insulting."

"Some people don't like it when you make it clear that certain behaviors won't be tolerated in the workplace," Mrs. Hortensis said, looking straight at Nick with that clear focus in her eyes when she was passionate about something. "People can make a real kerfuffle about those kinds of things, but every gardener knows that under the cloak of winter lies a miracle."

"Do you mean that sometimes we have to make things worse to get them better?"

"Not necessarily worse, but out in the open, which might possibly create tension in the process."

"I created tension all right. Cindy and I had to hold meetings to facilitate the apprehensions. At least now I know people are more aware of behavior that will no longer be tolerated."

"That kind of message is always hard to deliver, especially if you've never sent it before. Usually, in the end, the clarity of what is expected calms everyone down. As long as you are applying the rules in a fair and consistent manner, you shouldn't have any more problems."

"Speaking of that, the reference section in one of your articles assisted me in doing research on problem solving. I came up with new basic steps we've incorporated into the CPI program."

"What are they?" Mrs. Hortensis inquired.

"First, understand the reason for the problem. Is the process deficient (a common cause), or is there something unusual happening (a special cause)? The key becomes defining the problem as an imbalance between what should be expected and what is happening."

Mrs. Hortensis nodded her head. "That's an important stage. It's where you verify the problem, get the facts, and analyze them to determine the cause. I used to call it 'a dissatisfaction with the current state.'"

Nick agreed, "You don't know how many times I've said, 'Don't rush this stage.' It seems like everyone wants to just take action."

"Isn't that your behavioral style?" Mrs. Hortensis smiled, looking at him directly.

Nick tilted his head slightly. "Like I said, I'm working on that." He continued, "Studies in effective problem solving call it 'solution-mindedness.' That is, most individuals confronted with a problem feel a strong internal pressure to find a solution. Once a person discovers a solution, there is no encouragement to seek a second or third. Most just grab the first solution and run. Once a judgment is made, we tend to preserve it, even when evidence overwhelmingly indicates that we are wrong."

"That is why bad habits are repeated. Individuals attack new problems with methods they've used before," Mrs. Hortensis added.

"That's right. That's why we incorporated various practical skills into the CPI program. While teams are working on real issues, they are using new tools to break old habits."

"Good strategy. By formally focusing on improvement you are also addressing the main issue with effective problem solving."

"What's that?" Nick asked.

Mrs. Hortensis looked Nick straight in the eyes and said with more emphasis than he had ever heard, "Making time for it."

"I never thought about it that way," Nick said. "It does make it easier to solve problems when you get support from your management. Making the time for improving processes is something that we stress in the CPI program."

"Tools and time, that's all most people need," Mrs. Hortensis said.

"We provide several tools. We use process flow mapping and cause-and-effect analysis, which focus on obstacles and deviations. Teams look at either what is preventing the desired effect or causing the undesired effect. We also introduce CPI members to several soft techniques, like *six why analysis*, *pet peeve review*, and *imagery partnering*. We provide opportunities to use these and other tools to understand the issues. I've found that most problems tend to fall into one of three categories: people, technical, or operational.

"Yes, I would say those cover most issues," Mrs. Hortensis said. "So what's the next step after problem identification and analysis?"

"The next step is really important. It's the decision-making step. Just like during root cause analysis—separating causes from symptoms is critical—during this step, establishing criteria to evaluate alternatives is important."

"Did you notice the gardening term you just used, Nick?"

"No. What?"

"*Root* cause analysis." She smiled.

"I missed that," Nick said grinning as he continued. "This step is where we incorporated several techniques to fuel the creativity of a process team. We wanted team members to ask questions that explored functions, performance, costs, modifications, and combinations."

"Is this the brainstorming stage?" Mrs. Hortensis asked.

"Yes. We even use a technique called brainstorming. At this point we wanted CPI participants to generate, evaluate, and select. The main challenge with this step is that choices need to be made. The challenge of effective decision making in many organizations is a collective and often muddled phenomenon."

"If nothing else, it is predictably unpredictable," Mrs. Hortensis added.

"Our goal was to explore certainty, risks, and ambiguity. We decided to treat the decision process as if it were a sequential and linear progression. We also realized that decision making was an iterative process of clarification and reformulation, with complex decisions requiring the gradual blending of technical data. Then before making a final decision a review of the stakeholders concerns and preferences, both external and internal, was needed. We introduced the team to techniques that used both decision-relevant information as well as techniques to continually define the problem."

"What type of techniques?" she asked.

"Consensus mapping, cost-benefit analysis, influence diagrams, and risk analysis, to name a few."

Mrs. Hortensis raised her eyebrow. "Those are new. I would have incorporated some of those techniques when I was managing." She thought for a minute. "How about individual behavior? There are certainly a number of personality variables in decision making."

"Yes, and it goes beyond just Freud, Jung, and Maslow. It's the effect of different backgrounds and cultures on the way individuals process and act on information."

Mrs. Hortensis agreed. "Indecisive people are usually afraid of the unknown or of making the wrong decision."

"Yes, and that's why we created a structure for the process team activity."

"What do you mean?"

"The process improvement teams still go through the ten-week agenda, but now we bring in an outside facilitator to assist in integrating the new tools. We wanted the new tools to fit naturally into the process."

"Why?"

"So that the team members don't feel like they were being *taught* the tools, but instead they were learning to *apply* the tools. To them it seems like part of the process."

"That makes sense," Mrs. Hortensis said thoughtfully.

"The team also picks a team leader and the facilitator coaches that individual throughout the whole process. This allows us to incrementally increase the skills of someone selected by his or her peers as well as expands the "committed 10 percent" you talked about some time ago. They become the new change agents."

"You have thought this through, Nick."

"Thank you. You were an enormous influence." Nick let the words hang in the air as long as he could before he continued. "Understanding that solving problems is simply identifying the causes and making effective choices has helped teams with their final presentations. They can present recommendations that show how they analyzed the issue and made certain decisions."

"Remind me again what the final presentation is about?" Mrs. Hortensis queried.

"A final presentation is made to the resource team. This is where the results and resources come together. The process teams are asking for support and implementation of their ideas and recommendations. The outside consultant spent extra time with our resource team to make sure this step was handled appropriately. He pointed out that the resource team should focus on clarifying what resources are needed to implement suggestions and spend less time at the presentation scrutinizing how the team came up with the results."

"Create an atmosphere of support instead of one that appears to be an inquisition," Mrs. Hortensis expressed with conviction.

"Yes, the resource team has plenty of time, after the presentation, to look at the suggestions in more detail. It is better to critique after time is spent discussing and understanding the suggestions made."

"Do the teams ever present solutions that are out of scope with the original goals?" she asked.

"On more than one occasion, the resource team has been requested to attend meetings to provide clarity to the team's objectives."

"So team objectives are well documented." Mrs. Hortensis's tone of voice indicated this was important.

"The resource team develops a detailed objective statement explaining the scope of the team, the issues, and the expected deliverables. There haven't been any real surprises yet. The resource team members take turns attending team meetings as silent facilitators."

"And what is a silent facilitator?"

"They sit at the back of the room, away from the table, and observe the meeting. They become the eyes and ears of the team leader. Then, after each team meeting, the facilitator coaches and counsels the elected leader. If the team is starting to drift, they usually get right back on track. Remarkably, it has also helped some of the resource team members become better at listening to, observing, and coaching individuals."

Looking straight at Nick, Mrs. Hortensis added, "Probably the biggest challenge was sitting through the meeting without interrupting."

Nick knew she was addressing his interactive style. "You would be happy to know I'm much better at that now."

"This is really well thought out," Mrs. Hortensis expressed, acknowledging the obvious hard work.

"CPI only gets support because it gets results," Nick said. "Measurable results. Since part of the presentation breaks the proposed solutions into a manageable size and prioritized actions, I had the resource team select one of its members to facilitate the implementation and make sure we accomplish the results. That member would own the success of the team suggestions. The outside consultant stressed that how we supported and implemented team suggestions determines the ongoing participation and quality of the program."

"So how do you know process improvements are a success?" Mrs. Hortensis asked.

"We also refined measurements to identify if we are successful. Information is collected on the amount of time new changes are taking, the reduction in the number of customer complaints, and the overall level of involvement of employees in the CPI process. The resource team member assigned the responsibility to support the implementation reports periodically to the resource team on the implementation status. I constantly remind them, 'Make team successes visible.'

"You would be proud. I used a gardening example to make my point with the group. I referred to rain meters and small weather stations. I asked, 'How can a gardener make plans if he or she has no record of what happened in the past? With information about weather, rain, and temperature, a gardener can predict outcomes, seasons, and unique conditions more accurately.'"

"Nick, do you see that book over there on the self next to the refrigerator?"

"Yes."

"Could you bring that over here?"

Mrs. Hortensis showed Nick a logbook dating back to May 17, 1949, where she recorded rainfall, temperature, wind velocity, and frost warnings every year to the present. Nick was amazed with the detail and consistency of the records and told her it belonged in a museum. She brushed off the compliment and reminded him it was just a tool that illustrated the importance of keeping a visible history. To Nick, it definitely exposed Mrs. Hortensis's scientific background.

They also discussed team leadership. Mrs. Hortensis pointed out there had been extensive research by Carroll Shartle at Ohio State University in the forties and fifties on leadership. Shartle found that leadership behavior could be classified into two independent dimensions called "initiating structure" and "personal consideration." These later were altered slightly by William Reddin and labeled "task orientation" and "relationship orientation."

Mrs. Hortensis asked Nick if that sounded familiar.

Nick removed a piece of paper from his wallet and showed Mrs. Hortensis a small card. He carried it with him everywhere and pulled it out occasionally as a reminder.

THE LANGUAGE OF LEADERSHIP

Task Orientation: The extent to which an individual directs his own and his subordinates' efforts; characterized by initiating, organizing, directing, controlling, monitoring, and confronting.

Relationships Orientation: The extent to which an individual cultivates personal work relationships; characterized by listening, trusting, encouraging, empowering, coaching, and supporting.

"I use this card to remind myself I need to do both," Nick said.

Mrs. Hortensis expanded on research by Merrill, Reid, and Reddin, indicating that there is a third dimension to leadership that was not part of a style type, but an indicator of whether a style was being used well. The third dimension referred to versatility and readiness. "You have to be strong as a leader, but there are many kinds of strengths." She referenced Lin Yutang's translation of *The Wisdom of Lao-tse,* where the ancient Chinese sage Lao-tse stated that power could be characteristic of people not perceived as being overly forceful or directive. "The softest substance in the world goes through the hardest. The persistent dripping of water erodes the hardest rock."

"That's why we incorporated leadership coaching into the improvement efforts," Nick said. "Many of the individuals being elected as team leaders only know one primary way to get through the hard spots. That's with a jackhammer."

Mrs. Hortensis reflected for a moment on some of the abrasive individuals she used to deal with.

"As I grow in my understanding of good leadership, I am realizing it is my responsibility to shape other leaders in my group as well. Not only those in management positions, but those with influence."

"There has been a lot of debate over the last fifty years about what makes a leader," Mrs. Hortensis expressed with curiosity in her voice. "Is leadership innate and characteristic-based, or principles that can be taught?"

Nick offered, "I've been doing some reading in this area lately. According to Peter Drucker, the whole discussion of characteristics and traits is a waste of time. Leadership characteristics at best should be viewed as yardsticks with which to measure how to improve leadership abilities. They are not a mandatory list, essential to leadership, but instead as a way to understand natural strengths and weaknesses. Currently three major leadership shifts are occurring in modern organizations. They are the shift from: strategist to visionary, commander to storyteller, and system architect to change agent and servant."

"Drucker seems to be closer to reality than most of the theories I've read," Mrs. Hortensis shared. "However, there are a few characteristics that many leaders hold in common, such as the desire to lead, the willingness to take risks, and a need to achieve. However, these characteristics aren't necessarily shared by all leaders."

"I agree," Nick jumped in, "there are also some characteristics we would like leaders to have, such as honesty, ethics, and concern for others. Warren Blank suggested we might understand leaders better if we focused less on the traits of the leader and more on the relationships between the leader and followers. That was one of my underlying intentions behind the CPI program, to demonstrate visible support and concern from management for those struggling with real everyday issues."

"If you look at some of the greatest leaders in history, they did have one thing in common."

"What's that?" Nick asked.

"Willing followers. That is one thing that clearly differentiates leaders from nonleaders."

"That's what Warren Blank said," Nick exclaimed. When we focus on the leader–follower relationship rather than on the leader's personal traits, we develop a new insight into leadership. He calls this perspective the 'nine natural laws of servant leadership.'"

Mrs. Hortensis nodded. "The idea of the servant-leader was actually drawn from the teachings of Robert Greenleaf in the mid-1960s. Greenleaf was so inspired after reading the work of Hermann Hesse, *Journey to the East*, that he began to focus on a new approach to leadership. The story is about a servant who does all the menial chores, yet also uplifts those around him with his spirit and song. He is a person of extraordinary presence. Later, we discover that the servant was in fact a great and noble leader."

"I read Greenleaf's book *Servant Leadership*," Nick added. "Traditional leaders ask questions about results, while servant-leaders asks questions that help uncover what he or she can do to help. When I read that, I understood why our CPI program was so effective. At the core of it lies the question: What can I do to make your job easier?"

Mrs. Hortensis reflected for a moment. "I guess the ultimate understanding about leadership is that it can and must be experienced. We can learn the techniques, skills, ways of communicating, and master theories and strategies. These become the tricks of the leadership trade, the polish that brings out the leadership shine. It is through our actions and primarily our failures that we refine the leadership role. It is through understanding the forces impacting the leadership experience that determine if you have the passion for leadership." She smiled. "Leadership, unlike instant tea, must be slow brewed for perfection, like our tea from the garden. The leadership learning process is a lengthy one and requires, at times, being in hot water."

Nick laughed. "Recently I've been wondering about the forces that shape the leadership experience. In the *Harvard Business Review* classic article on "How to Choose a Leadership Pattern," Nick stopped himself in midsentence. "See how you have rubbed off on me! I walk around quoting information like this all the time."

"Well, you could have picked up worse habits from me." Mrs. Hortensis winked, clearly trying to fight back a gleam in her eyes that radiated a sense of pride.

Nick continued, "The article explains that the key to successful leadership lies in an individual's ability to assess relevant forces within himself, others, and the situation. Success becomes the ability to be creative, visionary, innovative, and flexible in responding to these forces. Of the factors or forces a leader should consider in deciding how to lead, three are of particular importance. They are …" Nick remembered the binder he brought with him. "This is the "Essential Skills of Management" binder I told you about," Nick said as he retrieved the binder from the bureau by the back door where he placed it earlier while helping Mrs. Hortensis to the kitchen table.

Nick turned to the section on leadership. "These are the elements that need to be managed for effective leadership," Nick said.

FORCES IN THE LEADER
- Own value system
- Confidence in the subordinates
- Own leadership inclinations
- Feelings of security in an uncertain situation (releasing control reduces outcome predictability)

FORCES IN THE SUBORDINATES (what behavior on the part of the manager will enable subordinates to act most effectively). If the below conditions do not exist, the boss tends to make fuller use of authority.
- Interest in problem and the feeling it is important
- Necessary knowledge and experience to deal with problem
- Learned to share in decision making
- Strong need for independence
- Readiness to assume responsibility
- High tolerance for ambiguity

FORCES IN THE SITUATION
- Type of organization
- Group effectiveness
- The problem itself
- Pressure of time

Nick turned to another page. "This information discusses traits versus style and leadership characteristics." They reviewed it together.

Leadership: Traits versus Style
Early theorists believed that the primary factors in leadership effectiveness were the leader's personal characteristics or traits.

TRAITS (who the leader is): drive, intelligence, energy, tact, persuasiveness, humor, courage, optimism, and creativity
- The inability of trait concepts to account adequately for leadership effectiveness led to a focus on the leader's behavior or leadership style. After three decades of research

from the University of Michigan and Ohio State, behavior was divided between (1) behavior that focuses primarily on task accomplishment and (2) behavior that emphasizes building a strong relationship between the leader and team members.

STYLE (how the leader behaves)
- Although there is inconclusive research about which behavior style leads to high performance, several findings have surfaced. There is a positive correlation between employee-oriented leadership and team member morale, but even this does not hold in all situations. Experiments indicate that low-performing subordinates caused their superior to behave less considerately and autocratically.

They turned to another page.

LEADERSHIP ATTRIBUTES TO ENHANCE OR DEVELOP
- *Integrity*: Keep promises. Do not abuse position of authority.
- *Vision*: Perceive importance of long-range goals. Do not use excuse of future uncertainty to avoid planning and setting goals.
- *Analytical skills*: Analyze what is preventing programs from succeeding.
- *Communication skills:* Communicate effectively, avoiding personal attacks, intimidation, provocation, and anger.
- *Sensitivity*: Listen to not only what is said but also what is not said.
- *Ability to solve problems:* Participate in the process of solving problems, not simply taking a position on it.
- *Mentor:* Enjoy identifying and developing the best in others.
- *Always a leader:* Lead even when not in a position of authority.
- *Sense of humor:* Never take yourself too seriously.

Nick continued to flip through the book, and Mrs. Hortensis reinforced several sections with her own experiences..

LEADERSHIP INFLUENCE

Group performance is closely related to the quality of leadership. Through leadership, an individual secures the cooperation of others in accomplishing an objective. Leadership then is a social talent that of bringing out the best effort from group members.

CORE BELIEF

Leadership is "the privilege to have the responsibility to direct the actions of others in carrying out the purpose of the organization, at varying levels of authority, with accountability for both successful and failed results" (Wess Roberts, Leadership Secrets of Attila the Hun).

NINE CORE LEADERSHIP COMPETENCIES

- *Loyalty:* The ability to influence or discourage disloyalty; to know when to remove those whose disloyalty cannot be changed.
- *Courage:* Leaders must be fearless and have the fortitude to carry out assignments given to them and the gallantry to accept the risks of leadership.
- *Desire:* Leaders must have strong personal desires and an inherent commitment to influencing people, processes, and outcomes.
- *Emotional stamina:* Leaders must have the stamina to recover rapidly from disappointment, to bounce back from disappointment, and to carry out responsibilities without becoming distorted in their views and without losing clear perspective.
- *Decisiveness:* Leaders must be decisive, knowing when to act and when not to act, taking into account all facts bearing on the situation.
- *Competitiveness:* An essential quality of leadership is the desire to win; a leader without a sense of competitiveness is weak and easily overcome by the slightest challenge.
- *Accountability:* Leaders must never heap blame on others for what they themselves achieve or fail to accomplish, no matter how glorious or grave the consequences.

- *Responsibility:* Leaders must accept full and unconditional responsibility to see that actions are carried out and directions followed.
- *Stewardship:* Subordinates are not to be abused. They are to be guided, developed, and rewarded for their performance. Punishment is to be reserved as a consequence of last resort and sparingly applied only when all other attempts have failed. Leaders are caretakers of the interests and the well-being of those and the purposes they serve.

"You have been doing some in-depth reading," Mrs. Hortensis declared as they continued their discussion about leadership. Finally, it was clear that Mrs. Hortensis needed to rest.

Mrs. Hortensis said she would be gone again but would be back in a month or so. She had to go through more medical tests. "Frankly, I think I get worse with each examination," Mrs. Hortensis said, shaking her head. "I sure would like to apply the gardening metaphor to the medical industry."

They agreed to meet on August 28. Mrs. Hortensis requested that Nick come straight to the back door the next visit, knock, and just come in.

Nick volunteered to look after the garden again while Mrs. Hortensis was gone and promised not to spray any chemicals on the plants.

Mrs. Hortensis reviewed what needed to be done while she was away: maintaining, harvesting, and preserving.

She also had several more articles for Nick to read and shared the titles out loud: "Laws of Nature" and "Force Field Analysis."

Nick took two articles he had copied for Mrs. Hortensis from the "Essential Skills of Management" binder and gave them to her. One was an article on horticultural therapy, and the other was called "In Search of Exotic Plants."

"Thank you," Mrs. Hortensis said. "I will read them while I sit around waiting for those doctors to determine what they plan to do with me next."

DIFFICULT PEOPLE

Nick posted signs on the different types of pests and weeds typically found in business, along with strategies for dealing with what was called "difficult people."

Some people don't like it when it is made clear that certain behaviors won't be tolerated and are inappropriate in a healthy work environment. That kind of message is always hard to deliver, especially if it has never been sent before. In the end, the clarity of what is expected calms everyone down as long as the rules are applied in a fair and consistent manner.

Lesson learned: When making changes in an organization, do not do things that will destroy the good that exists just to squelch the bad.

PROBLEM SOLVING

Solving problems is simply identifying what are the causes of the issues and utilizing effective decision making when selecting an appropriate solution.

Key question to ask: Is the process deficient (a common cause), or is there something unusual happening (a special cause)?

Most problems tend to fall into one of three categories:

- people
- technical
- operational

CPI addresses the main issue with effective problem solving, and that is making time for it.

Problem Identification and Analysis Step

Good problem identification and analysis starts with understanding the dissatisfaction with the current state. Verify the problem, get the facts, and analyze them to determine the cause of the current situation. Process teams should look at what is either preventing the desired effect or causing the undesired effect.

Decision Making Step

Once the problem is properly identified and analyzed, it is time to make a choice.

Compare the alternatives using establish criteria, and then begin taking action.

RESOURCE TEAM

Once issues have been identified as "process" problems, the resource team forms a group of individuals to work on resolving the deficiencies.

The resource team develops a detailed objective statement explaining the scope of the team, the issues, and the expected deliverables.

Some of the tools used by a process team can include: six why analysis (technique used to probe deeper into the assumed cause), imagery partnering, consensus mapping, cost-benefit analysis, influence diagrams, risk analysis, root cause analysis, brainstorming, process flow mapping, and cause-and-effect analysis, which focuses on obstacles and deviations.

After ten meetings, the process team presents their analysis and solutions to the resource team. This is where the results and resources come together

The resource team also establishes measurements to identify if the CPI efforts are successful. Information is collected on the amount of time for new changes, the reduction in the number of customer complaints (internal as well as external), and the overall level of involvement of employees in the CPI process.

LEADERSHIP

To increase the benefits of process team interaction, leadership coaching is incorporated into the program. During the first meeting, each process team selects an individual to lead. The leader is provided coaching after each session and support material on how to:

- run meetings.

- address team performance issues.

- hold team members accountable.

- guide using the different tools of CPI.

Leadership coaching reflects some of the changes occurring in organizations, such as the shift from strategist to visionary, commander to storyteller, or system architect to change agent and servant leader.

Traditional leaders ask questions about results, while servant-leaders ask questions that help uncover what he or she can do to help.

The Nature of Understanding

"Look deep into nature and you will understand everything better."

—Albert Einstein

August 28

Nick continued to be productively engaged at work, his activities seasoned with new challenges and discovery. He was promoted to director of the company's first "lean" initiative and quickly realized many of the strategies employed in CPI were essential to the new program's success.

Nick computerized his skill matrix inventory and established regular training sessions for key skill sets. Because of demand for some of the classes, a waiting list was established, and management took notice that Nick's group was a place to which people wanted to transfer.

To be able to provide more classes, Nick developed a mentoring program that allowed individuals proficient in certain skills to teach others. As an incentive to conduct the training, Nick created a pay scale that allowed individuals to earn extra money as instructors.

Nick established a standard amount he paid all instructors regardless of their current salary, and some individuals were making three times their normal rate. When he explained the pay scale to his boss, Nick justified the expense because of experience. "These people know the company and can teach information in a way that is relevant to our environment. As long as they are good at instructing, then we have a great mix of knowledge and experience."

Nick also implemented a basic train-the-trainer boot camp to assist some individuals in polishing their natural skills.

Most of the classes were offered at the beginning or end of the normal workday, but a few individuals had asked for evening classes. One group even requested a Saturday session where they planned to cover key topics while kayaking. Nick was skeptical about the practicality of a Saturday class, but interaction with participants afterward convinced him they really applied themselves. The instructor had used kayaking as a metaphor for the learning points of the day.

To ensure classes remained effective, the participants evaluated the sessions and instructors. Attendees determined what classes and instructors were available in the future. To maintain content consistency and instructor commitment, Nick and Cindy periodically audited classes to evaluate progress.

There was no grading of attendees, but individuals received credit for participation in a skill development database maintained by human resources. Some selected skills required additional capability verification as a follow-up to the class, and Nick developed a qualification program with simple proficiency checklists. These were to be completed by the participants' area management after the class. The qualification checklists became a tool to assist and encourage frontline management to be a part of the ongoing coaching efforts.

Individuals applying for openings in management and other positions were given additional consideration based on their documented skills or classes taught.

Workers could teach as many classes as they wanted, provided their immediate management approved. Teaching commitments were limited to just a few hours a week, because this was to be viewed as something special and not to compete with normal work activities. To guarantee support from the top, managers were evaluated on how many individuals participated as instructors.

In his mind Nick kept reviewing the articles Mrs. Hortensis shared with him as he headed to her home. He found the information opened up new understandings as well as questions, and he was looking forward to some interesting discussions.

As he knocked on the back door, Nick could see Mrs. Hortensis comfortably huddled, with a dark blue afghan cocooning her shoulders, sitting at the kitchen table reading.

Nick opened the door slowly, as if some force was gently pushing against it. "Hello. What are you reading?" he asked, being graciously considerate as he entered.

Mrs. Hortensis carefully turned and looked up. "Hi, Nick, I was rereading some of the papers we exchanged. I enjoyed reading about horticulture therapy. Never heard of it before. Did you find time to read the information I gave you?"

"I sure did." He had looked forward to reviewing with her one article in particular, "Laws of Nature." "Is the 'Laws of Nature' article where you began to formalize your thoughts on gardening as a metaphor for management?"

Mrs. Hortensis nodded slowly. "It's where I tried to explain the natural forces shaping human interaction. The garden was merely the bridge. Richard Feynman said it best: 'There is a rhythm and a pattern behind the phenomena of nature, which is not apparent to the eye, but only to the eye of analysis; and it is these rhythms and patterns which we call Physical Laws.'"

Nick thought for a moment and then related, "It is interesting that the forces of nature are so powerful and yet simple at the same time. There is so much to understand about the hidden forces that impact us all. For example, you mentioned the concept of cognizantability, the capacity to concentrate on any given thing and establish different channels of communication."

"Yes, the transmutation of creative energy. How about we review it over a cup of tea?" Mrs. Hortensis asked. "You wouldn't mind making us some, would you?"

"Are you kidding! Anything special you want in it?"

"See if there is any licorice mint left."

Nick ventured into the garden and collected the leaves for tea. He prepared the leaves, put them in a pot, and poured hot water on them. As the hot water released the fresh aroma, Nick exclaimed, "How refreshing is the smell of nature."

As they drank their tea, Nick and Mrs. Hortensis discussed the esoteric laws regarding the transmutation of creative energy. Mrs. Hortensis referenced a step Nick used when making tea and compared the transmutation of energy—how the boiling of water into steam transforms it to give water an even greater power.

In that same context they discussed how understanding leadership is really the discovery of your inner self. As you analyze your leadership triumphs and failures, you become aware that you, and you alone, are responsible for your shortcomings and your successes. During a leadership journey, questions arise, such as "Why do we react as we do?" Mrs. Hortensis related that one of the basic human desires is to know oneself: "As Socrates said 'Know thyself; know your strengths and your weakness; your potential, your aims and purpose.'" As an individual unfolds this understanding, the forces of nature are slowly brought under conscious control. Aphorisms become the result of activities experienced, not just dreamed, and a realization that through everything we place into action we have reacted and enacted the results. Mrs. Hortensis quoted a saying:

> According to the seeds that you sew,
> So is the fruit you reap,
> Those of positive, will gather positive,
> Focus of the negative, negativity keeps.

"In your article ..." Nick said, placing the "Essential Skills of Management and Leadership" binder he brought with him on the table and turning to the article on "Laws of Nature." He pointed to a red underlined paragraph and read it out loud, "... when we engage in managing and leading, there are fundamental natural laws that impact our outcomes. There are predictable occurrences or happenings that manifest with some regularity. These activities might appear to be irregular, like the variation that occurs with weather, but underneath it all are some simple and general laws governing the predictability of the event."

"Identifying the laws of nature can be challenging," Mrs. Hortensis said, pointing at the article.

Nick responded, "In the article you pointed out that the laws of nature can be divided into fundamental laws and those less fundamental or derivative."

"You did read the article," Mrs. Hortensis exclaimed, smiling. "Mankind has always known that there was some order in the natural world. For example, the tides rise and fall, the moon has four phases, and persons grow older, not younger. Modern science is slowly attempting to reveal that order through physics, chemistry, biology, economics, sociology, psychology, neuroscience, and geology, to mention a few. With untrodden understanding comes a fresh metaphysical challenge: can we explain the existence of this pervasive order? Contemporary metaphysics ultimately splits into two competing theories regarding the laws of nature. On one account, the regularity theory is that the laws of nature are statements of the uniformities or regularities in the world; they are mere descriptions of the way the world is. On the other account, the Necessitarian theory states that the laws of nature are the principles, which govern the natural phenomena of the world; that is, the world obeys the laws of nature. Regularists account that there are virtually limitless number of laws. We explain events every day in circumscribed generalities without supposing the principles we reference are in any sense necessary. You don't wake up in the morning and ask, 'Which natural laws will I break today?' No, you ask yourself, 'What will I do today?' Regularists point out that human beings have for thousands of years been successfully explaining environmental events—a casting cracked because it cooled too quickly—without understanding fundamental laws."

Nick pointed at the article. "Whereas the Necessitarians believe that the laws of nature can be used to explain the occurrence of events. Certain propositions impose their truth on events. To them there are only a small number of laws, and those are the most fundamental laws."

"They both agree that to be a law of nature, theories must be factual, universal, and conditional. From the Necessitarians' view, the laws of nature govern the world. The Regularists insist that the laws of nature do no more than correctly describe the world. The heyday of this dispute was the 1940s and 1950s. But, the point is," Mrs. Hortensis said, returning the discussion to her original thought, "humans have always looked for patterns in nature. Are these patterns fundamental laws? From the point of view of the practical scientist, it doesn't mater. So long as the laws we devise give correct predictions, we assume we are right. For the current moment they become the discovered truths."

"You made that clear when you stated that Galileo's law of free fall, and Kepler's laws of planetary motion were eventually found to be special cases of Newton's laws of motion. However, when they were first proposed, they were determined to be fundamental laws or discovered truths."

Mrs. Hortensis looked at Nick with clear eyes. "Yes, those discovered truths evolved, but at one time they were essential for explaining natural events in a simple fundamental way."

Nick shrugged his shoulders.

"It is difficult to prove that any law is truly fundamental," Mrs. Hortensis continued. "For example, Newton's laws of motion were eventually replaced by more fundamental laws, laws of relativity and quantum mechanics. Some question if these then are the ultimate fundamental laws."

"Are they?"

"I don't think that should be the point. We needed the original understanding to be able to progress to the next level. It only becomes an important question when viewed from the context of a limiting paradigm.

"A what?" Nick asked.

"A construct or rule that prevents you from looking for and accepting other alternatives, or when we stop challenging fundamental laws."

"Then there are no fundamental laws," Nick retorted.

"Nature is inescapably committed to behaving in accordance with its laws and cannot behave otherwise. Fundamental laws became a way to explain the unexplainable."

Nick focused on every word, like a cat observing the fluttering of a butterfly.

Mrs. Hortensis continued, "To be effective in managing and leading, key principles should be understood in terms of the basic natural laws that are governing the situation."

Nick quickly countered, "Are these the ultimate fundamental laws?"

"They are, to our current understanding. My article attempted to answer the question: are there natural laws that apply to human interaction as well?"

"But science is a limited method and does not have the means to deal with the imaginary. It would be like performing a chemistry experiment to test the laws of logic."

"Yes," Mrs. Hortensis said, impressed by Nick's insight. "Do natural laws exist that impact effective leadership? This is a philosophical position. Scientific methods don't rule them out of existence, merely out of science."

Nick responded, "Do you mean laws governing interaction between people in organizations defy scientific assumptions? If you can't empirically prove something, then it doesn't exist."

"The laws of nature are simply the way things behave because of what they are. They are descriptions of aspects of the nature of Mother Nature. It is the basic law of causation: a thing *does* what it *is*."

"So that's why in leadership we search to understand who we are, and by understanding this we learn to manage our strengths and weaknesses. I need some time to reflect on that," Nick said, wanting to return to the article. "You also explained there are only a few fundamental laws that govern our physical world. In physics they are conservation of energy, conservation of momentum, laws of motion, and laws of force. You indicated that physics is the study of the behavior of matter and energy and related that to understanding group dynamics."

Nick had underlined in red the specific paragraphs he wanted to discuss with Mrs. Hortensis. "Here." Nick pointed to a paragraph and read out loud, "'In physics, energy is defined as the product of force times the distance in which the force moves.' Does that mean we achieve more by simply increasing energy?"

"Unfortunately," Mrs. Hortensis took a deep breath, "organizations teach us to work harder, apply more energy, without providing alternative approaches to improve work efforts. The focus should not be on applying more effort but providing the proper direction for the effort. Efforts committed to a common direction are an aligned energy."

Nick pointed to the article again and said, "Explain what you mean by aligned energy."

Mrs. Hortensis thought for a moment. "In physics, energy must be defined in a way that allows us to measure it. The law of conservation of energy states that in any isolated system the total amount of energy remains unchanged. There are basically two kinds of energy: kinetic and potential. Kinetic energy is equal to the work done to set a body in motion and can be measured in terms of mass and velocity of the body itself. All potential energy can be thought of as energy stored in a field of force."

Nick quickly interjected, "I'm not a scientist, so go easy here."

Mrs. Hortensis smiled. "Potential energy is stored energy. Take a spring, for example. When compressed, it stores potential energy. When it expands to release, there is kinetic energy of the mass in motion."

Nick rubbed his head and queried, "So the total energy of a system is potential energy plus kinetic energy?"

"Yes, the connection between the two is given in Einstein's famous formula, $E = mc2$. Conservation of energy remains one of the cornerstones of modern science."

"So ..." Nick sounded perplexed. "In relation to team dynamics, in every group there is kinetic and potential energy. Potential energy is the: understood team purpose, demonstrated commitment, motivational environment, undiscovered capability, goals and objectives, and leadership opportunities. Kinetic energy is the everyday actions and reactions. Using the law of nature, dealing with conservation of energy, the direction of energy in most organizational efforts is often dispersed and conflicting."

"Yes, this happens primarily because people do not understand why they are doing the work and how it fits into the organizational scheme, the potential energy. They have some sense of the organization's strategy to achieve its goals, but this strategy is rarely discussed. Sometimes individuals know their own part but might not understand how others fit in."

"Without increasing the potential energy, you can't increase the kinetic energy," Nick exclaimed.

Mrs. Hortensis nodded.

"So that's the law of nature I addressed almost a year ago when my group was struggling. Individual goals were in conflict with group goals. When conflict arose, it was easy to blame others. The focus became who sabotaged the efforts, which reinforced counterproductive behavior."

Mrs. Hortensis continued, "Under those circumstances, applying basic management techniques only makes the problem worse. Kinetic energy isn't aligned with internal processes and is creating a misalignment between customers. That's like expecting a spring to recoil farther with the same amount of pressure; it just can't happen. Asking employees to work harder when misalignment exists only increases burnout, worker apathy, and unnecessary costs."

Nick smiled. "That's something you stressed when we first met. Organizational alignment must start at the top. Now I get it, by understanding and investing in potential energy. It is difficult to get an organization pulling together and moving in the same direction when the leadership of the organization is fractured or in conflict, only demanding more kinetic energy output."

"The leaders must create a vision of organizational potential and then inspire the members to achieve it. That is one of the secret ingredients in leadership and the key to managing change. Sometimes it's as simple as 'For every action there is an equal and opposite reaction.' Potential energy and kinetic energy—it's what should drive the corporate bottom line."

"I'm afraid to ask about the laws of motion and the laws of force," Nick said with a grin on his face.

"The application of those laws is quite clear in regard to change management." Mrs. Hortensis pointed to Newton's three laws of motion:

1. To change a body's momentum or direction of motion, an outside force must be applied.
2. The change is directly proportional to the force and the time over which it is applied.

3. Every force involves an action and equal and opposite reaction.

"For change to happen, it's simple: force equals mass times acceleration divided by the square root of one minus the ratio squared of the object's velocity to the speed of light."

"Stop already." Nick grinned. *At ninety-one, her mind is more intact,* he thought, *than mine could ever be.*

Mrs. Hortensis smiled. "The article attempted to discover the relationship between known fundamental laws and laws of human nature and determine if certain meaningful leadership principles could be developed. The premise wasn't completely new. In Germany during the early 1800s, there was a philosophical movement known as Naturphilosophia. It sought a simple, unifying principle for all natural phenomena. Recently there has been a new branch of science, known as systemics, which addresses holistic systems and their application to human beings. Principles like entropy and the new principle of enformy are discussed.

"I've heard of entropy before," Nick said, relieved he could finally contribute to the conversation. "Entropy, the condition where chaos reigns. The measure of the unavailability of a system's energy for conversion into mechanical work."

"Yes, very good." Mrs. Hortensis added, "... and enformy is a principle that imposes nonrandomness on elements of nature."

Nick sat silently for a moment. "I think I need some time to contemplate all of this."

"It's simple. We continually struggle to define the ultimate forces at work, learn from our failures, or become doomed to repeat them," Mrs. Hortensis said.

Nick sat quietly for a few moments, reflecting on their conversation. "Sometimes you can learn an awful lot from failures. When we were looking for a new manager in my group, a corporate headhunter shared an interesting insight with me. She looked for people who had experienced setbacks in their careers and viewed them as stronger candidates. Of course, the type of setback was considered. Those representing certain character flaws, such as embezzlement or harassment, were different than a downsizing in an industry, changes in top management, and relocation issues. In general she saw a plus in a person based on unplanned career changes. She was looking for individuals who through these changes could regroup, rebuild, and again become successful."

"Now that's making a positive out of a negative."

"Some individuals in corporate life have never failed, had the same job for years, and moved up as others moved out. The headhunter wondered whether they would know how to rebuild again if a major setback happened. Failure is not necessarily a sign of weakness; it's what we learn and do with that experience that is important."

"From the dry desert comes some of the strongest plants," Mrs. Hortensis said.

"In my group, I used to think some would never bloom. There are people who just won't make the effort."

Mrs. Hortensis smiled. "Do you remember the rain last week? Let me show you something interesting. I really haven't been out in the garden much except when you are here. Could you help me up?"

The treatments were starting to visibly affect her movement. She leaned heavily on Nick as they walked slowly through the garden. They stopped several times and rested on benches, and Mrs. Hortensis pointed out different stones Nick hadn't noticed before.

Nick knew Mrs. Hortensis preferred not to discus what was going on with her. She had made it clear that she was content with whatever happened and wanted to enjoy the moment instead of focus on the negative. He could see in her eyes the delight she was experiencing being again in her garden.

"This garden is amazing. Each time I discover something new."

Mrs. Hortensis offered a faint smile. "I can't take full credit. Some of it I planted, and some are nature's surprises. Despite a gardener's best intentions, nature will improvise. It is the serendipitous essence of the unexpected revelation. Just like managing people, your contribution may lead to new discoveries, some of which were totally unpredictable. That's what makes it so intriguingly exhilarant. You never know what discoveries wait once you plan the garden. It is one of the reasons that gardening and management are similar. There can be so many wonderful surprises with the little effort you start."

"Definitely, there can be surprises working with projects and people."

At the farthest part of the garden, Mrs. Hortensis stopped by an old wooden fence overgrown and well hidden by honeysuckle vines laced with clemantis and *passiflora edulis*.

"Nick, look over the fence and tell me what you see." The fence separated her yard from her neighbor's.

Nick climbed on a rock near the fence. "I never realized those trees in the distance weren't part of your yard."

"The Japanese call it *shakkei*, or borrowed view."

Looking over the fence he recognized the backyard of the Garlands. They were never home. Both had very successful careers and worked long hours. Their yard appeared neglected and tired.

"What do you see?"

"A lot of work," Nick replied. "Mostly dirt and sand. They're never home."

"Look closer."

Nick looked closer and noticed a few small flowers sprouting. "I don't believe it. How can they survive without any support?"

"Even in the worst of conditions, some plant types can survive. However, in most cases only temporarily. Some die out just as soon as they bloom. Just like the willingness to improve and excel found in all organizations and individuals. The initial excitement that blooms naturally will disappear if not supported."

On the fence, partially overgrown with vines, were several motivational plaques. One read: *Even in the harshest of conditions there is a desire to succeed.*

"I read that in Hiroshima, after the bomb, they thought nothing would ever grow again, but the very next spring, the grass began to sprout."

"Yes, exactly. Remember the rain we had the other day?" Mrs. Hortensis motioned again toward the Garlands' backyard. "With a little attention, even the most neglected areas can still bloom." Mrs. Hortensis pointed to another plaque on the fence partially covered:

MANAGEMENT'S LAWS OF NATURE
All living things require:
Belonging
Development
Fulfillment
Believing

"That's fairly simple and requires some explanation," Nick said, looking over at Mrs. Hortensis.

"All living things want to belong. Those that don't posses the ability to reason still group themselves in like collections. Creatures clearly function in clusters, hives, pods, flocks, gaggles, and communities. Throughout the animal kingdom there is clear evidence that comfort and survival is found in numbers."

"That's why we created a purpose statement so team members understood they belong to something," Nick said, nodding his head.

"Living things also seek development. Again, for those lacking reasoning we can view their growth as an evolutionist might. There is a constant adjustment in responding to the forces around them, or development as part of survival. More intelligent creatures practice to become more proficient, making a key component to survival the ability to grow and adapt—survival of the fittest."

"Therefore, the coaching and skill development efforts," Nick shared.

"Fulfillment can be as simple as the transformational mitosis of a cell, seasonal germination of plants, or cyclical gestation in insects and animals. Whether executing natural instincts or cognitively pursuing specific goals, achievement of purpose is fundamental to nature."

Nick added, "Those species with the ability to make choices require motivational forces to assist in fulfillment."

"Yes, and finally believing. All living things need to believe. With those incapable of rational thought, we can view believing as a reaction to a natural force greater than themselves. In humankind, it is the belief that there is some force greater than ourselves. This believing becomes the recognition of the definable, and the explanation for the undefinable forces influencing and impacting us all. For the spiritualist, it is God's will, for the scientist, forces of nature."

Nick suggested, "In group dynamics those basic belief systems would include trust, fairness, expectations of higher authority, equitable rights, and just rewards."

Mrs. Hortensis pointed to an area farther to the right where Nick helped remove a thick growth of vines revealing two additional plaques side by side.

NATURAL LAWS OF LEADERSHIP
- Fear is managed and comfort created, by knowing purpose.

- Commitment is a visible affirmation of understood purpose.
- Development of self and others is a responsibility and obligation for survival.
- Establishment and maintenance of environments for success allow new challenges to flourishes where failures are learned.
- Survival instincts are destructive when cornered, and constructive when focused.
- Followers want to choose and believe in leaders, who provide for individual and group needs.

PRINCIPLES OF LEADERSHIP
- Set the example for others to follow.
- Build pride, develop purpose, and establish trust.
- Reinforce and respect self-worth and contributive value.
- Observe behavior. Continually improve.
- Reinforce positive *voices*. Manage the negative.
- Open minds. Seek alternatives.
- Visualize the future. Share the present.

Nick wrote down the messages on a piece of paper while Mrs. Hortensis rested on a nearby bench. Mrs. Hortensis reinforced the message by referencing Thomas Jefferson. She said, Jefferson would define social architecture today as the wisdom of the universal revealed in natural order used for the planning and enhancement of human fulfillment. A learning culture is one where collaborative creativity in all contexts, relationships, and experiences is a basic purpose of the culture. It is a culture where the measure of success is the combined wisdom of groups and synergy, leadership, and service of the organization as a whole.

Finally, they slowly meandered back to the house. They agreed to meet next month. Mrs. Hortensis was sure that by then, the medical testing and treatments would be over and they could start planning the garden for next year.

SKILL DEVELOPMENT

Establish a database maintained by human resources.

Develop information-exchange classes based on employee knowledge to expand the team skill base. Some selected skills require additional capability verification as a follow-up to the class and develop a qualification program with simple proficiency checklists. These are to be completed by the participants' area management after the class. The qualification checklist is a tool to assist and encourage frontline management to be a part of the ongoing skill development efforts.

LAWS OF NATURE

As leadership triumphs and failures are analyzed, one becomes aware that you, and you alone, are responsible for your shortcomings and your successes. During a leadership journey, questions arise, such as "Why do we react as we do?" One of the basic human desires is to know oneself, and as an individual unfolds this understanding, the forces of nature are slowly brought under conscious control. We search to understand who we are, and by understanding this, we learn to manage our strengths and weaknesses.

When we engage in managing and leading, there are fundamental natural laws, which impact our outcomes.

TEAM DYNAMICS

In every group there is kinetic and potential energy. Potential energy is the understood team purpose, demonstrated commitment, motivational environment, undiscovered capability, goals and objectives, and leadership opportunities. Kinetic energy is the everyday actions and reactions. Using the law of nature dealing with conservation of energy, the direction of energy in most organizational efforts is often dispersed and conflicting.

Leaders must create a vision of organizational potential and then inspire individuals to achieve it. That is one of the secret ingredients in leadership and the key to managing change.

MANAGEMENT'S LAWS OF NATURE

All living things require:

BELONGING: *All living things want to belong.*

DEVELOPMENT: *Living things seek development.*

FULFILLMENT: *Whether executing natural instincts or cognitively pursuing specific goals, achievement of purpose is fundamental to nature.*

BELIEVING: *All living things need to believe.*

In Every Winter There Is a Spring

"Gardening is a way of showing that you believe in tomorrow."

—Paul Allman

September–October

It was an unusually blustery day as Nick leaned forward to steady himself, nearing Mrs. Hortensis's house. Just last week it was warm and balmy, and today the wind was uncomfortable an-d inconvenient. He braced as the force of nature pushed from behind, encouraging him to journey faster. Nick smiled to himself as he thought, *The conditions were much like this a year ago when I first encountered Mrs. Hortensis.* He remembered a weather lore Mrs. Hortensis shared then: *No weather is ill, if the wind is still.*

Nick knew that a day like this wouldn't normally keep Mrs. Hortensis from working in the garden. He hoped that the medical treatments had resolved her issues and once again she could enjoy the magical oasis she had created. Gardening meant so much to her.

Nick arrived at the time they had agreed on, but Mrs. Hortensis didn't answer the door. He tried to open it as he looked through the window, noticing she wasn't sitting at the table, but it was locked. Nick knocked several times and waited, remembering a prior visit when impatience resulted in Mrs. Hortensis first going to the front door and then to the back. During their last meeting she had seemed so fragile and weak. *Maybe she just needs a little more time to get to the door,* he thought as he continued to wait. Finally, Nick walked out into the garden and called her name. *Maybe she is feeling better and already working in the yard.* But no one answered his call.

Nick checked for the key to the back door under the gardenia pot on the porch, but it had been removed. *That's strange*, he said to himself. *That key has always been here.* He knocked several more times and waited on the porch. Finally, he headed home. "I only pray she is okay," he said out loud as he felt the windy force of nature pushing against him, as if to say, "Stop, turn around, go back."

Over the next few weeks, Nick walked by Mrs. Hortensis's house every chance he had, but she wasn't working in the yard. Each time he stopped and knocked, waiting a long time for a response, but she never answered.

He even left a note with contact information. *Funny*, he thought to himself, *in all the time we had spent together, we had never exchanged phone numbers or my address.*

After leaving his contact information, Nick received a very nice letter from Mrs. Hortensis's daughter explaining that her mother had been admitted to a local hospital. Mrs. Hortensis's daughter had traveled from up north to look after her mother and was now staying in a hotel near the hospital. She had heard about Nick but, until his note, had no way to contact him. She thanked him for the message and wondered if he could continue to look in on the garden once in a while. She had used a key, from under the gardenia pot, and would put it back in the same spot.

That weekend Nick jogged to the garden. He missed sitting in the kitchen drinking tea after working in nature. Surrounded by harmony, time disappeared. Among plants he found moments to think, and the reflection many times led to discovering new solutions to formidable work challenges.

There wasn't that much work to do in the garden now. He had harvested the vegetables and done weeding throughout the summer and fall. He did some light trimming but primarily dressed the garden in preparation for the winter and its well-deserved rest.

The harvest had been spectacular and the tomatoes were better than Nick had expected. With Mrs. Hortensis's help, he had learned how to can and preserve food from the garden. He created a label called "Natural Selection" and used several jars as a CPI raffle item. They were a big hit.

Nick enjoyed sitting on a bench in the backyard, sipping tea, relaxing, and reading. At the back of several of the articles from Mrs. Hortensis there were numerous reference sources, and Nick had systematically begun reading them to better understand the subjects.

However, after all of Mrs. Hortensis's insightful discussions, he was still most fascinated with the concept of managing others based on understanding essential natural laws.

Nick did a force field analysis of his group to identify situations that contributed to problems (restraining forces) and the actions necessary to counter these problems (the driving forces). Kurt Lewin had developed the technique to better understand where the energy for movement came from. Driving forces move a situation toward change while restraining forces inhibit or block movement. Nick had discovered that when the restraining forces were stronger than the driving forces, change did not occur. To accomplish change, the challenge was to reduce the restraining forces, strengthen the driving forces, or both. Usually, the most effective tactic was to diminish or eliminate the restraining force. The force field analysis encouraged individuals to think creatively together and agree on the most important process that needed to improve. The results were something he wanted to share with Mrs. Hortensis.

A few days after the correspondence from Mrs. Hortensis's daughter, a letter arrived asking if Nick would come and visit her mother in the hospital. She hoped he would come as soon as possible and left her phone number. Nick called her immediately to arrange a visit.

Nick had feared the worst since his last meeting with Mrs. Hortensis. It was clear that she was dying, and Nick had tried to respect her wishes and not make her illness a part of their conversations. He was thankful and felt fortunate to have met this incredible individual. Even though she was comfortable and resolved that the end was near, Nick did not easily accept that he would soon be without a true friend, a friend who had led him down a path of growth and development yet never really demanded that he take a single step. What a loss to the world such a person would be. He had really grown accustomed to their discussions, her insight, but most of all her support.

In the morning, prior to the visit, Nick stopped by the garden to make a special bouquet of fresh cut flowers. Nick could only imagine how much Mrs. Hortensis had missed her garden, and if she couldn't come to it he would bring it to her. There was always something in bloom, and Nick marveled at how well thought out it was.

It was a long way to the hospital, but Nick decided to make the trip on foot to help ease his tensions.

As he turned the corner and approached the building, it seemed to take forever crossing the expansive grass front lawn. He smiled to himself as he recognized the ground covering as a combination of blue grass and a dwarf broadleaf fescue. Not long ago he would never have noticed—such a wonderfully fulfilling thing, the gift of awareness. He remembered a quote by Thoreau 'The art of awareness is the art of learning to wake up to the miracles all around.'

As he entered the building his feelings began to tug on his thoughts. He did not look forward to seeing Mrs. Hortensis in her current state of suffering, but at the same time he couldn't wait to visit with her. Nick hesitated a few minutes outside her room. Finally, he knocked, extending the bouquet of flowers out in front as he slowly entered.

As the door to her room opened, Mrs. Hortensis smiled. "I recognize those roses," she said softly. "Hi, Nick. How is the garden looking?"

"Fantastic," Nick said, trying to hide his emotions. "I tilled the soil where the vegetable garden was and started pruning some of the rose bushes. I canned the vegetables as you showed me and even brought you one of the jars."

Nick gently sat the jar and flowers on the bed stand. "I noticed the Myoporum trees had developed curly growth on the new leaves, so I released some *encarsia formosa* to help. Beneficial organisms and biological control, just like you said were best."

"My, you sure have become quite the gardener, Nick," Mrs. Hortensis said, taking a long deep breath. "And things at work?"

"Well, my team completed three more key improvement projects. There are several active CPI groups now, and from all of them our team was nominated for the new People's Choice Award."

"Sounds impressive. What is the People's Choice Award?"

"Do you remember that award my group started a while ago? Well, management decided to make it an award for the whole company. Award winners are nominated and selected by the workers."

Taking another long, slow breath, Mrs. Hortensis strained to exert herself. "Your team is having quite … a meaningful impact. I hope you know it is a reflection … of their leader. Their successes are yours."

"Thank you. I think I'm beginning to realize what you meant when you said I was responsible for the performance of the team. They should take more of the credit, and I should accept much of the blame when it comes to performance. I couldn't have done it without your help."

"Nonsense. I think you would have. It just would have taken longer." Mrs. Hortensis was showing the signs of struggling as she breathed.

Nick quickly kept the conversation going. "I've been doing a lot of reading about management science. Edgar H. Schein, Chris Argyris, Carl R. Rogers, Douglas M. McGregor, Warren Bennis, and several others," Nick said with a tone of pride in his voice.

Mrs. Hortensis listened patiently as Nick continued on about the new information he was learning. Finally, Nick's enthusiasm slowed, and he just looked at her and smiled.

"So what do you think, Nick? Has becoming a gardener helped you in your efforts to manage people?" Mrs. Hortensis asked, visibly defying her discomfort.

"Definitely. I had no reference point to make complex issues easier to understand. It's ironic that we already know many of the key principles. The gardening metaphor—or as the team at work calls it, corporate gardening—really helped me recognize what I already knew. I just didn't know how to express and use it."

Nick continued, "*When gardeners garden, it is not just plants that grow, but the gardeners themselves. So plant your own garden and decorate your own soul, instead of waiting for someone to bring you flowers.* That's from one of the stones I found hidden in the garden."

Mrs. Hortensis slowly nodded.

"You know," Nick said, trying to lighten things up, "you are a real gardener when you think compost is a fascinating subject."

Mrs. Hortensis smiled weakly. "Thanks for the flowers, Nick. I have something … for you as well." Mrs. Hortensis slowly paused for a breath, gently raising herself on one elbow. "It's something I've been working on … a long time."

Mrs. Hortensis gingerly pointed to a bag laying on the chair in the corner of the room. "I had my daughter bring it over when I knew you were coming. You just missed her. She went out to get me a cup of tea."

"What is it?" Nick picked up the bag and gently pulled out an old, thick musty book from inside. It was handmade and leather bound. Beautiful hand-stitched signatures were interspersed with loose-leaf papers. The writing on most of the pages was recognizable to Nick. It was the same elegant calligraphy he had seen on the note pinned to the screen door several months ago. "What is it?" he asked again.

"It's what we've been talking about for the last year. I looked everywhere but just couldn't find it. My daughter located it when she was going through my late husband's papers and clearing out parts of the house. Somehow it must have gotten mixed up with his stuff. You know, besides being the discoverer of coenzyme Q_{10} in 1957, he was also a fantastic gardener." Her words trailed off softly at the end. Mrs. Hortensis paused for what seemed a long time. "He used to refer to this book all the time."

Nick slowly sat down in the chair, looking at the book the whole time.

"It's over thirty years of notes and thoughts. We called it the 'Gardener's Companion Guide to Management.'" Mrs. Hortensis's voice again trailed off at the end of her sentence.

Nick began to thumb through the journal. "This is great information, *Motivational theory and group dynamics based on companion planting and crop rotation.*"

Nick slowly turned to Mrs. Hortensis. "I can't take this."

Mrs. Hortensis uttered a weak "Nonsense." Slowly she said, "Nick, you have come a long way in understanding the principles of nature and applying them to managing a team. It is your turn to pass the information along to others."

Nick gently placed the book on his lap and looked at Mrs. Hortensis.

"You know, during our last sessions together, I was learning from you, Nick. There is so much information being developed all the time. I am glad you will continue to collect, understand it … and share it …"

There was a long pause. "Nick, I need to rest now," Mrs. Hortensis said, closing her eyes. "Can you promise to plant some licorice mint this year for me? I love it in my afternoon tea."

"You mean *agastache foeniculum*?" Nick asked with a warm tone to his voice.

Mrs. Hortensis strained a smiled that lingered a long time.

"Sure thing," Nick said. "I'll stop by next week with some fresh leaves."

That was the last time Nick talked with Doctrina Hortensis, but he knew she would always be a constant reference.

When he first experienced Mrs. Hortensis's garden, it had made a significant impact on him. He didn't know it then, but through his understanding of the garden, he would learn the secrets of managing and leading others. The garden had now become a magical place for Nick. He realized that anytime one can discover and learn the elementary essence of something, it is truly magical.

Applying the fundamental laws of nature to the challenges of corporate life provided Nick with a way to understand that his struggles with group dynamics were nothing really new, and simply represented some underlying basic and powerful principles.

Nick reflected using the gardening analogy: *When it comes to gardening, there is no problem unique to you.* Once the basic principles were understood, it was easy to see that corporate gardening has gone on—and many times been misunderstood—for a long time. Like all gardens, some are successful, some not, some open to the public, some very closed and private.

When it comes to corporate life, Nick usually asks others who are struggling with managing their groups, "How does your corporate garden grow?"

Today Nick owns a consulting business and still uses the companion guide as a reference source for coaching and organizational development assignments. Currently he is working on publishing the guide so others can enjoy the benefits of understanding the relationship between nature and organizational life.

Nick, to this day, is amazed at the initial resistance to gardening as a metaphor for management. "It just seems too obvious" is the usual response. "Just too plain corny."

Since Mrs. Hortensis's daughter lived out of the area and had no interest in the house, Nick bought it from her and continues gardening there to this day. He has been approached several times about subdividing the lot, but he has no intention of changing this magical place.

Mrs. Hortensis had said many times that finding the meaning behind things was one of the most exciting parts of management. She frequently used puns to illustrate her point. Cleverly she would convey different meanings with usual words.

Nick frequently reflects on his own journey and is thankful that he learned the obvious relationship between gardening and management, *just in the* NICK *of time.*

FORCE FIELD ANALYSIS

Identify situations that contribute to performance problems and the actions necessary to counter these problems.

What are the restraining forces?
What are the driving forces?

Leaders are responsible for the performance of a team. The team should be given credit for much of the success, and the leader should accept most of the blame when it comes to poor performance.

LAWS OF NATURE

Applying the fundamental laws of nature to the challenges of corporate life provides a way to understand that managers and leaders struggling with group dynamics is nothing new, and simply represented some underlying basic and powerful principles.

Appendix:

AUTHOR'S NOTES:

<u>Latin References:</u>

Doctrina (Trina for short) = teaching, instruction, learning, such as *animos doctrina excolere*

Hortensis = of or belonging to a garden

The main character Doctrina Hortensis means learning from the garden.

<u>Key Characters:</u>

Nicolas Avtid = *Nick of time*: Nick has established one of the best consulting firms in the business. His moto is, "I'm not afraid to get my hands dirty." He guarantees that he can dig-up and resolve the most stubborn issues, while redoing the organization's landscape. He specializes in trimming the organization to the right size, eliminating unwanted pests, and replacing existing structures with more natural flora.

Fritz Morgan: Known for running a "tight ship" is a decendent of the famous Sir Henry Morgan (better known as Captain Morgan – 1635 to 1688), one of the most notorious, successful and dangerous pirates who worked the Spanish Main. John Steinbeck's first novel *Cup of Gold* (1926) is about Henry Morgan's life.

Cindy DeConfianza: Eventually went on to do her own consulting specializing in company turn-arounds. She was instrumental working with Conseco, Lehman Bros., and WorldCom, finally ending up at Enron where she retired. She now resides in Costa Rica and has not visited the US since quickly leaving the country.

DIRECT GARDENING REFERENCES:

Being a pest = annoying behavior
Blooming inspiration = finally motivated
Blossoming individual = growing stronger
Branching out = expanding effort
Busy as a bee = a lot to do
Check the temperature of the group = current state of affairs
Climbing the ladder = individual growth
Clouds over work environment = poor group dynamics
Cloudy issue = lack of clarity
Cultivating ideas = develop understanding
Digging up issues = looking for problems
Digging in = committed action
Fertilizing = stimulating
Flowering prose = colorful writing
Fruits of your labor = end results
Getting the dirt on someone = finding the real story
Germinating ideas = beginning the future
Going out on a limb = adventurous
Grafting on to something = unplanned additions
Grass is always greener = Things look better from a different perspective
Gravitating toward = moving in a direction
Harvesting ideas = gathering the benefits of past efforts
Low-lying fruit = easy issues to resolve
Organic flow = natural order
Organizational tree = group structure
Organizational branch = specific subset of group
Peel back one layer at a time = reference to an onion
Plant seeds of .... = starting the change process
Planting ideas = beginning a new direction
Plow through it = determination
Propagate understanding = spreading clarity
Reaping the rewards = benefiting from activity
Root cause = finding core issues
Seasonal issues = periodic problems
Shady deal = unfavorable outcome
Smell like a rose = individual success
Sprouting ideas = beginning to think about something

Testing the soil conditions = looking for ways to improve team environment
Transplanting = relocating
Weeding out the bad = eliminating unfavorable
Whichever way the wind blows = indecision
You bug me = bothersome behavior

If you have others please submit to www.teampts.com. We are compiling a" growing" list.

READING LIST:

<u>General:</u>

Abrams, R., *Wear Clean Underwear*, 1999
Allman, P.G., *Time Management and Prioritizing Skills* (www.teampts.com)
Argyris, C., *Understanding Organizational Behavior*, 1960
Argyris, C. and D. Schön, *Organizational Learning II*, 1996
Blake and Mouton, *Grid Organization Development*, 1969
Blanchard, K. and S. Johnson, *The One Minute Manager*, 1982
Bolton, R. and D. G. Bolton, *Social Style / Management Style*, 1984
Collins, J. and J. Porras, *Built To Last*, 1997
Gladwell, M., *The Tipping Point*, 2000
Gray and Starke, *Organizational Behavior*, 1984
Hennig and Jardin, *The Managerial Woman*, 1977
Herzberg, F., *Work and the Nature of Man*, 1966
Hesse, H., *Journey to the East*, 1956
Hortensis, D. (Paul G. Allman), *The Laws of Nature* (www.teampts.com)
Jowett, B., *Machiavelli's: The Prince*, 1513, translation 1885
Mayo, E., *The Human Problems of Industrial Civilizations*, 1933
McClelland, Atkinson, and Clark, *The Achievement Factor*, 1953
Peters, T. and R. Waterman, *In Search of Excellence, 1991*
Roethlisberger and Dickson, *Management and the Worker*, 1939
Stogdill, M., *Leadership Behavior: The Description and Measure*, 1957
Teeguarden, R., *Chinese Tonic Herbs*, 1984
The Encyclopedia of the Social Sciences, 1937
Vroom, V., *Leadership and Decision Making*, 1973

Specific:
<u>COACHING:</u>

Allman P. G., *Discovering the Talent Within*, 2005 (www.teampts.com)

<u>COMMUNICATION:</u>
Allman P. G., *Behavior Interaction as Represented by Plants*, 2009 (www.
    teampts.com)
Bolton, R. and D. G. Bolton, *Social Style / Management Style*, 1984
Brinkman and Kirschner, *Dealing With People You Can't Stand*, 1994
Fournies, F., *Why Employees Don't Do What They're Supposed To Do*, 1988
Gill, L., *How To Work With Just About Anyone*, 1999

<u>CUSTOMER SERVICE:</u>
Albrecht, K., *At America's Service*, 1988
Collins, J. and J. Porras, *Build to Last*, 1997
Lareau, W., *American Samurai*, 1991
Desatnick, R., *Managing to Keep the Customer*, 1987

<u>GARDENING:</u>
CERES, *Herbal Teas, Tisanes and Lotions*, 1981
D.K., *Encyclopedia of Gardening*, 1993
Kaptchuk, T., *The Web That Has No Weaver*, 1983
Pest Publications, *The Shepherd's Purse—Organic Pest Control Handbook*,
1987

<u>LEADERSHIP:</u>
Bennis W. and B. Nanus, *Leaders: The Strategies for Taking Charge*, 1997
Blanchard and Hersey, Situational Leadership theory
Blank, W., *The Nine Natural Laws of Leadership*, 1995
Covey, S., *Seven Habits of Highly Effective People*, 1989
DePree, M., *Leadership Is an Art*, 1992
Drucker, P., *Concept of the Corporation*, "Leadership: Can It Be Learned?"
    Forbes, April 8, 1996
Drucker, P., *The Practice of Management*, 1954
Gardner, J., *On Leadership*, 1990
Greenleaf, R., *Servant Leadership*, 2002
Harvard Business Review, *Leadership that gets results*, D. Goleman, 2000

Harvard Business Review Classic, *How to choose a leadership pattern*, R. Tannenbaum and W. Schmidt, 1973

Kets de Vries, M., *Life and Death in the Executive Fast Lane*, 1995

Kotter, J., *The Leadership Factor*, 1988

Kotter, J., *Leading Change*, 1996

Nanus, B., *Visionary Leadership: Creating a Compelling Sense of Direction for Your Organization*, 1992

Roberts, W., *Leadership Secrets of Attila the Hun*, 1987

Stogdill, R., *Handbook of Leadership*, 1974

Wheatley, M., *Leadership and the New Science*, 1994

MANAGING CHANGE:

Allman, P., *Organizational Dynamics: Understand Natural Laws* (www.teampts.com)

Buckingham, M. and C. Coffman, *First, Break All the Rules*, 1999

Champy, J., *Reengineering the Corporation*, 1995

Drucker, P., *The Practice of Management*, 1956

Galpin, T., *The Human Side of Change*, 1996

Gladwell, M., *Tipping Point*, 2001

Goldratt, E., *The Goal: A Process of Ongoing Improvement*, 1984

Jacobs, R., *Real Time Strategic Change*, 1994

Johnson, S., *Who Moved My Cheese?*, 1998

Kotter, J., *A Force for Change*, 1990

O'Toole, J., *Leading Change*, 1996

American Society for Quality, *The Quality Toolbox*

Pasmore, W., *Creating Strategic Change*, 1994

Pressfield, S., *The War of Art*, 2002

Tarlow, *Navigating the Future*, 1998

Tichy, N., *Control Your Destiny or Someone Else Will*, 1993

Weibord, M., *Discovering Common Ground*, 1992

MOTIVATION:

Daniels, A., *Performance Management*, 1989

Flannery, Hofrichter, and Platten, *People, Performance and Pay*, 1996

Herzberg, F., "One more time: How do you motivate employees?" *Harvard Business Review*, Sep/Oct87, Vol. 65 Issue 5, p. 109–12

Gilbert, T., *Human Competence*, 1978

Maslow, A., *Motivation and Personality*, 1954

McCelland, D., *The Achieving Society*, 1961

PROJECT MANAGEMENT:
Lewis, *The Project Managers Desk Reference*, 2000
Pinto, *Project Management Handbook*, 1998
Tinnurello, *Project Management*, 1999

RE-ENGINEERING:
Allman, P. G., *Structuring CPI For Success* (www.teampts.com)

TEAMWORK AND TEAM BUILDING:
Katzenback, J., *The Wisdom of Teams*, 1993
Lawler, E., III, *From the Ground Up*, 1996
Mohrman, A. and S. Mohrman, *Designing Team-Based Organizations*, 1995
Moran, J., E. Mussselwhite, and J. Zenger, *Self-Directed Work Teams*, 1996
Scholtes, P., *The Team Handbook*, 1996
Smith, D., Katzenbach, J., *The Wisdom of Teams*, 2003

THE LEARNING ORGANIZATION:
Argyris, C., *On Organizational Learning*, 1999
Kim, D., *Applying Systems Archetypes*, 1997
Kim, D., *The Link Between Individual and Organizational Learning*, 1993
Schein, E., *Building the Learning Consortium*, 1995
Schön, D., *Organizational Learning: A Theory of Action Perspective*, 1978
Senge, P., *The Fifth Discipline*, 1990

TRUST:
Allman, P. G., *Building Organizational Trust* (www.teampts.com)
Allman, P. G., *Foundational Trust* (www.teampts.com)

ABOUT THE AUTHOR

Paul Allman is an accomplished consulting professional in the field of Employee Skill Development and Organizational Development Strategies, with over 25 years of actual "hands-on" experience. Recognized as a strategic thinker and trusted business advisor by clients and colleagues with a demonstrated ability to provide "realistic" solutions to ambiguous human capital situations, he has influenced diverse, cross functional teams to achieve critical objectives.

Mr. Allman started PTS - Professional Training Services in 1988 and since then has successfully handled large-scale consulting engagements, managed collaborative teams, coached individuals and established measurable results with clients in a variety of industries such as Entertainment, Manufacturing, Aerospace, Health Care, Service Industries, and local government.

A partial list of clients include: Warner Bros., Northrop Grumman, Parker Aerospace, Getty Museum, University of Southern California, Screen Actors Guild, Writer's Guild of America, Golden State Foods, NEC, Bancomer, Teledyne, Los Angeles Aquarium of the Pacific, and the City of Los Angeles.